Warzone Speedway

The Story of Armed Forces Racing

Trevor Davies

First published 2008

Trevor Davies Publishing
21, Gatton Way,
Hucclecote,
Gloucester, GL3 3DG.

British Library cataloguing in Publishing data.
A catalogue record for this book is available from the British Library.

ISBN 978 - 0 - 9558624 - 0 - 3

Graphic Design and Print Management by
Print by Design Ltd., Bodmin, Cornwall, UK.
www.printbydesign.co.uk

Printed in Malta

Contents

Foreword

My sixteen year professional speedway career (1947-62) will always be a time I remember with fond memories. Riding for the Wembley 'Lions', five world championship finals, representing England in test matches and defeating Jack Parker for the Golden Helmet match race title are times I recall with great pride.

When the author of **Warzone Speedway** contacted me for an interview I had almost forgotten my Army speedway career which was to lead to me becoming a professional rider. The research by Trevor Davies for this book brought back memories of a period in my life in WWII which still fills me with pride. My time in North Africa (Royal Fusiliers) and Italy Palestine, Germany (Royal Electrical Mechanical Engineers) was one of mixed emotions. Sixty years ago danger death and fear was on the mind of every soldier in uniform. Army speedway racing with its crude bikes and rough tracks, was a welcome diversion and relaxation from the ravages of war. It is my opinion that **Warzone Speedway** is a significant part of the history of the sport of speedway which uniquely records rare Army meetings, riders and machinery as well as tracking some of the military campaigns from an era in speedway history largely forgotten or overlooked.

Whilst I was aware of forces speedway in Italy and Germany, I am amazed at the detail the book uncovers. I was totally unaware of warzone speedway events in Libya, Austria, Egypt, Palestine, and Malaya and these events have lain largely uncovered for over sixty years. Some of my happiest days were in the early post-war days when I learnt to ride speedway on the Vomero stadium track in Naples, Italy. But for that experience it is unlikely I would have turned professional in 1947.

I am pleased to commend this book to you as a dedication to all soldiers who rode in khaki between 1939-1955.

Squire Francis 'Split' Waterman

NERJE, SPAIN, JANUARY 2007

Acknowledgements

During the two years of research for Warzone Speedway many forces veterans, speedway historians and Army archivists have generously assisted this author. Unique memories, photographs and records have been willingly shared to help tell "the forgotten speedway story".

I am particularly indebted to members of the WWII veterans associations who have unselfishly raided their personal war memorabilia.

It should be remembered many of their pictures from the early years were carried by soldiers as personal keepsakes. Their reproduction quality, whilst variable reflects the challenging conditions under which they were taken. Archivists Tim Stankus (Royal Corps Signals) Major D R Gilliam retd (Royal Electrical Mechanical Engineers) and Annice Collette (Vintage Motor Cycle Club) have also given me access to their historical records. The loan of unique historical data is fully recognised and thanks go to Dennis Egan and the late Colin V Morgan (Air Formation Signal Association), Barry Stephenson, Geoff Bennett, Alan Johnson, Roy Andrews, Peter Nuzum and others from around the world who responded to my call for information.

I am proud there are so many pictures to illustrate Warzone Speedway, most of them taken under difficult circumstances and most never before seen in print. For the use of these my gratitude goes to: John Somerville (Wright Wood collection), Ron Pope, Reg Fearman, Don Hardy, Barry Duke, Geoff Bennett ,Jim Gregory, Ian Moultray, Chris Illman, Chris Holifield, Eric Boothroyd, Bert Loader, Jimmy Gooch, David Hurrel, Basil Sheppard, Don Francis, Arthur Hewitt, Tom Fearnon, Ron Fitton, Bert Steddy, Chris Collier, Rob Wallis, Billy Bales, Ron Walton, Harry Mappin, Len Baker , Jimmy Green, Ray Cook, Tom Taylor, Les Mullins, Len Brace, Alan Clark, Jack Uglow, Graham Plant, Mrs Farrant, Terry Palmer, John Hart, Peter Nuzum, Split Waterman, Terry Stone, Vic Gooden, Noel Clarke, Ron Stone, Eric Wood, Dave Collett, Mike Exton, Dusty Miller, Frank Gale, Gordon Milne and Bernard Crossland, James Bond, Eric Wood. Every effort has been made to identify all photographers and credit is given to their work.

My final thanks must go to Glynn Shailes, John Jarvis and Jim Henry whose encyclopaedic knowledge of speedway history I have often called upon to verify a date, identify a rider or just to chat and revive my flagging spirit during what has proved to be a project of mammoth proportion and complexity.

Bibliography

Speedway News, Speedway Star, Stenners Annuals, The Craftsman, Speedway Gazette, Belle Vue Bulletin, The Wire, Motorcycling, Speedway Express, History of Australian Speedway, British Forces Motorcycles 1925/45, To War on Two Wheels, Picture Post, History of Exeter Speedway and The White Ghost.

Introduction

Whilst researching for '**Speedway Flyers**', a tribute to RAF speedway riders, many WWII veterans of the British Army contacted me enquiring "what about the lads in khaki? Don't forget the Tel el Kabir 'Dons', Hanomag 'Saints' or the Suez 'Lions'. How could I ignore the Middle East Championship and what about the team events in Libya?" It usually started with a phone call, e-mail or letter. All of a very similar tone. "I don't suppose this will be of much interest to you but......................." was the message. And so the snowball had been pushed down the hill and I had no idea where it would take me.

This then was how Warzone Speedway, the sequel book to 'Speedway Flyers' was born. Official records show that WWII was declared on September 3 1939, league speedway and the imminent Wembley World Championship final were both abandoned. When war was declared BelleVue headed the First Division, one point ahead of Wimbledon, whilst Newcastle were well on the way to the Second Division title. Southampton's, Cordy Milne was due to take eight bonus points from the qualifying rounds into the final, due to be staged on Thursday September 7 and with Bluey Wilkinson, the reigning champion having retired to manage Sheffield, a new World champion would have been crowned at the Empire stadium.

The last recorded meetings in Britain in 1939 were amateur meetings on November 5 at Dagenham and Oxford. The Speedway News, generally regarded as the voice of speedway at the time, printed its last edition on September 9 and it was not to appear on the news stands until April 10 1946. A government directive discouraged the staging of sports which attracted large gatherings as potential German bombing raids were anticipated. That, the speedway world thought, was that! Before starting our search for warzone speedway, i.e. racing on loose surfaces, on an oval in an anti-clockwise direction, using clutch starts as the criteria for qualification as 'speedway', firstly a short history lesson.

The British Army connection with speedway racing can be traced back to 1927 at Camberley Heath overlooking the famous Royal Military College at Sandhurst. The Camberley motor cycle club was already established, having staged the Southern Scott trial on the Heath and claimed to have staged the first Scramble in Great Britain . The club was incidentally at one time led by E.O Spence who became the pre-war driving force at Belle Vue Manchester. Motorcycling, the contemporary magazine of the time, carried news of the May 7 meeting in its May 11 issue under the headlines 'First British Dirt Track meeting'. The meeting, which pre-dates the High Beech official start of speedway racing on these shores by some 9 months, received an Auto Cycle Union permit for racing on a sand surface quarter mile circuit with racing clockwise, ie right handed bends, with three riders competing each race. C Harman (349cc OK Supreme) won the 350 and 500cc classes, with Fay Taylour later to be interned in WWII amongst the competitors.
Forward now to 1939 and what to many were the forgotten speedway years of 1939-45. Most of the sports aficionados will know that the Zoolological Gardens at Belle Vue Manchester ran meetings throughout the war years, utilising riders on leave from the forces and other home based pre-war speedsters involved in war work. Fewer will know that meetings were held in the war years at Harringay, Crystal Palace, Oxford, Glasgow, Southampton, West Ham and Rye House before peace time racing returned in 1945.

The technical development of motorcycles during the 30s was recognised by the War Department in preparation for the expected conflict.The horse played a key role in WW1, offering mobility, speed and manoeuvrability for the troops.The motorcycle, thousands were ordered by the WD in the build up to war, was to supersede the horse and this fundamental decision led to a whole generation of soldiers learning motorcycling skills which would prove crucial as 'speedway' became a recognised forces sporting activity. Europe, the Middle East, North Africa, Europe and Far East all took their turns as theatres of war.The 'phoney' war of 1940, the Battle of Britain, Dunkirk, D-Day and the fall of Berlin all occupied the speedway family of fans and riders alike for over five years. By late 1944 however, with the war turning in favour of the Allies, it fell to troops in Italy, under the direction of Major A.E Simcock and Flight Sergeant Harry Whitfield (RAF), the pre-war Wembley rider, to introduce racing on the first true warzone speedway at Trani, an East coast Italian town where racing was used to entertain injured soldiers from local hospitals. October 29 1944 was to ignite the fire, with tracks being constructed across the warzones as fighting gradually ceased.The formation of the Bar-None Motorcycle club in Egypt in that same year was equally important and saw the club initially staging time trials for despatch riders in the desert.'Sand track trials' (speedway) meetings followed for troops in the Western desert and led to a near ten year spread of Armed Forces racing to some 30 locations wherever the British Army was deployed.

This book endeavours to document the facts, capture the enthusiasm, fill the historical void and uncover a story which has been left largely forgotten for over 60 years. Over six decades have passed since many of the events detailed in this book took place. Much of its content, both words and pictures, I am proud to say have never seen the public light of day.The traditional speedway press had closed for the duration of the war and so left me tracking down real war heroes, the veteran soldiers who rode, spectated, built tracks, printed programmes and generally organised racing under war theatre conditions. Chapters attempt to provide facts, statistics and the spirit of the forces champions.A rider directory, listing as best as possible, riders who rode under official conditions between 1945-52 is believed to be a unique first.
I am truly indebted for the help I have received from a generation of men and women who fought to preserve this countries freedom.Thank you ladies and gentlemen!

Trevor Davies

War Time Britain

By mid September 1939, the government was discouraging the gathering of large crowds at sporting events, fearful of air raids by the Luftwaffe on British towns and cities. With Wembley, Belle Vue Manchester, West Ham and some Second Division tracks attracting crowds which compared with and often exceeded football league attendances, speedway racing very quickly came under this restrictive edict. The last professional meeting to be held in Britain was at Belle Vue on September 30 when the aptly named 'Farewell Trophy' was won by Frank Varey. Amateur racing continued at Oxford and Dagenham until bonfire night when the lights went out on racing for 1939.

It was anticipated that Luftwaffe raids were imminent. There were indeed isolated air attacks, an early example being a Heinkel 111 raid on Rosyth in Scotland on October 16 which had a fascinating speedway link. The late Flt Lt George Pinkerton, who rode for Glasgow in 1930, flew a Spitfire in defence of HMS Hood which was in dock at Rosyth. He was awarded the Distinguished Flying Cross (DFC) for his brave action in a dog fight. In spite of the government's early stance on large sporting gatherings, pressure for the staging of sporting activities (including speedway) came from the Mass Observation Organisation. Formed in 1937 to record public opinion, they reported "*Sport has an absolute affect on the morale of people*" and they continued "*Probably does more to affect the countries spirit than the recent poster campaign urging cheerfulness*". Regionalisation enabled the introduction of a war time football league which commenced on October 21 1939. Transportation and fuel was to prove the biggest challenge, a problem which was to hamper speedway racing throughout the war period. This more flexible approach from the authorities encouraged speedway promoters, mostly under the auspices of a local motorcycle club, (Belle Vue and Rye House were two good examples of this) to run meetings between 1940-45, often in aid or war charities.

Rationing of fuel, food, clothing and general shortage of spare money would, you'd have thought, have extinguished all prospect of speedway on the home front until Mr Hitler had been dealt with! In what was dubbed the 'phoney war', a period between late 1939 and mid 1940, any invasion of German Forces on British soil seemed unlikely and the only awareness most people had of the war was the fact that the relatively small British Expeditionary Force was out in France at the sharp end of the conflict in Europe. The Luftwaffe began air raids on London September 7 1940 and during the first day of the 'Blitz' dropped 300 tonnes of bombs on the civilian population in the capital. By October 31 the Luftwaffe had lost 1,733 aircraft at the hands of the RAF in the famous Battle of Britain. However despite the RAF losing some 1,379 aircraft itself and Londoners suffering some 57 consecutive days of bombing raids the countries spirit was not broken.

A mass evacuation of children living near vulnerable targets such as docklands, railway marshalling yards, and war production factories was implemented. The East End of London, in and around the location of the West Ham stadium at Custom House, proved a particularly good landmark for incoming German fighters and bombers. From the air, the distinctive oval was used as a landmark to target specific locations felt by the Germans to be strategically significant. Bombings of other speedway centres such as Coventry, Southampton, Glasgow, Liverpool, Manchester, Hull, Birmingham, Bristol , Plymouth and Cardiff brought the war to the front door step of many speedway fans. In these modern days of relative plenty, technological advances and almost endless choice it is perhaps appropriate to examine the war time life style and record the war-time exploits of a few of the speedway family. Many speedway venues were requisitioned by the forces as part of the war effort and used as holding areas for British troops awaiting embarkation before later becoming Prisoner of War camps. The Southampton Bannister Court stadium was home to French forces as was Arlington stadium in Eastbourne, the County ground at Exeter became home to American GIs (including boxer Joe Louis) and the Empire stadium at Wembley was turned over to the war effort including hosting many of the Dunkirk evacuees in May 1940.

Whilst many of the fans favourite riders were away fighting on foreign soil, those left at home were not immune from the impact of the conflict. As early as July 1939, trial black outs and air raid exercises were staged in most towns with the Air Raid warden being almost as feared as the local policeman. Crime grew dramatically, burglaries in particular, as under the cover of the black-out conditions the criminal element plied their trade, as well as developing a black market in goods that were in short supply. In 1941 the Morrison shelter was issued, which was a steel cage arrangement in which families slept to protect them from falling rubble in the event of their home being hit by a bomb. Incendiary devices containing magnesium were feared by the National Fire Service (NFS) as they spread fire at a tremendous rate and volunteer fire watching became a normal part of war-time life. 'Dig for Victory' and 'Make Do and Mend' were just two of many government initiatives to overcome the shortages, as shipping bringing 60% of the countries needs from overseas came under attack from German U boats. With most men at the battle front, women were urged to begin work in the factories to stem the shortfall in manpower. The aircraft industry and munitions factories were particularly grateful for the influx of women workers and so quickly was their impact that by 1942 a Lancaster bomber was being completed every two hours. Travel was greatly restricted, with the railways becoming the main arteries across the country. London based riders travelling North to Belle Vue by train for the war-time meetings would stow their bike and gear in the baggage van, sometimes only after some argument with railway staff. Petrol was in limited supply with the equivalent of just 200 miles worth per month being allowed, this being reduced in March 1942 when petrol was completely withdrawn from private use. A black market in fuel existed, with a red dyed version designated for official and commercial use changing hands at 6s 6d (32.5p), four times the official price.

THIS IS HOW THEY STOOD WHEN WAR BROKE OUT

NATIONAL LEAGUE: FIRST DIVISION

Track	Matches Played Home	Matches Played Away	Won	Lost	Drawn	Points For	Points Against	Match Points
Belle Vue	9	7	12	3	1	762	575	25
Wimbledon	9	9	12	6	—	807	695	24
Wembley	11	8	11	7	1	874	716	23
West Ham	9	10	9	10	—	766	819	18
Harringay	8	8	7	8	1	659	674	15
Southampton	8	9	5	12	—	611½	808½	10
New Cross	8	11	4	14	1	695½	887½	9

NATIONAL LEAGUE: SECOND DIVISION

Track	Matches Played Home	Matches Played Away	Won	Lost	Drawn	Points For	Points Against	Match Points
Newcastle	6	9	10	5	—	675	574	20
Hackney Wick	7	6	7	6	—	567	512	14
Norwich	7	5	6	6	—	501	493	12
Sheffield	4	4	6	2	—	361	302	12
Bristol	8	6	5	9	—	561	596	10
Belle Vue II.	6	8	4	10	—	490	678	8

UNION CUP: SECOND DIVISION

NORTHERN SECTION

Track	Matches Played Home	Matches Played Away	Won	Lost	Drawn	Points For	Points Against	Match Points
Newcastle	4	4	5	3	—	355	303	10
Sheffield	3	4	5	2	—	294½	290½	10
Edinburgh	4	4	3	4	1	347	308	7
Belle Vue II.	3	3	2	3	1	241½	254½	5
Glasgow	3	2	1	4	—	64	246	2

SOUTHERN SECTION

Track	Matches Played Home	Matches Played Away	Won	Lost	Drawn	Points For	Points Against	Match Points
Hackney Wick	2	1	2	1	—	117	134	4
Norwich	1	2	1	2	—	140	110	2
Bristol	1	1	1	1	—	77	90	2

THE ACES NEVER CLOSED

It was Belle Vue, under the control of E.O.Spence and the 'first lady' of speedway Alice Hart who decided that war would not deter them from entertaining the Northern speedway watching public by deciding to stage war-time meetings. Records show that some 29 meetings were staged at the Zoological Gardens in 1940.The Manchester club were not alone in keeping the speedway flame burning and in the same year some 34 other meetings were held at Crystal Palace 2, Glasgow White City 6, Harringay 1, Rye House 11, Southampton 2,West Ham 4 and Oxford 8. One of the leading 'black out boys' who regularly made near impossible journeys by train to ride at the Zoo on a Saturday night was Canadian Eric Chitty of West Ham. Eric had tried to enlist in the Army, Royal Navy and RAF before reputedly becoming a war time policeman in his spare time away from his war work. It was Eric who went to discuss the prospect of racing with the Belle Vue management. So the story goes, on his return journey home to London after meeting with Miss Hart, he decided to call in on his children who had been evacuated to Derbyshire. His car broke down and the garage called to assist was that of Wilf Plant who had ridden pre-war for New Cross, Wimbledon, Middlesbrough and Edinburgh. It was whilst the vehicle was being repaired that the subject of racing at Belle Vue came into the conversation. Plant revealed he had 250 gallons of racing fuel stored at his workshop. Not only was this Wilf's passport to Belle Vue bookings (he brought the nights racing fuel with him) but the availability of this fuel ensured racing continued throughout the war years.

BELLE VUE WAR TIME CHAMPIONS

British Ind. Champ.	**Northn. Champ.**	**Grand Prix**	**Empire Best pairs**	**Nat. Trophy**	**Track Champ.**
1940 E.Chitty	B. Kitchen	Langton/Varey	_____	_____	_____
1941 E.Chitty	O. Hart	B Kitchen	Langton/Varey Kitchen/Hart	Kitchen/Hart	_____
1942 E. Chitty	E, Chitty	E. Chitty	Varey/Kitchen	R. Johnson	O. Hart
1943 R.Clarke	N. Parker	N. Parker	Kitchen/Hart	Parker/ Wotton	F. Varey
1944 F. Varey	N. Parker	N. Parker	Chitty/Clarke	E. Chitty	E, Gregory
1945 B. Kitchen	A.Statham	T. Price	J. Parker/ Pitcher	_____	N. Parker

Speedway Derby	**England Best Pairs**	**Speedway cup**	**100 Guineas**
1940 J. Parker	Langton/Varey	_____	_____
1941 F. Varey	Johnson/Chitty	Kitchen/Hart	_____
1942 B. Longley	Kitchen/Hart	Langton/ Varey	E, Chitty
1943 _____	Chitty/ Tuck	F. Varey	_____
1944 N. Parker	_____	Hart/Wotton	_____
1945 J. Parker/T. Price	Johnson/ Statham	_____	R. Johnson

The Belle Vue claim that "we never closed" played a major part in keeping the sport of speedway racing alive in the black out years. Other clubs ran ad- hoc meetings, with riders becoming available on forces leave at short notice, and sharing of equipment being quite normal as most machinery was mothballed for the duration of the war. Norman Parker was reputed to having stored many of his competitor's machinery in his workshops awaiting the day their owners returned from the war.

The Manchester staged meetings were thankfully recorded in the Belle Vue Bulletin which was a magazine, come programme which was sold at meetings. With the speedway press closed, the Bulletin became the voice of British speedway and was often sent to pre-war fans in uniform around the world to keep them abreast of their favourite sport. As early as August 30 1939 the Bulletin was rallying supporters for the war effort. Under the headline 'Belle Vue mobilised for Victory' the Bulletin said *"What with the crisis and Hitler and Russia and all the rest of it, we are all having a harassing time these days. Its only natural that people should ask us what is happening in speedway racing and how is it affected by the International position? Well at the time of writing, the position may alter at any moment before publication, we can say the Belle Vue team are being mobilised. They are being called up to win the championship of the National League, the National Trophy and the World Championship."*

On a more serious note the Aces management said *"The position is quite simply explained. In these trying times, more than ever the vast speedway public must have something to divert their minds from more serious thoughts and the best service we can do for everybody is to carry on just as if nothing extraordinary was happening. If war comes, we frankly do not now what will happen. In these circumstances we wait until some expression of the government's opinion. The matter is entirely out of our hands."*

Eric Chitty leads a war time race at Belle Vue

The Belle Vue management were always keen to assist in the local war effort and during the 1940 season they offered free admission to all troops in uniform. This regularly attracted hundreds of soldiers , the lads in khaki coming prepared for all eventualities watching racing from the stands wearing their tin hats with rifles at the ready.

Later in that same season the Bulletin was used to call all motorcycling 'Aces' fans to arms. Major Becke, Chief Constable of Cheshire, issued an appeal through the columns of the Manchester 'Evening Chronicle' and 'Evening News' for up to 3,000 motor cyclists to be trained as despatch riders for Home Defence. Writing in the Bulletin, the Major said *"Particular appeal is directed to all motor cyclists with racing experience, either in trials, grass track or speedway racing. That does not mean that unless you have had experience of this kind you are not eligible"*. The Major wanted every man who had a motor cycle to attend a meeting at the Cheshire Police training school ground on the following Sunday. *"As long as you have some qualifications for the work and a bike, other difficulties such as petrol, oil, licenses etc., will be swept away"*. Some weeks later he returned asking for further help in the City of Manchester locality. *"Most of you here tonight live broadly within the City precincts. The defence of the City is everybody's business and every man who is now ready to offer his services in this capacity mentioned will be worth three or four in a month's time"*. Said the Major *"Many of you older motor cyclists feel that you have forgotten more than some of the younger generation are likely to learn about motors- even some of the speedway riders! Well here is a chance to show them how"*

MEMORABLE MATCH DAY

Crystal Palace Whit Monday 1940

Archie in Wimbledon colours

Archie Windmill, the pre-war Hackney 'Wolves' rider who went on post-war to ride for Wimbledon, Walthamstow and Aldershot was one of the few surviving riders who competed in the last ever speedway meeting at Crystal Palace during the war. Shortly after this interview Arch sadly passed away aged 92 years old. His memories of the day are a fitting memory to riders who overcame impossible odds to compete in order to entertain the fans in those grim times.

The Crystal Palace 'Glaziers' originally rode as a league team between 1929- 33 and in 1939 before war was declared (open meetings were staged between 1936-38). Archie who was President of the Veteran Riders Association in 2001, was waiting for his RAF posting in May 1940 when the surprise offer arrived from Fred Mockford to ride in an ENSA organised combination meeting at the famous South London circuit. *"I remember receiving the booking to ride in a Cavalcade of Speed type meeting. I had my JAP bike at home stored behind the wardrobe not expecting to use it again until after the war, but I was pleased to get some racing action. It was a combined car, bike meeting and from memory Ron Johnson (New Cross), Ken Brett (Hackney), George Craig (Bristol), Phil Hart (Hackney), Keith Harvey (Palace), Les Trim (Palace), Fred Tuck (Stoke) and myself all rode in the afternoon meeting".* This was to be the last time the Crystal Palace track heard the roar of speedway engines as the War Department requisitioned the whole area for a military tank park with the consequential damage to the track and surrounding grounds,

Archie's memories of this war time meeting were remarkably vivid, *"I can distinctly recall one race where I was following Ron Johnson who was such a good and safe rider and I thought if I follow Ron I would be OK. He suffered a puncture right in front of me and I barely missed him as he struggled to control his bike!"* The RAF occupied most of Archie's time from 1940 onwards and he served at Cardington, Wilmslow, Weston-Super-Mare, and RAF Syreston before a brief period in Scotland. *"If I have one regret about the war years it is that I was unable to ride in any Belle Vue meeting* "explained Archie " *but the RAF were very good with weekend passes and I was able to ride in many of the Rye House meetings organised by George Kay on behalf of the Harringay Speedway motor cycle and light car club.* In 1943 Rye House ran a Whit-weekend Sunday and Monday event named the Reunion Cup when a team captained by Arch rode against a Geoff Godwin team. These spasmodic meetings were used to raise funds for the Prisoners of War Parcel Fund organised by the British Red Cross.

For the record during the 1941-44 war time seasons, Belle Vue again led the way staging meetings each year but they were not completely alone:

> 1941 - Belle Vue held 29 meetings, Rye House kept the Southern flag flying with 14 meetings ranging from Individual championships, three team tournaments and even a challenge match against Norwich. Harringay, Oxford 2 and West Ham also staged meetings.

1942 –Another full Belle Vue programme of 27 meetings included an England v Overseas test in June which was supplemented by Harringay, West Ham and Rye House 5 meetings.

1943 - Only Belle Vue 24 and Rye House 5 were able to stage racing.

1944 - With the war turning against Germany it was left to Belle Vue to keep speedway alive staging a 26 meeting season starting in March and concluding in September with the aptly named Victory Trophy Final won by Oliver Hart.

Grass track 'Speedways' were very much in vogue pre-WWII with team and individual meetings attracting many conventional 'dirt speedway' riders to the events. Although, like professional speedway clubs, prevented from staging regular meetings during the war due to petrol shortages and the inevitable lack of competitors, spasmodic grass track speedway was possible between 1940-45.

Probably the best known of tracks, Farleigh Castle Speedway in Wiltshire, staged a meeting in May 1940, but the rigours of war closed the club for almost six years. There were no meetings staged during 1941 and it was left to the Chard, Somerset club to revive the sport with two meetings in 1942 involving several 'dirt' riders including 'Bronco' Slade, Fred Tuck, Reg Lambourne and Ron Clarke. In 1943 the Worcester club staged two meetings in aid of the local 'Infirmary Appeal' to start a trend for war time meetings to be used to raise funds for local and national war time charity appeals. By 1944 the concept of 'Holidays at Home' weeks to avoid unnecessary travel, saw grass speedway meetings attract crowds of 5,000 plus. Such meetings were held at Bristol (Filton), Pontypool, Gloucester, Dursley, Coventry and Hereford.

LADY SPEEDWAY RIDER INTERNED FOR HER BELIEFS

After the outbreak of WWII, combatant nations arrested and held without trial 'enemy' aliens. Internment, as it was called, was also the fate of service personnel who found themselves in a neutral country. In the autumn of 1939 it was estimated there were 80,000 potential enemy aliens in Britain, who it was feared could be spies. Following the failure of the Norwegian campaign in 1940, increasing numbers of German, Austrian and Italian nationals plus sympathisers were rounded up and sent to camps on racecourses and unfinished housing estates throughout the UK. Peel, Douglas and Port Erin on the Isle of Man were also locations selected for internment camps.

Speedway's best known lady rider Fay Taylour, born in Ireland, was to suffer the fate of internment after she attracted the attention of the security services by becoming enamoured with the extreme right British Fascist party led by Sir Oswald Moseley and his infamous ' brown shirts'. Recently released public records revealed correspondence which led to Miss Taylour's internment in the IOM. One letter intercepted at the time quoted Fay as saying *" I love Nazi Germany, the German people and their leader and this war seems terribly unfair"* Port Erin records leading up to her release described her as *"one of the most pro-Nazi individuals in the camp"*, Fay having acquired the habit of hoarding pictures of Adolf Hitler! Fay was released by the Home Office in October 1943 against the advice of the security services and returned to Ireland.

Born Francis Helen Taylour, Fay quickly became the star lady rider along with Eva Asquith riding in both England and Australia between 1928-30. Post WWII Fay travelled to America and discovered midget car racing on the dirt tracks of the United States and was still racing 500cc Coopers at Brands Hatch and Silverstone in the 1950s, competing against the emerging young Grand Prix drivers such as Stirling Moss and Peter Collins. Fay eventually died in Blandford, Dorset aged 80 in 1983.

WEMBLEY PLAYED ITS PART

Sir Arthur Elvin MBE

When the lights went out on the 74-33pts Wembley Lions defeat of Southampton on August 31 1939, just three days before war against Germany was declared, most expected that when war came Wembley stadium would be mothballed for the duration. Arthur Elvin, Managing director at the Empire stadium and his management team however had other ideas! Whilst key stadium staff enlisted in the Armed Forces (riders Lionel Van Praag and Morian Hansen being examples who joined the RAAF and RAF respectively), plans were made to ensure the Wembley facilities didn't go to waste. Elvin was determined that Wembley would play its part in the war effort by maintaining its reputation as an entertainment centre but also supporting both the local community and the general war effort wherever possible. The initial government ban on large public gatherings for fear of bombing raids, meant an immediate cessation of speedway and other sporting events. Autumn 1939 through to the spring of 1940, saw some relaxation of this ban. With team speedway abandoned and riders away fighting for King and country, only weekly greyhound racing, ad-hoc football matches (normally involving inter-forces matches) and some indoor events at the Empire Pool were possible. Elvin, by now Commander of a Wembley division of the Home Guard, was quick to offer the vast stadium facility to the War Department.

The evacuation of troops from Dunkirk gave Wembley its first opportunity to help, with thousands of troops returning from France spending their first days back home sleeping in the corridors of the cavernous stadium. Hospitality for troops and local children in the Wembley area were a regular occurrence, with Christmas being particularly popular with soldiers who were given free lunch in the famous Terrace Restaurant overlooking the speedway start line, where the annual reception was held following the World Championship final each September. Refugees arrived almost daily from war torn Europe and Scandinavia making their homes at Wembley before moving into more permanent homes in the local community. The Civil Defence, Fire Service and the Home Guard were regular users of the hallowed turf for training exercises of some description. With the war reaching its peak in the autumn of 1944, Wembley stadium itself looked to have avoided the ravages of the London bombing, until a stray 'Doodlebug' flying bomb landed on the greyhound kennels in the car park. Some sixty dogs panicked and escaped into the local area and it took a week to re-capture them!

During the 1939-45 period Arthur Elvin successfully managed to provide the public with some sporting entertainment, offer invaluable emergency accommodation for thousands of troops from across the globe and amazingly still donate £140,000 to many charities. In 1943 he was made an Honorary Freeman of the Borough of Wembley, in 1945 he was awarded an M.B.E and a year later was knighted by the King at Buckingham Palace. Sir Arthur Elvin M.B.E died on a cruise in early 1957. The Wembley Lions withdrew from the league the same year!

VIC'S SECRET WAR

Over 30 years after the end of WWII , the role and significance of 'Station X' at Bletchley Park in the war was made public. Bletchley Park mansions and its grounds near to modern day Milton Keynes, was the home from 1938 of the Government Code & Cypher School, the fore-runner of today's GCHQ. Some 10,000 military and civilian personnel worked there in secret supporting mathematicians, cypher code experts and even crossword specialists who were tasked with cracking the Germans communications codes, in particular the Enigma machine which played a pivotal role in the Nazi war machine. Restricted for many years by the Official Secrets Act, team members who worked at Bletchley Park couldn't tell their story. Amongst those number was post-war rider and later speedway promoter Vic Gooden who can now reveal his memories of his time as part of the team.

Vic, pictured in uniform was born in Huntingdon in 1921 and was a product of the Rye House training school of 1947, but was hampered by a broken leg. In 1948 he secured a team place with Essex team Rayleigh, a club he was to manage in later years. Lance Corporal Gooden serial no 2597579 joined the Army in May 1940 and was selected for the Special Communications Unit based at 54, Broadway in London opposite St James tube station. Vic's role as a driver may on the surface seem pretty mundane until you realise that MI5 and MI6 were co-located alongside the SCU in the same building. Vic's unit operated under special rules status, known as ERE (Ex Regiment employed) giving its members different conditions of operation from main stream soldiers .The SCU main role was to gather short range signals communications using aircraft and torpedo boats in Norway, Denmark, and even Germany for much of WWII. Part of Vic's duties was to transport the sensitive information gathered to Whaddon Hall, near Bletchley Park for examination and analysis. Recalling those days Vic remembers *"I was often sent to RAF North Weald to pick up reconnaissance information from incoming planes and I was present the night a damaged aircraft tried to land with a damaged tail plane. It overran the runway and burst into flames after crashing into a hangar. I was privileged to serve with some great guys and even met Peter Scott, son of Scott of the Antarctic, when he was a Commander of one of the torpedo boats"*. After spending most of the war riding despatch bikes and driving cars to and from Bletchley, Vic enjoyed a successful speedway riding career with Rayleigh followed by a period at West Ham and eventual retirement after a season with Aldershot.

Vic , centre, team manager Wimbledon 1966

Vic entered speedway promoting at Rayleigh in Essex before moving on to run the Poole and Ipswich clubs. One of Vic's proudest moments in speedway was as England team manager on tours to Sweden, Poland and Russia. *" I was responsible for the transportation of bikes, managing the team during meetings, in fact most of the organisation admin when England travelled abroad, I'm proud to have held that position, although I never received a penny piece as payment"* says Vic who also went on to manage the Wimbledon 'Dons' in the 60s.

Away from speedway, Vic's other passions were his American Oldsmobile car and show jumping. The Oldsmobile was used in the Stanley Baker film Hell Drivers, whilst his equine skills saw him enjoy success against the likes of David Broome and Harvey Smith, both world class show jumpers of the time. Vic also became an accomplished musician playing the organ, piano, clarinet and even the bag pipes. History shows that the work at Bletchley Park shortened the war by several years and was an essential part of the D-Day landings by solving the Enigma machine codes used by the Germans. Bletchley is also recognised as the birth place of the first programmable computer, the fore-runner on the modern day personal computer.

PETER'S UNDERGROUND WAR EFFORT

Peter Orpwood scored 352 league points for Tamworth in 1949, assisting the 'Hounds' to third spot behind Yarmouth and champions Hanley in the National league Division 3. This feat, although memorable, is overshadowed by Peters' war effort. As the conscription programme gathered pace in the early 40s and increasing numbers of young men joined the forces, a major short fall in coal miners became apparent. By the end of 1943, Ernest Bevin, the Minister of Labour and National Service in the war time coalition government recognised the threat this presented to industry at home and decided that a percentage of conscripts would be directed to work in the mines rather than be sent to fight on the battle front. Selected by a numbered draw almost 48,000 were chosen, including a young Peter Orpwood.

Peter went underground between 1943-47 before starting to ride in novice events in June of 1947 at the newly opened Tamworth track near to his Burton-on-Trent home. 'Bevin Boys' did not wear uniforms and being of military age and without uniform were often stopped by police and questioned about avoiding the call up! They received no medals, nor did they have the right as the troops to return to their pre-war jobs. Peter's below ground comrades included DJ Jimmy Saville, comedian the late Eric Morecambe and actor Brian Rix. In September 2007 the Government announced it was going to formally recognise the war efforts of the surviving 'Bevin Boys'. Badges showing the pithead gear of a colliery with the words Bevin Boys-Veterans were going to be awarded at a ceremony in March 2008 to mark the 60th anniversary of the end of the scheme.

Jack sitting with brother Norman

PARKERS HELPED THE RAF EXPAND

Many pre-war riders were prevented from joining the armed forces, whether by age or being in reserved occupations such as skilled engineers. The Parker brothers, Jack and Norman who starred immediately before the war with Harringay, were amongst the second category of rider whose war efforts were concentrated on home soil. As early as 1934, the Air Ministry Aerodromes Board was formed and was part of the RAFs Expansion Plan to increase the number of airfields in Britain, to recognise the relatively new 'Flying Forces' key role in the future defence of the country and to provide locations from which sorties to Europe could be made if required.

When WWII was declared, the Parker family, amongst other business interests, ran a haulage business. They quickly converted their fleet of transport into mobile forges and welding stations and joined the 'army' of some 60,000 employed to quickly expand the number of airfields throughout Britain. To put into context the results of this construction force, which created typical airfields with a 2,000 yard runway (initially grass but then concrete), some 120 new RAF stations were built in 1942 alone, with a total of over 600 airfields being available to the RAF at the end of WWII in 1945.

Both Jack and Norman continued to ride after the war for Belle Vue and Wimbledon respectively, Jack's career of 27 years ending in 1954 through injury, whilst brother Norman also retired from racing in 1953 after a series of racing crashes including a fractured skull.

WHAT OF 1945?

By the winter of 1944 with the US 8th Army on German soil and with the Nazi forces on the run in Poland, Greece, Italy, Bulgaria and Belgium there was only one outcome possible to the war. With an Allied victory in Europe almost assured, thoughts turned to the return of normality, with speedway's power brokers considering the issues surrounding the resumption of racing. **Arthur Elvin** (Wembley) had already made arrangements to lease the Dicky Case track at Rye House under the guidance of manager Alec Jackson to find new talent. News of the scheme had already reached North Africa, Italy, France, and India with letters from Army despatch riders flooding in requesting trials.

Major C Kenneth Duthie (Secretary, Speedway Riders Association) was expecting many of the pre-war old hands to retire and a new generation of riders to come through. When comparing the restart to the earliest days of racing in 1928 he felt the sport was better prepared with regulations and structure to the sport which would cope with the anticipated influx of new tracks. Pioneer Australian promoter **Johnnie S Hoskins** was promoting the need to give new blood a chance and put some spectacle back into the sport. In favour of softer tracks with a surface loose and deep, Johnnie also suggested putting the old hands in the second halves of meetings to allow the new riders to blossom.

Money was a key agenda item with the existing prize money under ACU regulations being for league and cup fixtures: 25 shillings (£1.25p) per point per home match or 27s 6d (£1.37p) away for the winning team and 20s (£1.00p) for the losing team. Test match rates were 30s (£1.50p) per start whilst Second Division league rates were 10s (50p) per start and 10s per point. It was not surprising therefore that squaddies, used to 3s (15p) per DAY, would consider using their new found Army motorcycling skills on the speedways. **Mr E 0 Spence** (Managing Director Belle Vue) agreed that many hundreds of new riders would be available, as 'fit as fiddles', after their intense Army training. Not surprisingly Spence preferred the wide open bowl tracks such as his own Belle Vue to the tighter circuits inside greyhound tracks and remarkably he called for the introduction of a white surface material which would reflect the lights and add to the spectacle. **Fred Mockford** (Joint Managing Director New Cross Speedway) was calling for more new tracks and felt adequate public transport, sufficient to enable ten or twelve thousand people to get to a track within 20 minutes was required.

Mr Victor Martin (Engine tuner and pre-war co-promoter at West Ham) was turning his skills to the mechanical requirements of the sport. He was considering a 350cc engine which he claimed he built for 1938 world champion Bluey Wilkinson before the war which would improve the sport. Racing fuel would not be a problem as even during the war his company was supplying a wood alcohol product at 98% pure to the United States. Some 500-600 gallons had been imported just before the war started and remained unscathed on the dock side all through the London 'Blitz'. **Ronnie Greene** (Wimbledon promoter and Assistant Fire Force Commander) explained that a number of the National Fire Service despatch riders had approached him for rides. He promised to supply the initial bikes and the mechanics to look after them using the workshops he had pre-war at the Wimbledon stadium which was badly damaged by a bombing raid.

As London and other speedway centres prepared for the return of racing it is remarkable to note that the last V2 rocket raid on the capital took place on March 27 1945 in Stepney, barely 3 months before nearby New Cross reopened its gates to speedway staging a Victory Cup meeting on June 27,won by Jack Parker.The East End in particular had taken the brunt of the V1,V2 rocket damage with some 2,500 deaths being caused by these devices. By Easter 1945 the country was re awakening to some austere times. People were looking for some relief and entertainment from the war years and speedway was preparing for a boom. News was still being censored as the Far East war continued until August, but light entertainment in the shape of radio captured the public imagination.The 'Brains Trust','Music While You Work', and ITMA (Its That Man Again) were all family favourites. 56 million books were pulped to recycle paper, the lack of pulp being a major factor as to why the *Speedway News* did not re publish until April 1946. Even then it was limited to just 12 pages and could never print enough to satisfy demand and always sold out. An election in July 1945 saw a Labour Government replace Churchill's war time administration. A major debate over the introduction of mid week sport, including speedway, commenced with politicians concerned that it would detract the working public from the process of re- building a war torn Britain. Eventually league racing was to recommence in 1946 to enormous crowds but with a punitive entertainment tax on the sport many clubs still struggled to break even on crowds of over 7,000.

Whilst VE (Victory in Europe Day) was not until May 8 1945, an amazing variety of meetings were held as a prelude to a return to league racing the following year. Led by Belle Vue who staged an incredible 39 meetings including a three team tournament between GB v USA v Russia, some 123 meetings were staged throughout the country. As early as March 31 Belle Vue held a meeting followed within a few days by meetings at Newcastle. Tracks opened progressively across the country with Exeter, Bradford, Glasgow, Rye House, Middlesbrough, Holbeach, Sheffield and Norwich whetting the appetites of the speedway starved fans. The case for the first post war meeting in Britain is somewhat confused by the fact that the Japanese fought on after VE day. The formal Japanese surrender to General McArthur was September 2 on the US carrier 'Missouri' in Tokyo bay .VJ day (Victory in Japan) was however celebrated on August 15 which makes the Exeter Alphington Southern Championship meeting won by Bill Kitchen on August 16 the first official speedway meeting after full cessation of fighting.

SPEEDWAY FIXTURES 1945

	VENUE	EVENT
31/03/45	Belle Vue	Champions Trophy
02/04/45	Belle Vue	Even Chronicle Cup
07/04/45	Belle Vue	West Ham
14/04/45	Belle Vue	Speedway Derby
21/04/45	Belle Vue	Varey v Parker
28/04/45	Belle Vue	Best Pairs
05/05/45	Belle Vue	North v South
12/05/45	Belle Vue	Varey v Parker
19/05/45	Belle Vue	Grand Prix
21/05/45	Belle Vue	GB vs USA vs Russia
26/05/45	Belle Vue	Track Champ
02/06/45	Belle Vue	London
06/06/45	Belle Vue	Frank Varey Cup
09/06/45	Belle Vue	100 Guineas Trophy
16/06/45	Belle Vue	Supporters Trophy
23/06/45	Belle Vue	Northern Champ
27/06/45	Belle Vue	Oliver Hart Cup
30/06/45	Belle Vue	The Rest
07/07/45	Belle Vue	100 Guineas Trophy
11/07/45	Belle Vue	B Harrison Cup
14/07/45	Belle Vue	Empire Best Pairs
21/07/45	Belle Vue	British Champ Q R
25/07/45	Belle Vue	North v South
28/07/45	Belle Vue	Harringay v Rest
04/08/45	Belle Vue	100 Guineas Trophy
06/08/45	Belle Vue	Statham v Parker

	VENUE	EVENT
08/08/45	Belle Vue	Lancs v York
11/08/45	Belle Vue	Johnson v Parker
18/08/45	Belle Vue	Supporters Trophy
22/08/45	Belle Vue	Norman Parker Cup
25/08/45	Belle Vue	Stars Riders CH Q R
01/09/45	Belle Vue	Lancs v Yorks
08/09/45	Belle Vue	British Champ Final
15/09/45	Belle Vue	England v Overseas
22/09/45	Belle Vue	Star Riders Champ
29/09/45	Belle Vue	International TR Q R
06/10/45	Belle Vue	Grand National
13/10/45	Belle Vue	International TR FIN
20/10/45	Belle Vue	Golden Helmet
23/06/45	Bradford Odsal	A J Elvin Cup
30/06/45	Bradford Odsal	Newcastle
07/07/45	Bradford Odsal	West Ham
14/07/45	Bradford Odsal	North v South
18/07/45	Bradford Odsal	Eric Langton Cup
21/07/45	Bradford Odsal	Best Pairs
28/07/45	Bradford Odsal	Newcastle
04/08/45	Bradford Odsal	The Rest
06/08/45	Bradford Odsal	Empire Champ
11/08/45	Bradford Odsal	Glasgow
18/08/45	Bradford Odsal	Best Pairs
25/08/45	Bradford Odsal	North v South
29/08/45	Bradford Odsal	Wembley+Harringay
01/09/45	Bradford Odsal	England v Australia
05/09/45	Bradford Odsal	Inter Invit Race
05/07/45	Exeter Alphington	Individual
12/07/45	Exeter Alphington	Best Pairs
19/07/45	Exeter Alphington	England v Dominions
26/07/45	Exeter Alphington	Devon v Rest
02/08/45	Exeter Alphington	England v Dominions
09/08/45	Exeter Alphington	North v South
16/08/45	Exeter Alphington	Southern Championship
21/05/45	Exeter Exwick Field	Individual
15/08/45	Glasgow White City	London Select
22/08/45	Glasgow White City	Scotland v England
29/08/45	Glasgow White City	Newcastle
05/09/45	Glasgow White City	North London
12/09/45	Glasgow White City	Best Pairs
19/09/45	Glasgow White City	The Rest
26/09/45	Glasgow White City	RJ Sel v BK Sel
03/10/45	Glasgow White City	The Midlands
10/10/45	Glasgow White City	RJ Sel v BK Sel
17/10/45	Glasgow White City	Scottish Championship
30/09/45	Holbeach Bell End	Eastern Counties Ch

	VENUE	EVENT
29/09/45	Middlesbrough	Victory Cup
02/10/45	Middlesbrough	
09/10/45	Middlesbrough	
16/10/45	Middlesbrough	Golden Gauntlet
02/04/45	Newcastle	West Ham
21/05/45	Newcastle	British Champ
28/05/45	Newcastle	North v South
04/06/45	Newcastle	London
11/06/45	Newcastle	West Ham
18/06/45	Newcastle	Best Pairs
25/06/45	Newcastle	Bradford Odsal
02/07/45	Newcastle	Kitchen v Hart
09/07/45	Newcastle	North v London
16/07/45	Newcastle	Best Pairs
23/07/45	Newcastle	Bradford Odsal
30/07/45	Newcastle	
06/08/45	Newcastle	Norwich
07/08/45	Newcastle	Norwich
13/08/45	Newcastle	The Rest
20/08/45	Newcastle	British Champ
27/08/45	Newcastle	Other Tracks
03/09/45	Newcastle	Western Counties
10/09/45	Newcastle	Glasgow
17/09/45	Newcastle	The Best
24/09/45	Newcastle	Gala Cup Charity
01/10/45	Newcastle	Johnson v Kitchen
08/10/45	Newcastle	Best Pairs
15/10/45	Newcastle	Kitchen v Johnson
22/10/45	Newcastle	Match Race Night
29/10/45	Newcastle	Probable v Possible
27/06/45	New Cross	Victory Cup
04/07/45	New Cross	B Vue v Harringay+Rest
11/07/45	New Cross	Best Pairs
18/07/45	New Cross	London Riders CH
25/07/45	New Cross	Chitty v Johnson
13/09/45	Sheffield	Bluey Wilkinson Cup
20/09/45	Sheffield	Yorks v Lancs
	Sheffield	
	Norwich	
05/08/45	Rye House	V E Reunion Trophy
06/08/45	Rye House	
12/08/45	Rye House	
19/08/45	Rye House	
26/08/45	Rye House	
02/09/45	Rye House	
09/09/45	Rye House	

	VENUE	EVENT
16/09/45	Rye House	
23/09/45	Rye House	
30/09/45	Rye House	

1945 Fixtures List courtesy of Barry Stephenson.

Britain, post war was an austere place. Recovering from the ravages of war damage, continuing shortages and with rationing still in operation many ordinary people relied on 'Government Surplus' supplies for their everyday needs.

As can be seen from the adverts that appeared in the Speedway press of the time, many speedway fans were forced to purchase ex-forces supplied goods for their clothes. RAF trousers at 30/- (1.50p), Navy shirts at two for 14/6 (70p) and two panels of British nylon parachute material at 19/6 (90p) quoted as "Ideal for making undies, blouses, nighties, pyjamas and children's wear" demonstrates the shortages of new as the countries manufacturing industries struggled to get on it's feet!

To put prices into perspective admission to Harringay for a National League match at the time was 2/- (10p) 4/- (20p) with the best seat in the house costing 7/- (35p).The average weekly wage was between £4 - £5!

The Army Game

As war clouds gathered in April 1939, Prime Minister Neville Chamberlain was still hopeful of negotiating peace with Hitler, knowing that 645,000 men and women were already in uniform. By introducing limited conscription for 20-21 year olds as the militia, these men were allowed to state their preferred Army, Royal Navy , RAF postings and with the recall of reservists and supplementary reserves, by the out break of war (September 3), the British Army numbered approximately 1,065,000. On September 6, just 72 hours after war had been declared, the National Service (Armed Forces) Act was passed merging all forces into one entity, making all physically fit men between 18 and 41 years liable for military service. At its peak some 5,000,000 men wore the khaki colours of the British Army. A detailed overview of the organisation and workings of the British Army would require more pages than this book allows. However to put into some context the motorcycling and engineering links which attracted pre-war speedway stars to the Army and also developed a new generation of post - war riders, a brief synopsis of the key Corps and their military roles will help the reader.

ROYAL ELECTRICAL MECHANICAL ENGINEERS (R.E.M.E)

Until 1942 all inspection, repair and maintenance of technical equipment was the responsibility of the Royal Army Ordnance Corps. A Cabinet committee under the chairmanship of Sir William Beveridge was set up in 1941 and recommended that the repair services should be rationalised under R.E.M.E. The system and process for equipment was re-organised so that repairs could be carried out as far forward in the battle zone as was practicable. The Advance Base workshop concept was to be tested very shortly after the Corps was founded in the Battle of Alamein, with R.E.M.E becoming the largest technical Corps, extending its activities to include the manufacture of spare parts and maintenance of special equipment to a large scale. All R.A.O.C units with a workshop role were transferred to R.E.M.E as were Royal Army Service Corps Heavy Repair workshops with a ratio of one mechanic to every 100 vehicles. Skilled technicians had to have a range of experience to maintain equipment such as static engines, armament and fire control systems, radio and telecommunication, sound ranging and X-ray equipment as well as the conventional two, four wheeled and tracked motorised vehicles.

In addition to uniformed tradesman, the Corps was to employ thousands of civilians of many differing nationalities in its static workshops throughout the world. As the war progressed and reached a conclusion, the R.E.M.E workshops were to play a fundamental role in the building and development of racing machinery, track equipment and their officers provided the encouragement to form speedway teams.

ROYAL ARMY ORDNANCE CORPS (R.A.O.C)

The history of the RAOC stretches back to the 15th century and in WWII it was responsible for the procurement of all ordnance stores. A key role was the continuity of supplies via Ordnance stores, the aim being to keep supplies flowing freely from rear to front line so as to ensure stocks at all times in forward positions. Supplies included armaments (including RAF bombs), unit transport, radios and clothing amongst a vast range of goods required on the battlefield. In addition it was responsible for laundries across many war theatres as well as protection of its own installations. Some 130,000 troops and 8,000 officers ensured that the front line soldier was well provisioned.

ROYAL CORPS OF SIGNALS (R.C.S)

The Signals Corps was born in the Royal Engineers Signals service in 1920 and was responsible for Army communications including radio, wire, teleprinter and telegraph. The Royal Signals were also responsible for wire communications to RAF units allocated to the Army and the Air Formation Signals Regiment were to play a leading role in the birth of forces speedway in Egypt with their tracks at Maadi and later El Ballah. Despatch riders (DRs) who played a key role in communications in the early days of WWII operated the Forces Letter Service and it is rumoured that DRs were on occasions used as scouts on bogus message runs to establish a safe passage through particularly dangerous warzones! Although gradually replaced in part by jeeps, the solo motorcycle despatch rider was to provide a fast moving, flexible service unmatched by the four wheeled version.

The famous White Helmets motorcycle display team was formed in the late 1920s appearing for the first time at the Royal Tournament in1931. After WWII the team reformed at Catterick with 21 machines supplied by Triumph. At its height the Royal Corps Signals had 150,000 in their colours, with women forming 10% of the total being involved in Signals and Cypher offices.

ROYAL ARMY SERVICE CORPS (R.A.S.C)

The roots of the RASC reside in the supply of transport service dating back to 1794. In 1939 when the British Expeditionary Force went to France, this was the first time the RASC had taken to the field of conflict as a mechanised corps. The corps was responsible for the storage and issue of supplies and for the administration of barracks and HQs. Their service basically supplied the daily needs of the Army including food, hospital supplies and fuel for heating and cooking. In addition they had on their strength a range of civilian tradesman including butchers, bakers and clerks with drivers, storekeepers and mechanical transport specialists supporting the transport branch. The Mechanical Transport (MT) storage operation included all materials not supplied by R.E.M.E and gave access to motorcycles which made the RASC stores a popular haunt for any Regiment trying to form a speedway team and looking for bikes and clothing.

CORPS OF MILITARY POLICE (CMP)

At the outbreak of war some 3,500 'Red Caps' were deployed in areas of combat. On the battlefield their role was initially sign routeing and traffic control, when not performing more conventional policing tasks. Most were Lance Corporals mounted on solo motorcycles and a typical role was demonstrated in the Western desert at El Alamein where there was so much traffic in convoy trying to move forward that the CMP were tasked with creating six new tracks to relieve the pressure on the main coast road. Similarly in Normandy the CMP were responsible for the beach control and assembly areas. When Germany surrendered, some 7.7 million prisoners were held by the Western Allies with a further 3.7 million displaced persons presenting an enormous challenge for the authorities with the CMP on the front line when it came to keeping law and order. Although there is no record of the CMP entering their own team in speedway events from the earliest days 'Red Cap' riders used their motorcycling skills on warzone speedways as individuals.

THE LOCAL DEFENCE VOLUNTEERS (HOME GUARD)

The Home Guard probably conjures up images of the iconic television programme 'Dad's Army' rather than an organisation that activley promoted motorcycling to it's members.

Formed on May 14 1940 following an appeal by Anthony Eden for volunteers to join the Local Defence Volunteers (LDV), some 750,000 men between the age of 40-65 years old joined in the first month. The LDV, renamed the Home Guard by Winston Churchill, was a home based Army designed to delay an enemy invasion so enabling regular soldiers to establish a 'front line'. Remarkably the Guard members never fell below 1 million until the organisation was stood down in December 1944.

Most units had a despatch rider attached to it and a Specialist Training for Home Guard Despatch Riders manual was published by the *Motor Cycling* magazine for the princley sum of 1/3p. This formal structured training for motorcycling developed interest within the ranks throughout the war and when in 1944, the 'Holiday at Home' series of grass speedway meetings were announced, Guard members enthused by their last four years riding experience began to compete.

One of the most memorable of this series of war time meetings was at Westwood Heath, Coventry in September 1944 where Bugler Sgt Major Twineham of the Coventry branch of the Home Guard heralded riders into the arena for what the Coventry club described as 'The largest grass track meeting ever' with 'The finest entry of any grass speedway meeting ever promoted in Great Britain'. Some claim indeed, but looking at the entry field which included: Eric Chitty (West Ham), Fred Tuck (Belle Vue), Ron Clarke (New Cross), Reg Lambourne, Vic Worlock, Alex Gray, Louis Lawson, and Jack Parker (Harringay), the claim did have some credence.
Post war the Home Guard began promoting their own meetings, the Hawks in Cheltenham and the XT Tigers in Poole being the most prominent of organising clubs.

ARMY RANKS

As the warzone speedway story unfolds, rank will feature, especially in the rider index. A soldiers 'status' was of little significance on the track, his riding skill being the only measure that mattered. The Bar-None MCC in Egypt went one step further by becoming a no rank sensitive club, hence the concept of "no one barred" from competing whatever their rank or social standing. To illustrate the relationships between the ranks, below is listed in hierarchal order in the British Army, Private being entry level with Field Marshal the most senior officer.

Field Marshal
General
Lieutenant General
Major-General
Brigadier
Lieutenant Colonel
Major
Captain
Lieutenant
Second Lieutenant
Sergeant Major
Staff Sergeant
Sergeant
Corporal
Lance Corporal
Private

NATIONAL SERVICE

Throughout WWII all British men aged between 18ys and 41yrs were registered for National service. Post-war, conscription was extended to peace time. The plan was to prepare for any future conflicts and to provide protection as required to the Commonwealth. The 1948 National Service Act was introduced requiring all 18 year olds to serve 18 months in one of the armed forces followed by four years in the reserves. By 1950 with the Korean war erupting, the period of

National Service was extended to two years. Many young riders in the 1950s were required to 'join up' whilst trying to develop their speedway careers. Peter Craven (Army), Arthur Forrest (RAF) were just two of many who relied on co-operative commanding officers and 24 hour leave passes to complete far flung away team matches. Dennis Gray, when riding for Oxford, experienced some help from above whilst in the RAF. A far flung posting was overcome by being flown as near to Oxford as possible every Thursday to ride for the 'Cheetahs'. It is believed that promoter Les Calcutt, a member of the Chamber of Commerce approached the Oxford MP Quintin Hogg, later to become Lord Hailsham, who made the required phone call to ensure Gray was able to ride each week for the Oxford club.

'Call Up' ended on December 31 1960 in Britain, although Scandinavian riders had to contend with combining riding in the British leagues throughout the 70s & 80s whilst serving their compulsory service in uniform back home during the winter close season.

To accurately quantify the death toll of servicemen/women and civilians during WWII is impossible. Fifty million people is a conservative estimate. Millions of civilians were killed, with many of their names never being recorded, whilst many Army, Royal Navy and RAF personnel were recorded as 'lost in action' or 'missing'. The chart below whilst not definitive, illustrates the cost in human terms of a war which decimated a whole generation.

WAR LOSSES

Soviet Union	25,000,000	United States	300,000
France	420,000	Great Britain	305,000
China	13,500,000	Poland	6,600,000
Netherlands	250,000	Australia	34,000
Germany	5,250,000	Japan	2,600,000
Hungary	750,000	New Zealand	12,000

In The Beginning

Identifying the birthplace of warzone speedway does rather depend on your definition. At least two contenders can lay claim to the honour of being first to organise motorcycle 'speedway' racing to occupy fighting troops, at the same time as providing a training programme for despatch riders and motorcycle orderlies.

If you consider the formation of a structured motorcycle club which staged trials, timed hill climbs, and eventually sand track trials on oval race tracks, then the Bar-None M.C.C (Egypt) has a strong case. If on the other hand the first competitive meeting is your criteria, then Trani on the South East coast of Italy would get your vote!

Alan Johnson

Egypt in April 1944 was where Corporal Alan Johnson and Sgt Geoff Steer started organising motorcycle events for fellow despatch riders. Encouraged by their 'top brass', an inaugural get together was held in Kars-el-Nil barracks, where the Bar-None club (open to all ranks) was formed. A range of trials, hill climbs and eventually on September 23 1945, a sand track trial (speedway) meeting was staged at Almaza. At this event sixty riders from across the Middle East competed over fifty, three lap races in an individual meeting formula on a KO basis.

Arthur Simcock

The case for Italy is based on a meeting staged on October 29 1944 by Major A E Simcock who went onto to become the Australian team manager and British representative for Australia on the Speedway Control Board. With the assistance of Corporal Harry Whitfield (RAF) the prewar Wembley rider and S.Sgt 'Nobby' Stock, who rode for Harringay post-war, the Major staged racing on a specially constructed 440 yard track close to a hospital where injured soldiers were recuperating and speedway was considered suitable entertainment to keep up morale.

Before making your mind up, records do show that in the winter of 1928, RAF personnel from Heliopolis near Cairo (Egypt) took part in racing at Zamalek. This was the track built by pioneer riders Billy Galloway and Ivor Creek in conjunction with the Egyptian Greyhound Racing Association. Whether the area was in fact a warzone is open for discussion but the fact that British armed forces competed does in my view put this location in the frame as a contender. However....a fascinating story of 'sand racing' at an even more famous venue which would pre-date even Trani has been unearthed. In June 1940 on the beaches of Dunkirk, the British Expeditionary Forces were waiting to be evacuated back home to Britain following the fall of France. The flotilla of small ships was queuing up to lift troops off the beach as the Germans advanced. A more unlikely location for 'racing' it is difficult to imagine. The BBC WWII people's war recounts a remarkable story on its web site. A veteran recalls "Come the dawn and the only sign of shipping we could see was a distant destroyer hovering about outside the harbour entrance. Odd groups of troops started wandering about the beach searching for food or amusement. One or two despatch riders had got hold of a couple of motor bikes and enjoyed some sand racing until our Luftwaffe friends put a stop to that". Sand racing on motorcycles seems an odd way of spending what could have been the last few hour of your life. The provenance of this story, which took place over 67 years ago, is difficult to confirm, but it could just have been the seed which grew into competitive racing within the forces some four years later.

On balance my vote as to the birthplace of forces speedway goes to the Italian Trani track which opened in October 1944. Interestingly when Bari, another Italian coastal track opened in 1945, they proudly announced on its match programme cover **"In 54 area C.M.F, the birthplace of Army speedway"**

WAR DEPARTMENT TESTED FUTURE SPEEDWAY MACHINES

Military planners in the intervening war years (1918-39) had reached the conclusion, following experiences in WW1, that a move towards more mechanised transport and away from horse drawn modes of transport was inevitable in future conflicts. To this end in 1926 the Mechanical Warfare Experimental Establishment (M.W.E.E) was formed at Cove, nr Farnborough in Hampshire. MWEE's role was to assess and test for War Department suitability, a wide range of motor vehicles, including motor cycles. The need for speed, reliability, and flexibility in a range of motor cycle activities including despatch work, reconnaissance, convoy control, military police work and even small arms firing roles was to challenge the British motor cycle industry to provide the goods. Models were submitted for examination which included a 10,000 mile road test in both on and off road conditions, a quarter mile standing start sprint, a miles per gallon test as well as a full engine strip down to assess wear and tear.

The WD invited many British manufacturers to submit machines for test, looking particularly at size, weight, (under 300lbs was preferred), and ease of maintenance often in difficult war conditions. M.W.E.E which became M.E.E (Mechanical Experimental Establishment) in 1934 enlisted the help of selected Army units including the Royal Corps of Signals, and by the mid 30s Barnett, BSA, AJS, New Hudson, Matchless and Douglas were felt suitable up to 350ccc engine capacity. Triumph was added as a late addition, but many modified civilian road machines struggled to meet the exacting criteria. As Hitler prepared Nazi Germany for war, Ariel, BSA, Matchless, New Imperial, Norton Royal Enfield and Triumph emerged as front runners for war time duty with BSA, Triumph, Matchless and Norton eventually being selected as prime WD suppliers after some further improvements and modifications. The extensive range of solo machines used by the WD in WWII was also influenced by two separate initiatives. As early as the summer of 1939, the Army 'impressed' machines of various marques from High street showrooms across the country. This was followed, post the Dunkirk evacuation, by a government appeal to all motor cyclists to sell their machines to the armed forces to make up the short fall of equipment left on the beaches of France. When war broke, Britain was ill prepared for a full military offensive. The majority of motor cycles were still modified civilian models with the addition of extra tool boxes, a set of canvass panniers and the removal of rubber fittings and chromium plating being replaced by the utility Army khaki or olive green livery. These machines were delivered in their thousands and by 1944 were to become the raw material for the 'speedway' machines constructed from WD dumps of machines classified as BER, Beyond Economic Repair!

Lt.Col Vernon Brooke

The M.W.E.E organisation, not surprisingly, attracted some very able engineers from the motor cycle world. One such engineer was Lt Col Vernon Brooke CEng M.I.M.E. A.M.I.E.E who reached a very senior position in the organisation and had pre-war served the sport of motor cycling as a competitor and an administrator within the Auto Cycle Union. He was in fact the ACU representative at the first ever 'speedway' meeting held in Britain in February 1928. His task at that memorable meeting was to ensure that the meeting was run in accordance with ACU competition rules .The speedway rule book had not at that time even been written.The Lieutenant Colonel was actively involved in speedway from that 1928 date until 1962 after being appointed the Speedway Control Board Chairman!

The selection of BSA, Matchless, Norton and Triumph motor cycles as the main stay of the British Army two wheeled transport was to prove very significant as warzone speedway emerged in late 1944. Seasoned despatch riders I have spoken to always rated the Matchless with its power to weight ratio, girder forks and over all ease of riding as their favourite machine. Such however was the popularity of the Matchless G3 and G3L that many officers acquired them for their use leaving the heavier models for the Army's "professional motor cyclists".A later chapter is devoted to the variations, modifications and speciality of the machines raced on the army speedways.As a base line of understanding a brief overview of the standard issue WD models will put into perspective the ingenuity, imagination and engineering skills of the workshops who constructed the armed forces speedway bikes.

BSA M20

When war came the BSA factory in Birmingham shelved all motorcycle manufacturing apart from the M20 which allowed the company to divert the majority of its production capacity to military needs. The company went back to its manufacturing roots as British Small Arms making Sten, Browning, and Hisapano machine guns, ten million shell fuses, 750,000 anti aircraft shells and folding bicycles for paratroops.The factory suffered attack by German bombers and some 1,600 machine tools and much of the factory was destroyed in the early 40s.The M20 model was a stalwart machine for the despatch rider although its weight and lack of manoeuvrability had it's critics amongst the DR men.The M20 was in service with military forces until 1967, so taking the record for the longest serving bike in British military history.

Machine specification: 496cc, 13bhp, 392lbs, 55mph max speed

MATCHLESS G3/G3L

Associated Motorcycles, the manufacturer of the Matchless were delighted when the WD placed orders for as many model G3 (with girder forks) as the factory could produce. Even better news was to follow in 1941 when Matchless introduced unique teledraulic front suspension on the G3L model. Although not totally new, BMW and Norton had experimented previously, the Matchless forks design had particular benefits. Other manufacturers quickly followed the Matchless innovation, but the G3L forks proved highly suitable for a speedway machine and often they were rescued to be fitted on to a 'Bitsa' machine. As the demand to conserve aluminium alloy for aircraft production increased AMC experimented with the use of iron for gearbox and crankcases castings. Further experimentation saw a G3L produced with folding parts so that it could be packed into a parachute drop container, whilst fold away steel skis were added for models which were despatched to the Red Army for use in Arctic conditions.

Machine specification: 347cc, 16bhp, 330lbs, 65mph max speed.

NORTON 16H

The Norton factory had the production capacity to supply the WD with as many of the 16H model as they required. It was however a machine not really suitable for off road work and was difficult to handle. Although they gave solid service in a variety of war theatres and conditions such as the African desert as well as colder climates, they were not really suitable or sand trials 'speedway'. There were however some interesting combinations of Matchless bottom ends welded to Norton 16H heads to develop extra horsepower and engine torque.

Machine specification: 490cc, 12.5bhp, 389lbs, 60mph max speed.

TRIUMPH 3HW

The WD purchased the entire Triumph works stock of completed machine in late 1939, and the 350cc model was planned to eventually become the preferred choice for the Army. The original WD plan was to request a single military motor cycle model to be assembled at any available factory. The logic was this would make spare parts less of a problem than say four models and provide total compatibility. Triumph were weeks away from meeting the WD demand when the

Coventry factory was bombed in November 1940 and the idea had to be abandoned. By 1942 a new factory at Meriden had been constructed producing the 3SW and 3HW models. The Triumph models did appear on the warzone speedways, although not in great numbers due to the better performance of the Matchless machines.

Machine specification: 343cc, 17bhp, 375lbs, 65mph max speed.

EXCELSIOR WELBIKE

One of the most unusual of forces 'speedway bikes' that emerged from War Department issued motor cycles has to be the 98cc Welbike. This small machine was developed for the British Airborne Forces who needed a disposable, light and inexpensive to manufacture machine which could be parachuted in alongside airborne troops. Conceived in a military research establishment at Welwyn in Hertfordshire (hence the 'Wel' bike name), the small engine was not suitable for racing, but early post-war, several forces teams used them when modified, as bikes for their team mascots (usually the son of a serving soldier or airmen). The picture above, taken circa 1950, shows the mascot for the RAF 'Eagles' based at Kabrit in Egypt, aboard a modified Welbike. After the war the bikes, which were not road legal in Britain, were either destroyed or sent abroad. The

RAF Kabrit speedway team mascot on Welbike

bike eventually became the 'Corgi'and were common sights at RAF stations and Army bases as a simple and quick away of getting around.

Machine specification; 98cc, 2bhp (est), 70lbs, 30mph max speed.

The Warzone Speedways

WARZONE-TIMELINE

To provide the reader with an accurate timeline of 'warzone' speedways is as said before tinged with risk. What actually constitutes a warzone? How can a desert track, marked out and constructed by squaddies be compared with the more conventional stadium tracks of Hanover (Hanomag), Fayid (Olympia) and Naples (Vomero)? Before attempting a chronological timeline, perhaps a list of criteria for any track being included as a warzone speedway track would prove useful.

For the purpose of inclusion in the charts, the criteria which has been applied is one of a country, continent, area or region which staged speedway whilst some form of military activity was taking place:

1. An area where British forces were undertaking a 'policing' role eg. Ireland and parts of the Middle East.

2. The period of WWII where across the world British forces were in combat as part of the six years of hostilities.

3. British forces involved in a reconstruction role, post WWII, eg. BAOR Germany.

4. Non British riders competing in areas of civil war, eg. Hungary.

5. Areas which were occupied by British forces as part of that countries transfer to Independent country status, eg. Palestine.

6 Countries where insurgents, terrorists or guerrillas were threatening areas of strategic importance (Malaya) or which had political disputes with the UK eg. Rhodesia.

7. In the modern era, where speedway promotions were staged in the volatile Middle East (Egypt, U.A.E and in particular Kuwait) where the first Gulf war was to start in 1991.

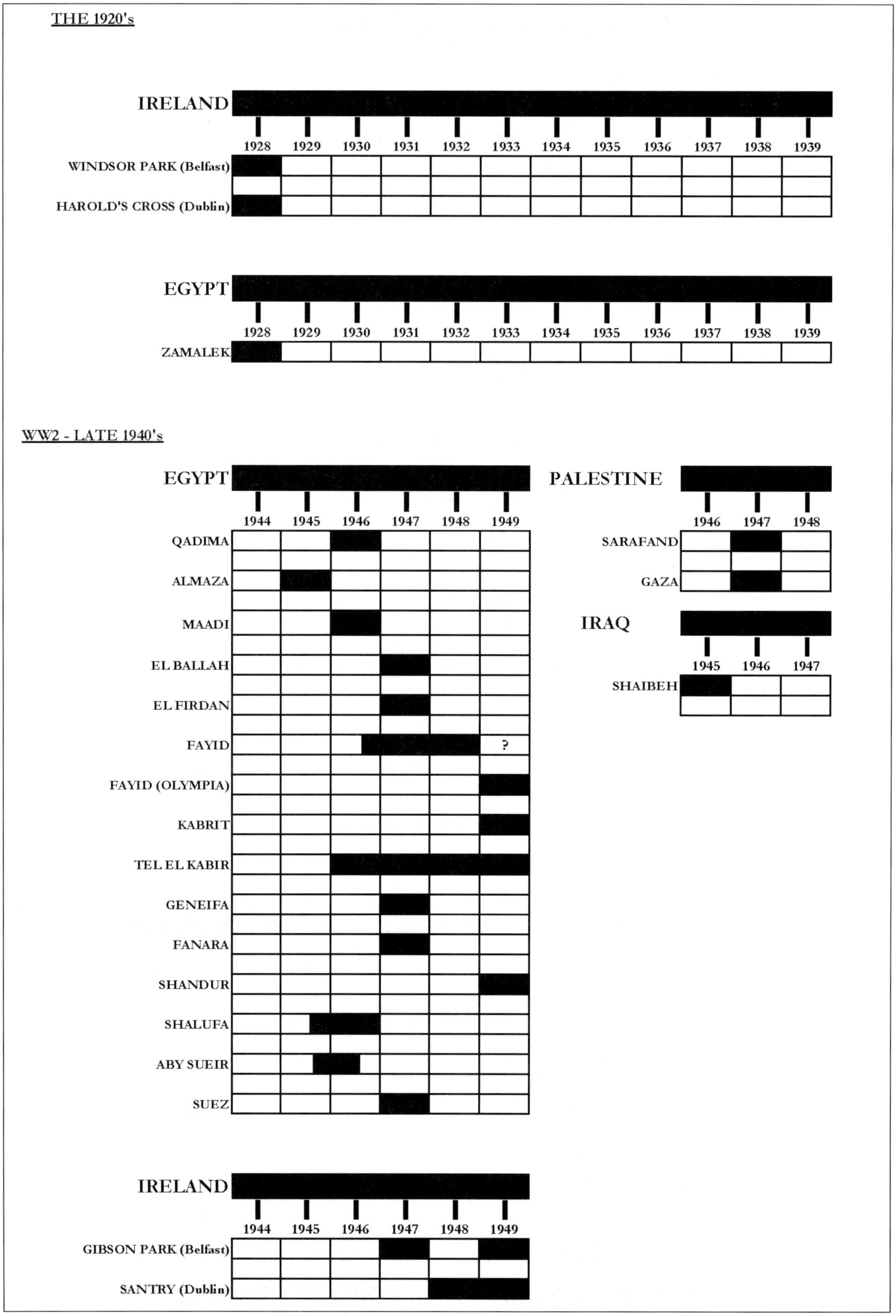
THE 1920's
IRELAND
1928 1929 1930 1931 1932 1933 1934 1935 1936 1937 1938 1939
WINDSOR PARK (Belfast)
HAROLD'S CROSS (Dublin)
EGYPT
1928 1929 1930 1931 1932 1933 1934 1935 1936 1937 1938 1939
ZAMALEK
WW2 - LATE 1940's
EGYPT
1944 1945 1946 1947 1948 1949
QADIMA
ALMAZA
MAADI
EL BALLAH
EL FIRDAN
FAYID
?
FAYID (OLYMPIA)
KABRIT
TEL EL KABIR
GENEIFA
FANARA
SHANDUR
SHALUFA
ABY SUEIR
SUEZ
PALESTINE
1946 1947 1948
SARAFAND
GAZA
IRAQ
1945 1946 1947
SHAIBEH
IRELAND
1944 1945 1946 1947 1948 1949
GIBSON PARK (Belfast)
SANTRY (Dublin)

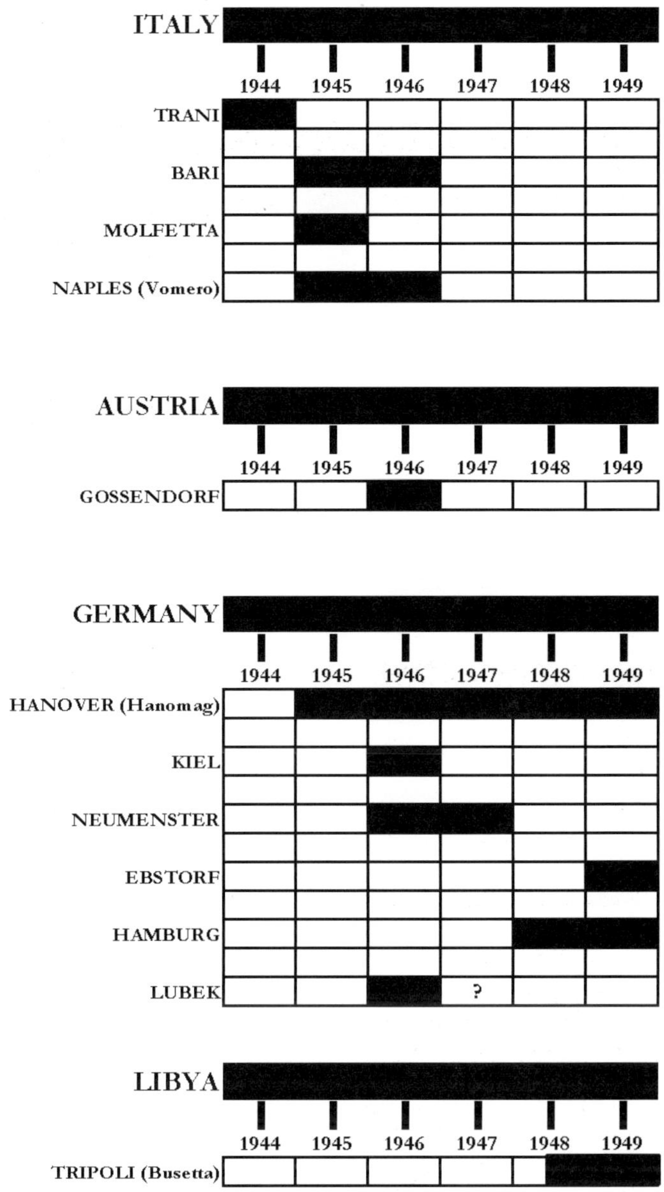
ITALY
1944
1945
1946
1947
1948
1949
TRANI
BARI
MOLFETTA
NAPLES (Vomero)
AUSTRIA
GOSSENDORF
GERMANY
HANOVER (Hanomag)
KIEL
NEUMENSTER
EBSTORF
HAMBURG
LUBEK
?
LIBYA
TRIPOLI (Busetta)

THE 1950's

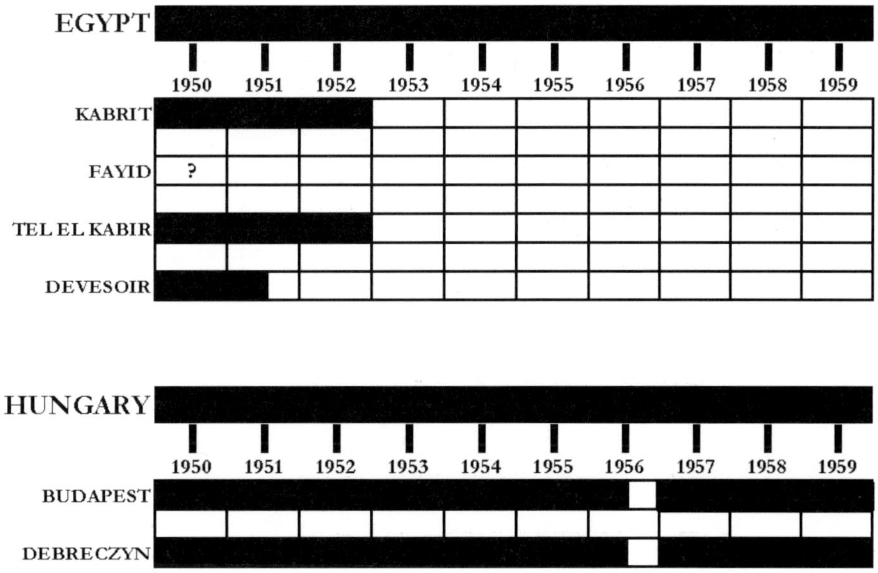
EGYPT
1950
1951
1952
1953
1954
1955
1956
1957
1958
1959
KABRIT
FAYID
?
TEL EL KABIR
DEVESOIR
HUNGARY
BUDAPEST
DEBRECZYN

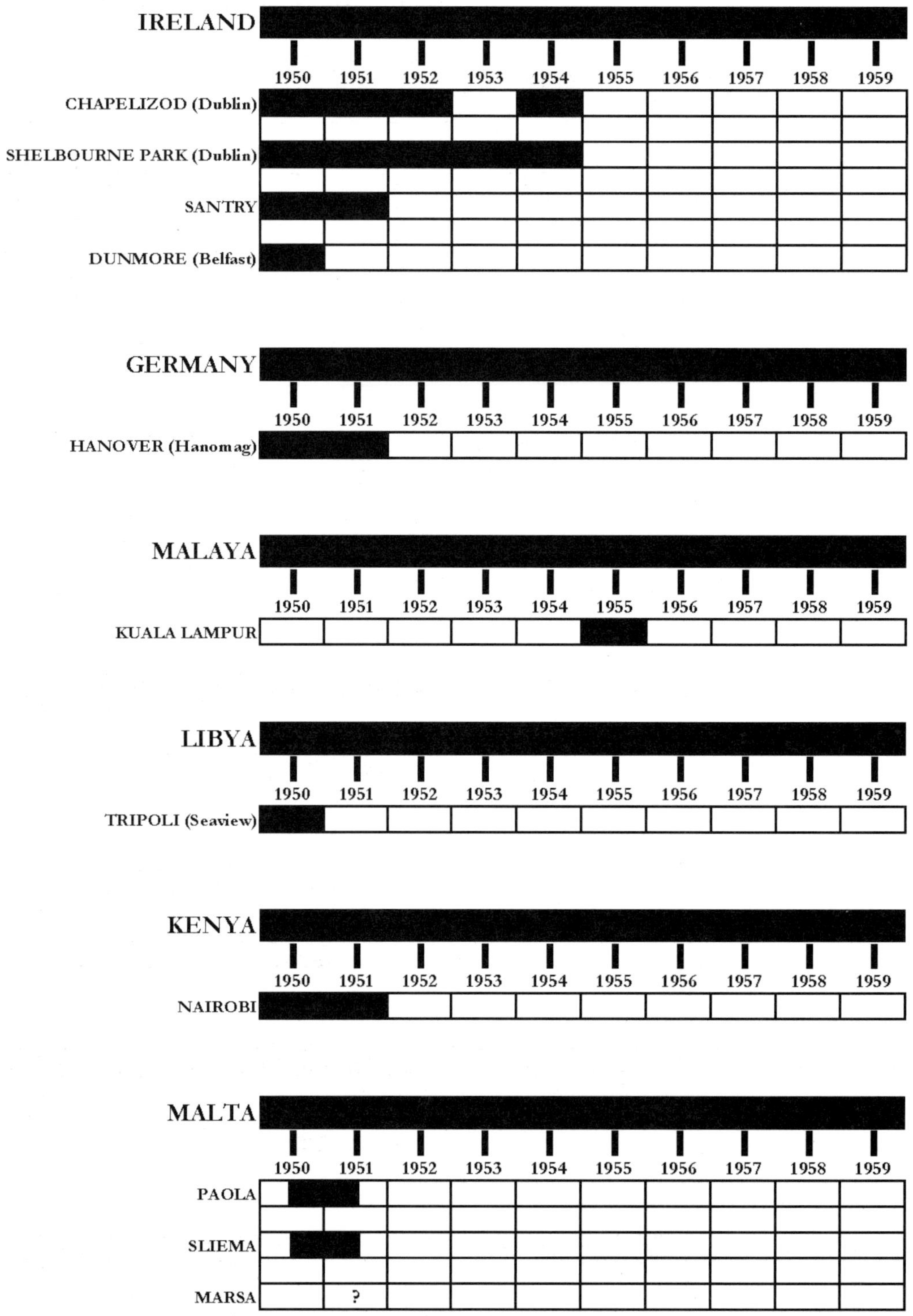
IRELAND
1950
1951
1952
1953
1954
1955
1956
1957
1958
1959
CHAPELIZOD (Dublin)
SHELBOURNE PARK (Dublin)
SANTRY
DUNMORE (Belfast)
GERMANY
HANOVER (Hanomag)
MALAYA
KUALA LAMPUR
LIBYA
TRIPOLI (Seaview)
KENYA
NAIROBI
MALTA
PAOLA
SLIEMA
MARSA
?

THE 1960's - 1990's

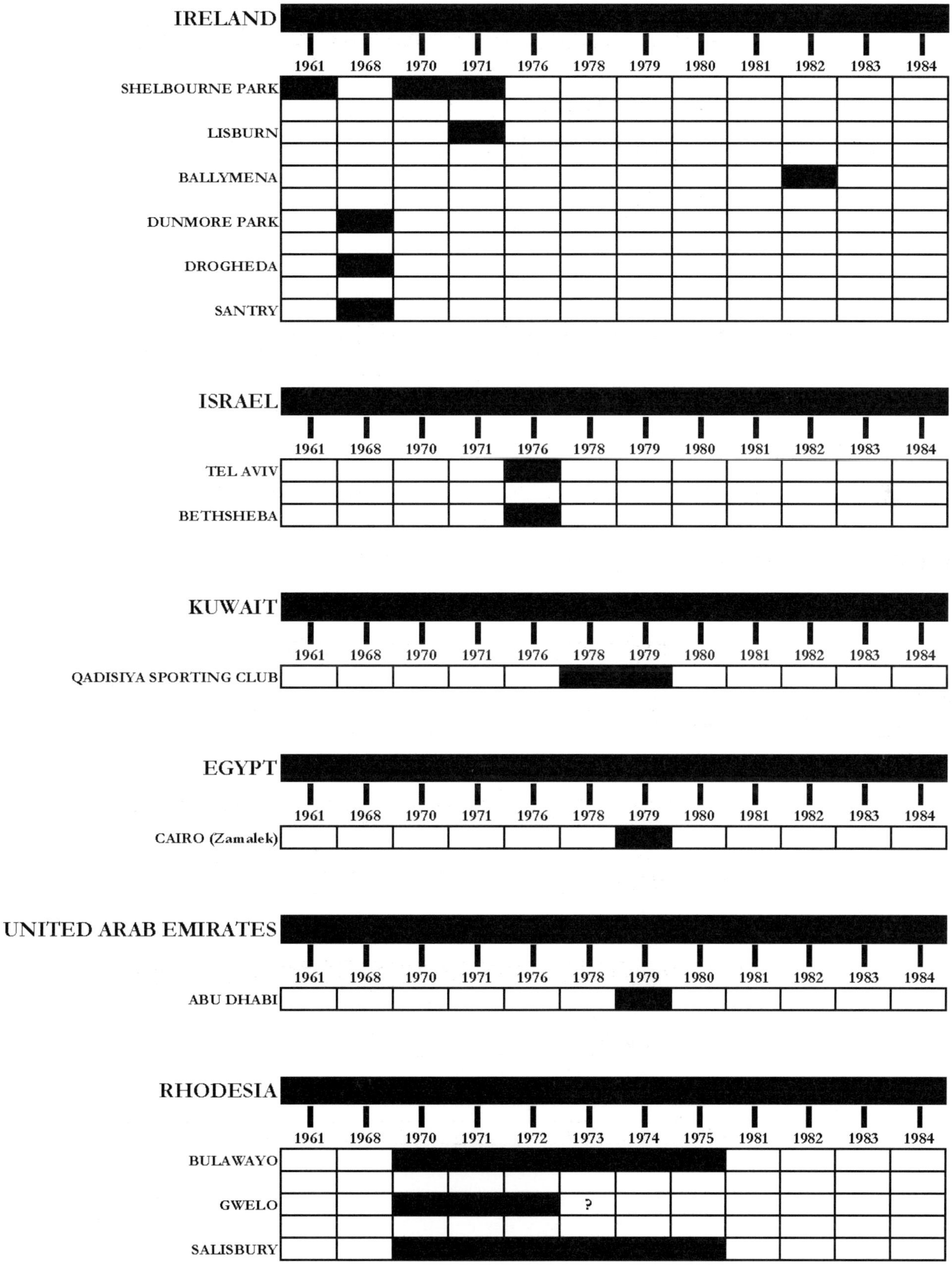

ITALY

The Italians, under the command of Benito Mussolini entered the war in June 1940 as Allies of the Germans. Italy's strategic position in the Mediterranean made the supply chain very difficult for the Western Allies.The Italian's presence in Libya and the Desert campaign was magnificently overcome by the British Army's of Wavell and eventually Montgomery who, with initially fewer men and even less equipment, out fought Mussolini's forces.The entry into WWII of the United States assisted the Allies push into Sicily and eventually Italy itself.As the war began going badly for the Italians, the Fascist Grand Commission restored King Victor Emmanuel to power, forcing Mussolini to resign. He was killed and duly hung and displayed in the streets of Milan. Italy then attempted to join the Allies against the Nazis in return for some post-war influence.The Americans entered Rome and it was declared an "open city" on June 4 1944 and whilst Germany held Northern Italy for another six months, Hitler retreated to try to defend his positions in France.

IN THE ZONE

With the Germans forces barely out of Southern Italy and with pockets of fighting in the North, it is staggering that on October 29 1944 a forces speedway event took place in South East Italy. Sergeant Peter Nuzum's account of events follows later in this chapter, suffice to say that Arthur Simcock, Harry Whitfield and 'Nobby' Stock all with pre-war links with professional speedway, built a track at Trani and staged racing against all the odds in what must rank alongside the historic events at High Beech in February 1928 when the sport was officially born in Britain. Freddie Smith won this opening Trani meeting and records show that a four team league consisting of teams representing Trani, Molfetta, Bisceglie and Bari was run on the Trani circuit in early 1945.

Racing at Molfetta 1945

Bari (San Spirito) transit camp, adjacent to the RAF Bari Airfield which serviced the whole of the Mediterranean, joined Trani in July 1945 as a speedway venue.A further 385 yard track at Molfetta opened in September, their team being pronounced league champions that year. Probably the most 'professional' speedway of this period was Vomero in Naples on the West coast which was a football stadium which housed an athletic track which formed the base on which the squaddies built their track.'Split' Waterman was to cut his speedway teeth on the Naples circuit which Geoff Bennett recalls was one of the roughest tracks he ever rode.The surface consisted of lava from the Mount Vesuvius volcano and was hardly ideal for broad-siding.Vomero was the venue for several Naples v Bari local derbies as the West v Eastern Italy 'bragging rights' were fought over in matches as fierce as any professional league match.

TRACK INDEX: Trani, Bari, Molfetta, Naples

FORCES SPEEDWAY IS BORN

By Sgt Peter Nuzum

Sadly very few veterans who experienced what was the birth of forces speedway now survive. Even less would have more detailed knowledge of those memorable days than Peter Nuzum from Devon who acted as speedway secretary for the 56 Area organising club. Some years ago Peter documented his Italian story in the Exeter Fanfare magazine. Peter kindly agreed to its reproduction.

"How long before age release group 28c are given tickets to board the weekly repatriation train for it five day crawl across a devastated Europe and home, to resume a civilised life again? This was the thought constantly in my mind as I went about my business at the Engineers store depot at Bari, South East Italy".

"One Sunday we had a delivery to make at the Convalescent hospital at Trani 20 miles up the coast and I decided to go along for the ride. After lunch, while waiting for the truck to start its journey back to Bari and hearing a strangely familiar sound, I went across to the sports field and discovered a bloke attempting to slide a heavy despatch riders bike around the cinder running track watched by a small group to whom I immediately attached myself. The rider was Sgt 'Nobby' Stock, pre-war with Hackney Wolves. Amongst the group watching was his Commanding officer Major A.E Simcock the Wembley clerk of the course accompanied by the top brass from the hospital. A rapid result of that meeting was the formation of a committee given the daunting but exciting task of organising speedway racing as entertainment for the wounded soldiers in the hospital. Most of the people on high were hostile to us and our crazy scheme, but like speedway folk everywhere we refused to be put down. Our enthusiasm and the interest we aroused was so terrific that we even amazed ourselves by staging the first ever services speedway meeting just six weeks later on a sunny Sunday afternoon (October 29 1944). I won't bore you with all the details, but you may well ask for instance, where did the machines come from?

A first bend faller at Trani Speedway

We obtained permission to visit the REME depot at Molfetta where there was literally a dump of despatch rider machines which had arrived from the UK minus parts which were supposed to be attended to when someone got around to it. After three hours of applied scrounging we drove off with about 25 of these machines plus a considerable amount of spares and anything considered useful, considerably in excess of amounts we had been officially authorised to collect. Nobby Stock, with willing helpers, built up four racing machines, stripped to the bare essentials, but still heavy by modern day standards. By the time they had finished that, another group had converted the running track into a passable speedway circuit, the top surface consisting of the residue of clinkers from the local soap factory. I acquired some scaffolding and boards from my own engineering unit and constructed a small grandstand and judge's bench. Somebody even came up with a design for a starting gate supported on tripods and activated by a multitude of saddle springs. We started by holding trials for aspiring riders with the four bikes we had. Early riders had to build their own bikes from the equipment we had gathered and later we insisted on a minimum of two practice sessions on their own machinery before being considered for public meetings. Needless to say our very first meeting contained at least four competitors who had never ridden before and used borrowed equipment. That first meeting was a really hairy afternoon I shall never forget and yet amazingly, despite many falls, no serious injuries resulted. One instruction to competitors was to take care coming out of the second bend as we had not yet had time to properly cover the water well situated in front of the orchard wall down the back straight. The highlight of the afternoon was a demonstration of how it should be done by Corporal Harry Whitfield (pre-war Wembley) who happened to be in the area and volunteered. He had retired from racing some years before the war and was so scared that his hands were visibly shaking as he mounted 'Nobby' Stock's machine

Cpl Harry Whitfield

In view of this I was surprised when after a couple of short power slides he suddenly turned the throttle on and did four laps flat out, it was a terrific performance and just what was needed to inspire our budding speedsters and show are spectators what was possible. We could never persuade Harry to get out on the track again although he often dropped into the pits to help out.

The first ever meeting was an unqualified success and in the series of fortnightly meetings that followed, until the weather got too bad, we made tremendous progress in all departments. By the time we started again in the spring of 1945 over a thousand spectators were driving up to Trani from the units sited around Bari and that produced our first crisis. In those days we received our pay in British Forces Voucher's or 'skrip' as we called it. It came in various denominations and we could only spend it in official service clubs. The local area commander, being a horse and hounds type, had somehow found himself a spare Indian mule pack company left over from WW1. In the interest of recreation he organised weekly mule racing in a waadi (a dry salt bed) outside Bari, complete with a betting totalisator. Bets could be made with Italian lira or BFVs and winnings were paid out in blank British postal orders. The possibilities of this arrangement can be imagined! When attendances at these meetings started to fall off badly, it was soon discovered that the missing punters at the mule racing were travelling the 20 odd miles up the coast to our meetings at Trani. Without warning, in the interest of economy! an area order was issued restricting the use of service transport for recreational purposes to within a radius of five miles from Bari without HQ authority. We were away and flying by this time, so nothing was going to stop us. After much wheeling and dealing and obtaining the services of an Italian POW volunteer work force, we were back in business within a month by building a new track in a sports ground by the sea at San Spirito (Bari), a staging post for personnel travelling back and forth to the UK from the nearby RAF station. This effectively overcame the five mile exclusion zone.

San Spirito-Bari 1946

Best of all, we were only half a mile up the road from the mule racing. A number of riders from those days went on to make the

grade at speedway back home. 'Nobby' Stock joined Harringay, and my good friend Geoff Bennett (who once scrounged an engine from the Norton factory whilst on leave, and lugged it back to Italy in his pack) rode with distinction for Birmingham although he was really more interested in the road racing scene. Another good friend from my own unit Ernie Rawlins, went on to become skipper of his home town team at Southampton before being tragically killed in a track crash. Another lad to make good was novice RAF aircraftman Eddie Rigg. Eddie turned up for a novice ride one day, lost control, went through the fence missing spectators and took off cross country ending up in a gorse bush a half mile away. In 1945 other tracks opened including Vomero in Naples where we travelled to see the spectacular 'Split' Waterman.

MEMORABLE MATCH DAY

What must be one of the most unusual three team tournament of all time took place at Trani in July 1945, when teams of Sergeants v Corporals v Privates rode against each other for the pride of their rank. Soldiers from throughout Southern Italy celebrated the end of the war by riding against their khaki colleagues after the RAF airmen in the area were refused permission to take part by their commanding officers.

Each team was split into two pairs, each rider having four rides. Unbelievably the meeting finished in Army rank order!, the Sergeants scoring 26 points ahead of the Corporals 24 and finally the Privates with 19. A Lieutenant Beardsmore of the RASC reported on the meeting for the motorcycling press, and there was no hint in his report that the finishing order was manipulated to avoid jankers or extra duties the next day. L/Cpl Davies was the star of the afternoon scoring three wins, only being beaten by S/Sgt 'Nobby' Stock who held the Eastern Italy championship at the time. S/Sgt Clarke and his partner Sgt Smith proved a strong pairing scoring 17 points between them with Craftsmen Drinkall and Driver Kemp, later to ride for Wembley and Oxford, showing good form. A novice competition followed the three team tournament, with Able Seaman Briley winning the event with a fastest time of 100.5 secs, only a couple of seconds slower than the experts over four laps. Stock, Davies and Drinkall made attempts on the flying lap track record of 22.7 secs held by Bill Kemp, but all were unsuccessful.

A silver trophy was presented for competition by Lt Col. Martin who had returned home to England. Three qualification races were won by L/Cpl Downham, S/Sgt Stock and L/Cpl Davies with a fastest second making up the grand final. Davies won the final in a time of 96 seconds with Clarke finishing second after 'paddling' his bike over the finishing line after it blew up 20 yards from the chequered flag.

I WAS THERE - Geoff Bennett

Geoff Bennett receives Italian silverware

Such was the rivalry between West and East coast forces speedway teams in Italy that a Southern Italy challenge cup meeting was staged to satisfy the 'bragging rights' between the troops. Bari (East coast) travelled to the infamously rough Vomero stadium to take on their West coast rivals Naples on Sunday March 10 1946. The Bari team was captained by post-war Harringay professional 'Nobby' Stock. But it was Geoff Bennett later to ride for Birmingham who top scored with maximum points in the 45-29 point win for the East coast side. Bari also comfortably won the return leg at San Spirito 50-32 points with Bennett and Stock scoring 12 points a piece. Geoff, pictured receiving the silverware, served in the Royal Corps of Signals between 1942-47 and was more of a road racing enthusiast, but he quickly took to oval racing on the speedways. The teams who competed in this Italian cup meeting were to produce at least six professional speedway riders including the 1951 & 53 World championship runner up 'Split' Waterman.

The teams were:
WEST ITALY (Naples) - Bill Carruthers (Norwich), 'Split' Waterman (Wembley), Don Hardy (Exeter), Sgt Edward, Cpl Heathcote, Sigmn Bevington, John Hancox (Exeter)

EAST ITALY (Bari) - 'Nobby' Stock (Harringay), Frank Holland (Cradley), Geoff Bennett (Birmingham), Don Drinkall, Sigmn Dagoni, Sigmn Gray

Geoff Bennett has particularly happy memories of 1946 when, apart from riding forces speedway he married his Italian sweetheart Vitoria, a trained opera singer who he met in her role as a translator. Remembers Geoff "*Riding speedway was really good for your Army career and I was surprised to be loaned the villa of an American army officer for the period of my honeymoon*". The Italian links continued for Geoff, and whilst riding for Birmingham he returned to the country to explore the possibility of promoting speedway. "*We looked at a horse trotting track*" explains Geoff "*and Les Marshall, the 'Brummies' promoter supplied all the ACU regulations regarding the construction and running of a speedway track which Vitoria translated into Italian for the local authorities. Despite all our efforts however, there was a lack or urgency shown by the Italian organisers so much so that we decided not to proceed with the venture*". Geoff and family went on to own a restaurant in Minorca for 17 years before retiring to Evesham, Worcestershire.

AIR CRASH STOPPED SPEEDWAY TOUR

Continuing his memories of his time as secretary of 54 Central Mediterranean Forces Area speedways Bari, Italy, Peter Nuzum recalls the occasion when all was set to see an Army speedway team from Italy travel to Germany to compete against a BAOR team in Hanover.

MAED V LAEE NR 52
FROM HEAVY WKSP COY BAOR 151Ø15A
TO SECRETARY 54 AREA SPEEDWAY BARI ITALY
M 12 HWC/226. YOUR BARI /SP/2 DATED 14 APRIL CHALLENGE FOR
SUNDAY 28 APRIL ACCEPTED SUGGEST 6 RIDERS AND 2 RESERVES.
FORWARD EARLIEST NAMES AND PARTICULARS OF RIDERS ALSO ETA TO
ENABLE ARRANGEMENTS TO BE MADE HERE
BT
SENT OF B
R NR 52 CRM 131Ø AR K

Official telex from BAOR Germany requesting team details for the ill fated Germany v Italy 'Army' meeting

"*In April 1945 we were hearing a lot about a successful track run in the BAOR in Hanover, so we issued a challenge which they accepted.* The teleprinter message, dated Sunday April 28 from Germany accepting the challenge and requesting particulars of riders and suggested dates is reproduced above. "*We were authorised to travel by RAF transport*" explains Peter "*and we were all very excited at the prospect of racing the most meaningful team match of our existence. Just three days before we were due to leave, a plane carrying an Army football team crashed in Austria. The top brass immediately put a freeze on the use of RAF transport for ser-*

vices sports teams. We were just choked up for there was no other way in those days for us to get to northern Europe. Some months later we had another bitter disappointment when an ENSA sponsored tour of professional speedway riders from UK visited troops in Germany. As the founder club of services speedway we felt we should have been first on the list for any official tour. We were told that as our area was being rapidly run down there would not be enough potential interest. In a way they were right and by early 1946 we were leaving Southern Italy on release or fresh postings in large numbers".

WARZONE MEMORIES

George Flower........ George, younger brother of Charlie Flower who rode at Lea Bridge, was a carpenter before he joined the City of London Yeomanry in 1940. Involved with the Maintenance Inspectorate, George saw action in North Africa, Italy and Austria and recalls two meetings at Naples and recalls watching 'Split' Waterman, Nelson Wilson and Don Hardy around the Vomero stadium speedway. When news of his demob came, George's lasting memory was a six day drive from Austria to Calais. He revived his speedway interest with trials at Yarmouth, Eastbourne and Rye House before captaining the High Beech team of 1949.

Jack Uglow.......Jack was with REME in Italy where the acceptance of motorcycle competition as a sport came quite early in late 1944, probably due to the enthusiasm from many ex-civilian works riders from the trials and scrambles world who had been called up for service with the Army. The machines used were created from Army issue 500cc side valve Nortons, 350 ohv Triumphs and Ariels salvaged from the workshop dumps. Bikes were suitably modified and the lads in the engineering sheds constructed specials including a 16H Norton bottom half sometimes with a solid bronze barrel mated with a Matchless cylinder head.

Jack Uglow on patrol in Italy

For speedway and grass track the girder forks were reversed giving a shorter wheelbase and more trail for cornering. How the machines handled on the straights is not recorded. Jack who retired to Devon well remembers riding against 'Split' Waterman in hill climbs, scrambles and grass tracks.

"Split was obviously set for great things "says Jack *"I well remember competing against him in a mountain scramble and whilst most lads took things steady around the tight mountain passes, he would broadside around totally ignoring the hundred feet drops on either side of the track".*

Frank Holland....... Frank, who went on to a professional speedway career with Cradley Heath and Tamworth recalls with fondness his Army speedway days in Italy. Riding in team events gained some privileges remembers Frank *"I was relieved of guard and driving duties and our Commanding officer insisted we had to have the best speedway team in Italy"*

Frank remembers fondly the bikes he rode which were named after wives and girlfriends. Dina, Elsie and Doris were often shared amongst the team.

Geoff Bennett.......... Riding in the Army speedway teams did have some status in 1946 and he recalls *"One day I was travelling on a troop train when a soldier introduced himself to me as Geoff Bennett the Army speedway rider, I showed him my ID and he was very embarrassed".*

Hugh Harben .... *"I was serving as a Lt Colonel at 750 Base workshops in Naples when 'Split' Waterman came to my attention as a very capable dirt track rider, performing mostly at the Vomero stadium in the suburbs of the city. I went to see him perform and it was obvious that he was an outstanding rider, with a very big gap between him and his nearest rival. 750 Base workshop comprised of several sections and I think he served in either D or E section. Speedway was getting very popular and even had an Officer element putting up a creditable show. Principal amongst those was Lieutenant Bert Trott"*

Don Drinkall........Craftsman Drinkall's health was the source of many soldiers interest as they prepared to sail home from Italy at the end of the war. A race meeting was staged at Vomero just days before the boat sailed for home. Don crashed badly after hitting a big hole in the track and missed the boat home as he spent five days unconscious in Naples hospital. Cfn, Drinkall eventually made it home to 'Blighty' some weeks after his mates.

Bob Friend.........Bob, an RAF 'Brylcreem boy', remembers fondly his friendship with Eddie Rigg who progressed to become a professional speedway rider with Bradford and England. Bob himself was banned from riding himself (many RAF Commanding officers would not allow flyers to take part in what they considered was a dangerous sport), spent many hours tuning engines and acting as mechanic for Eddie. *"I recall that Eddie spent a lot of time falling off"* says Bob *"but I was pleased and not surprised to hear he went on to a successful speedway riding career."*

EGYPT

Although not strictly at war, Egypt and the Middle East as a whole was an unstable area in 1928. British forces including the infant RAF (formed in 1918) countered a raid of 20,000 tribesman aimed at the Kuwait-Iraq border. In March of that year, the Egyptian government protested to Britain over interference in their affairs. The tension created was very real. By July, King Fuad in a Royal decree ended parliamentary government in Egypt, and suspended part of the constitution. Freedom of the press was suspended, elections were prohibited for at least three years as were public meetings by any opposition. Cairo (Helipolis) was to become a key staging post for the RAF's effort to establish an international reputation for long distance, high altitude, and high speed flying. The British government's desire was to establish commercial and transport routes across the Empire. The Empire Air routes had begun as early as 1921 with Cairo (Helipolis-Baghdad) becoming an early mail route. This route was so important and prestigious that it became the first overseas sector route for the internationally famous Imperial Airways.

Egypt's proximity to the Suez canal was always going to make the country a potential strategic war target in WWII. Italy entered the war in June 1940 as allies of the Germans, which immediately positioned some 500,000 Italian troops in Libya, facing a mere 50,000 British garrison in Egypt. Commanded by General Wavell, British forces secured the port of Tobruk in January 1941 capturing some 125,000 Italian prisoners. The German High Command gave General Erwen Rommel (later nicknamed the Desert Fox), the task of leading German troops fighting alongside the Italians. The collapse of operation 'Battleaxe' saw the removal of Wavell, with his replacement General Auchinleck sharing Prime Minister Winston Churchill's view that a victory over the axis power was possible. Operation 'Crusader' began in November 1941 and with far superior air power and previously unseen troop numbers, the allies appeared to have an easy victory in prospect. However Rommel's tactical know how frustrated the British and it was not until January 1942 that he was forced to retreat.

Battles for strategically important Tobruk on the Libyan/Egyptian border were legendary, but by June 1942 Rommel had reached El Alemain, inside Egypt. By now Bernard Law Montgomery was in charge of the 8th army and Operation 'Lightfoot' was delayed until he was sure the odds were overwhelming in his favour. Soon after, the United States entered the war following the Japanese attack on Pearl Harbor and American troops were committed to the North Africa campaign. Together with the British they delivered a crushing defeat to Rommel and the Afrika Corps. On May 12 1943, the axis empire in North Africa came to an end, allowing the allies to focus on their next objective, the Mediterranean.

IN THE ZONE

From the earliest days of WWII, the 'top brass' of the British Army in the Middle East were keen to formalise motor cycling as part of the forces training programme. This led to a variety of descriptions being used for motorcycling events which need clarification to establish a line in the sand as to when Army speedway started in this war theatre. 'Reliability Trials' were timed and observed events with up to 200 riders, run over a 10-15 mile length with points deducted at sections for 'dabbing' i.e. putting a foot on the ground, falling or stalling the machine. The competitor with the fewest dropped points was declared the winner. Only standard WD issue motorcycles were permitted in these events. 'Hill Climbs' as the name suggests were an individual against the clock timed trial up a steep incline with the quickest rider being the winner. The first recorded 'speedway' event was staged at Almaza on a 690 yard oval track which was advertised as Sand Trials. The term 'Sand Track Trial' was first used at RAF Qadima to describe a team match between the RAF and Army, with the term speedway first being used at a meeting at the El Ballah track outside Ismailia in May 1947. Tel el Kabir introduced yet another variation on a theme when advertising their regular Sunday afternoon racing events as 'Sand Speedway'.

Egypt has a strong claim as being the biggest and best in the warzone speedways world with some seventeen circuits being found to have staged practice, team, individual and even national championship meetings. Such was the sports standing, that the Egyptian championship was instigated in 1947 attracting riders and spectators from throughout Egypt. Its infancy can be traced back to the exploits of the Bar-None MCC, formed initially as a club for Army despatch riders and other motor cycle riders. Organised team racing started at RAF Qadima near Cairo when the Army defeated the RAF 73-67pts on June 2 1946. Several 'speedway' meetings at Maadi were followed by an eight meeting season at El Ballah where the 'Aces' organised by the Air Formation Signals group staged fortnightly meeting. The El Ballah season culminated in an Aces v Rest of Egypt clash which included the Middle East championship won by Craftsman Wright of REME. Using the criteria of staging competitive meetings involving serving soldiers, some twelve Egyptian forces tracks were constructed. This number increases to seventeen when training tracks such as El Firdan (1947), Shandur (1949) and Devesoir in the early 50s are included. Evidence of RAF types racing at Heliopolis taking part in racing at Zamalek in 1928 could legitimately take the grand total to eighteen.

The Bar-None Army team at RAF Qadima -Summer 1946

Pits scene at El Ballah

Racing venues not surprisingly followed the deployment of troops. Early post WWII saw a tremendous interest at Tel el Kabir, an enormous garrison with a reputed 25 mile perimeter fence which was responsible for almost all the Army's logistical support and equipment repair in Egypt at that time. By 1949 league racing was being staged at the Olympia stadium in Fayid, racing transferring from the early desert track originally used. At it's peak some 13 teams were competing at the Olympia stadium including:

The Dicers, TEK Dons, Suez Tigers, The Gunners, The Ciphers, The Ironsides, Argosy, Hell's Ladies, The Zodiacs, RASC, RAF Kabrit, The Pirates and Fayid Lions.

International meetings, Scotland v England and Wales v Ireland were particularly popular and no doubt reminded the troops of their roots back home. Moving into the 50s, RAF Kabrit was to stage further international meetings between England and Scotland with Billy Bales the Norwich and England star riding there whilst completing his National service whilst, at the same time riding professional speedway back home when on leave!

TRACK INDEX:
1.Almaza 2.Qadima 3.El Ballah 4.Aby Sueir 5. El Firdan 6.Fayid (desert) 7. Fayid Olympia, 8. Kabrit 9.Suez 10.Tel el Kabir 11.Shalufa12.Geneifa 13.Shandur 14.Fanara 15. Devesoir 16. Maadi 17 Suez.

SPEEDWAY BETTING FAILS IN EGYPT

Almost 17 years before the Bar - None MCC organised sand trials meeting at Almaza in September 1945, speedway had been staged in the land of the pyramids at Zamalek on the outskirts of Cairo. Barely nine months after the famous first ever British meeting at High Beech, Essex, pioneer riders Ivor Creek and Billy Galloway were recruited by an Egyptian dirt track syndicate to construct a 440yard race track inside the already laid greyhound track.

The intrepid pair enlisted help from the local Arabs, initially relying on manual labour with rake and baskets for the construction work. Time was running short, so a motor car with cricket pitch roller and eventually a heavy duty steam roller was used to create a smooth racing surface. Soft ground however saw the twelve tonne machine sink into the ground and the project looked doomed. Only the greatest of effort by all involved rescued the roller and enabled the opening meeting to proceed. With the track built, the touring riders arrived which included Les Brakebrough, Les Barker, Clem Cort, Tommy Croombs, Ivor

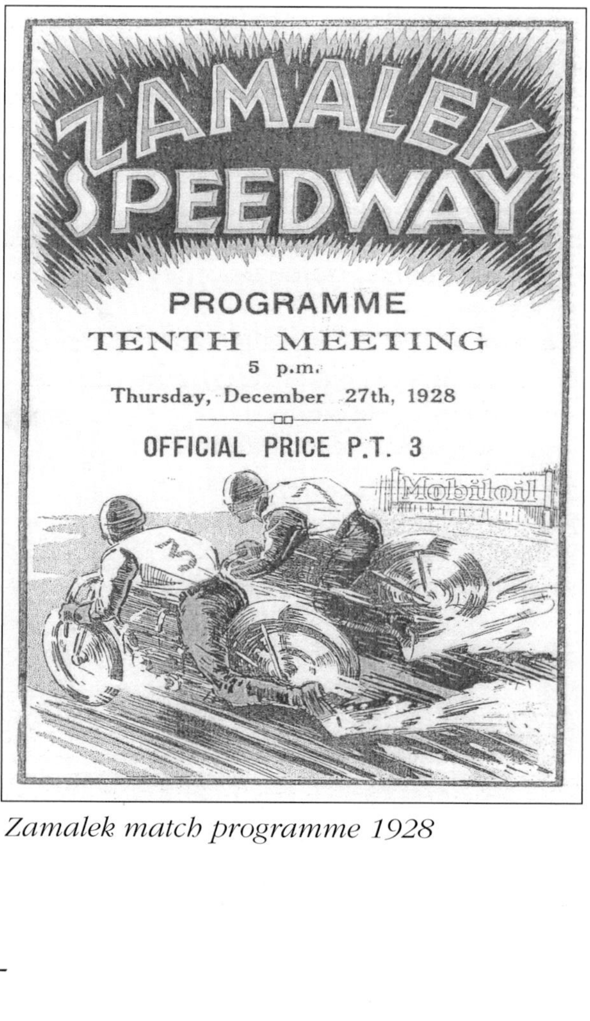

Zamalek match programme 1928

Creek, Colin Ford, Del Forster, Dudley Froy, Billy Galloway, Jimmy Hayes, Burn Hieatt, C. Pink, Smoke Robinson, Winks Rice and G.Betteridge.

The uniqueness of the venture was that racing operated under a totalisator regime, using a stadium bookmaker system called Pari-Mutuel. Meetings were run over a 9 heat formula with afternoon meetings commencing at 5pm, often following an afternoon greyhound meeting.The plan was no doubt designed to exploit the well known Arab love of betting. Curiously the whole venture had a definite Welsh flavour with officials including; W V Williams (starter), J L Davies (lap scorer), L Pugh (time keeper), J L Jones (Pit steward), W V Jones and B Griffiths (corner stewards). Although the commercial venture was eventually to fail, there is evidence that RAF pilots and air crew based at Helipolis airfield did practice on the track under floodlights. One of the most unique features of the Zamalek track was the 60 foot high palm trees growing on the centre green. Creek and Galloway remained in Egypt following the track closure, working at the Jowett and Austin Morris car factories respectively.

MEMORABLE MATCH DAY

Since it's formation in May 1944, the Bar-None Motor Cycle Club had been considering staging other forms of events in addition to their traditional hill climb and time trials. Talk of staging grass track racing appeared in the club's newsletter but proved impossible because of the obvious lack of a suitable location in the desert! This did however lead to the staging of the first Sand Trials meeting. This was the term initially used to describe oval racing, four riders in race over 3 or 4 laps, a speedway by an other name. And so it was that on September 23 1945, the first forces speedway meeting in Egypt was staged at Almaza near Cairo. Some 6,000 troops and locals from all over the Middle East arrived for a unique occasion comparable with the famous High Beech meeting in 1928 which marked the start of dirt track racing in England.

Flight Sergeant A.J.Tucker and Battery Sergeant Major M.L.Terrel, the joint organising secretaries on behalf of the Bar-None had no idea how many competitors would enter. They need not have worried with 35 rider entries being received from the Cairo based RAF and Army despatch riders, they being joined by 25 visiting riders from Alexandria, the Western desert and Palestine to take part in a knock out formula not unlike today's grass track system.

Crowds began arriving in mid morning of that Sunday over 60 years ago, with the main Cairo to Alamaza road experiencing a traffic jam of huge proportion. The four tenths of a mile to the lap (approximately 690yards) was oval shaped with bends of different shapes to fully test competitors. Waste water and engine oil was poured on to bind the loose sand surface ,with a natural sand bank grandstand providing good viewing for the thousands of expectant soldiers. The back straight was initially out of bounds but such was the size of the crowd that they quickly overflowed into this area. Three classes of event were offered for Cairo based riders, namely 350cc overhead valve, 500cc side valve and an unlimited cc class.

Bar-none MCC first sand trial meeting 1945

Racing began at 2 o'clock and the sand quickly cut up requiring some strong handling of machinery. Reports of the time described the standard of racing as extremely good. Three main riding styles were adopted: a. Square on the saddle left foot out and body out, b. Body back on the saddle, foot out and body in, and finally, c. Both feet up, standing on the footrests. The racing regulations give an insight in to how basic the equipment was in this unique 'first' meeting, another fascinating comparison with the High Beech meeting back in 1928.

1. Only WD (War Dept.) machines may be used, freak of Bitsa machines not permitted.

2. All electrics and non essential accessories may be removed but not modified.

3. Silencers may be removed and extensions fitted if required.

4. Machines must be equipped with TWO independent serviceable brakes.

5. Rear mudguards may not be removed from machines.

6. Machines will be fitted with round or oval number plates.

7. MT (Military Transport) fuel ONLY will be used (max 80 octane).

8. Standard engine sprockets will be used.

9. Any type of WD tyres may be used with the exception of competition tyres. Maximum size 3.50 x 19ins.

10. Competitors must be prepared to remove cylinder head or primary chain case after the meeting. Machines will be examined by a competent inspector prior to competing.

The Norton 16H and BSA 500cc machines were to dominate the event with their top end speed suiting the conditions best. The usual inter-force rivalry was much in evidence with the RAF providing all four finalists in the 500cc class, much to the Army's frustration. An unusual match race took place in the form of a challenge match race between Brigadier Hayman-Joyce (Army) and Air Commodore Oliver (RAF). The Air Commodore had previously beaten Hayman-Joyce at a Mena hill climb event, a feat he repeated at Alamaza, much to the excitement of the RAF personnel on the terraces.

In all some 60 races were run with average race speeds of 34mph being recorded by the fastest riders

The Almaza event enabled a cheque for LE 82,575 (local currency) to be donated to the Army Benevolent Fund and other charitable organisations.

I WAS THERE Colin V Morgan

May 18 1947 was scheduled as Colin 'Taffy' Morgan's last speedway meeting in Egypt as he was due to return home for demob from the Army. Colin, a despatch rider with the 18th Air Formation Signals, had been a leading rider in the El Ballah 'Aces' team formed in 1946. Following the successful team season during the winter of 1946-47, the club decided to stage a grand challenge match against the 'Rest of Egypt' over 16 heats as a swan song event before returning to the UK. In addition a seven heat 'Middle East Championship' for a silver trophy donated by Squadron Leader Barret from RAF Devesoir was to make it a truly memorable day.

GRAND
SPEEDWAY MEETING
AT EL BALLAH
ON
Sunday 18th May 1947
Commencing 2.15 p.m.

EL-BALLAH "ACES"
V
THE REST OF EGYPT
(Held under the auspices of the Bar None M.C.C.
and by kind permission of Brig. H.D.W. Sitwell, C.B. M.Ç.
Official Programme : - 5 P.T.

Programme from last ever meeting at El Ballah 1947

'Taffy' top scored for the El Ballah Aces with 8pts but the Rest of Egypt team, made up from the best riders in Egypt comfortably won the meeting 54-42pts. Colin's last ride in Egypt was the final of the Middle East championship when he came third behind Cpl Harry Mappin who won the Egyptian title in 1948 and the overall winner Craftsman Wright. Back home in England, the opportunity of a professional speedway trial with Harringay proved just too expensive, with a move to London and the purchase of a bike being beyond his financial means at the time.

EL BALLAH ACES 42pts - Bert Steddy 5pts, John Percival 6, Taffy Morgan 8, Spud Thompson 8, Dickie Bird 0 (Injured), ???? Hogg 3 (Replacement), Ray King 2, Ginger Pay 7, Bronco Fenner 3.

REST OF EGYPT 54pts - Ron Vallance 10pts, ???? Walley 3, Cfn Emmerton 6, Cpl Mappin 12, Cpl Wright 11, Cpl Ellis 4, Sgmn Beaumont 3, Cpl Brierley 5.

MIDDLE EAST CHAMPIONSHIP - 1st Cfn Wright, 2nd Cpl Mappin, 3rd Taffy Morgan, 4th Bert Steddy. Sadly Colin passed away during my research for warzone speedway. I am grateful to his wife Pamela for arranging for Colin's memoirs of his time with the El Ballah 'Aces' to be recorded for posterity.

Army trucks formed useful grandstands

"It was spring of 1947 and many of the chaps were preparing to be returned home to their loved ones and demob. Our play time was coming to an end so let's round it off with a major Middle East event" remembered Colin *"El Ballah Aces versus the Rest of Egypt was to be our toughest test to date, having to field 8 team riders and two reserves It was finally agreed and May 18th 1947 was the date arranged. Preparations went ahead with a great deal of paperwork involved, full programmes had to be produced with all officials knowing their duties. The day was of course fine and dry, the track looked wonderful and by the arranged start time the entire area was packed with spectators and supporters. The Grand Parade was a wonderful sight and all was set for racing.*

Colin Morgan racing at El Ballah speedway

From the first heat things seemed to go wrong for us, and when Dickie Bird crashed, receiving serious injuries followed by engine troubles, the battle began to go decidedly less in our favour .Our hard earnt glory faded rapidly away, and the final result did us little credit. However it was a good day, one set down in memory along with many others. On returning home I lost contact with many comrades with us all going our separate ways. A trial at Harringay speedway was suggested, which meant moving to London, with a speedway machine. and being available twice a week or more for practice. A tough decision! I had been away for nearly 5 years and my older brother had been killed in an RAF test flight in France 3 months after the end of the war. I chose to resettle at home in Wales and competed successfully in regular track and trials events as well as sand race meetings at Pendine and Aberavon beaches"

The meeting Colin Morgan described was the culmination of an historic 12 month period in Egyptian forces speedway with team racing becoming the staple diet for participating and spectating troops, especially those based near Ismailia, the nearest town to the El Ballah track. Comparable with the pioneer British professional season of 1929 when team events became the vogue, for the statisticians amongst readers, the results are detailed overleaf.

RAF QADIMA

2 June 1946 Army (Cairo)	73pts	RAF Qadima Q club	67pts	24 heats
18 August Army	66pts	RAF Qadima	35pts	18 heats

MAADI

8 September Air Formation Signals	59 pts	The Rest	45pts	18 heats
20 October Air Formation Signals	61pts	The Rest	44pts	18 heats
24 November 3 GHQ Signals	54pts	The Rest	51pts	18 heats

EL BALLAH

26 December Signals (Canal)	36pts	Signals (Cairo)	35pts	12 heats
12 January 1947 15/19Hussars	17pts	18th Air Formation	54pts	12 heats
9 February El Ballah 'Aces'	49pts	Tel el Kabir 'Lions'	35pts	12 heats
23 February 18TH A.F.S	49½pts	2nd Lincolns	22½pts	12 heats
16 March El Ballah 'Aces'	49pts	3 GHQ (Fayid)	22pts	12 heats
23 March 51 Coy RASC	???	7 GHQ Sigs	???	Result unknown
5 April Canal 'Lions'	42pts	Canal 'Tigers'	30pts	12 heats
18 May El Ballah 'Aces'	42pts	Rest of Egypt	54pts	16 heats

DID TEL EL KABIR SPEEDWAY HELP PREVENT AN ARMY REBELLION ?

Egyptian championship -Tel El Kabir 1947

On the road west of Ismailia, on route to Cairo, lies Tel el Kabir, commonly known in the mid 1940s by every soldier as TEK. With a perimeter fence estimated at around 25 miles, TEK was reputed to be the biggest British army garrison in the Middle East and possibly the world at the time. As a supply, repair, storage and distribution depot it's role was to ensure the front line supply chain was maintained with all required supplies and services.
From a speedway perspective, TEK holds a special place in Army speedway folklore, matching the Hanomag track in Hanover, Germany. In 1946 an oval race track was layed, and eventually grandstands and other facilities were constructed to make a venue which for some eight years was the location for most of the major Egyptian championships. It was also the home of the TEK 'Dons' team who could claim to be the premier Army team in Egypt based on track facilities and length of operation.
During my research I have uncovered a remarkable story the source of which I have decided to keep private but is 100% reliable, because the story teller was there when it happened..........

Stewards eye view

Egyptian championship trophies

It was in 1946, when many troops were waiting for demobilisation back home to Britain,that frustration was beginning to build as the process was being delayed. TEK was home to thousands of troops and with the war over they were desperate to go home to their families, but repeated delays led to serious unrest and anger amongst the ranks. Mutiny or rebellion are strong words, but my source tells me that born out of frustration, a significant number of troops approached the sports hall intent on tackling Officers about the delays. Armed guards quelled the revolt but it was obvious something needed to be done. To placate the troops, resources were allocated to provide a range of entertainments and sporting facilities to occupy the soldiers in the long days waiting for demob. Heavy plant for the building of a speedway, engineering equipment, WD motorcycles and specialist forces personnel were all made available by the Army. The facility was to attract crowds approaching 6,000 for major meetings and continued until 1952 when due to reducing troop numbers and the departure of key organising personnel the track closed.

Truth or fiction? You decide. I have no corroboration of the story, but have no reason to doubt the source who went onto to play a leading part at Tel el Kabir speedway!

WARZONE MEMORIES

Ron Stones

Ron was in the 312 tank delivery troop in Palestine when he was transferred to Shandur in the Canal Zone of Egypt. As a despatch rider he travelled extensively between Fayid, Suez, Port Said and Ismailia. *"Someone hit on the idea of forming a speedway team"* explains Ron *"and our Regimental Sergeant Major 'Nobby' Clark took a hippo (the nickname for a heavy transporter) to Tel el Kabir and rescued a load of damaged motor cycles in various states of repair. A 500cc Norton 16H was tested with the side valves cut off and a 350cc Matchless head grafted on. It went like a bomb and when the front forks were reversed we found this improved the steering"*

Ron Stones in the colours of Shandur 'Argosy'

Geoff Bland

Geoff and buddy Ron Ottaway became aware of forces speedway after a visit to El Ballah, close to Ismailia. Keen to ride and possibly form a team, as luck would have it RAF El Firdan where they were based had a rugby pitch which had been constructed by a keen Officer *" I recall they had laid special sand, watered it with saltwater and rolled it firm, but it turned out no one wanted to play rugby! It stood unused until we suggested building a speedway track around the pitch on the very firm base"* says Geoff *"We used it for practice and everything seemed ready to form a team until a novice suffered a broken thigh."*

The RAF hierarchy were not impressed and refused permission for their personnel to use the track on the basis that an injury in what was a warzone could have been construed as being 'self inflicted', an offence punishable by court marshal.

Lt Col Penfold MBE

Lt Col Penfold spent 1946-49 at TEK as a REME Inspectorate Sergeant ensuring the engineering work was up to the very exacting standards set by the Army. He well remembers his Sunday afternoon visits to the speedway with crowds of 6-7,000 not unknown. So popular was the Sunday racing, that so much income was derived from the admission and programme sales that money became a problem. To overcome this embarrassment of riches the lucky programme prize was often a return ticket with BAOC to London from Cairo or a new Triumph motor cycle to disperse the funds. All warzone speedway events were run in aid of Army charitable funds and there was a keen eye kept on finances to ensure that War Department funds were used appropriately.

Eric Robinson
A veteran of the Suez campaign, Eric's story first appeared in the Suez veteran's association newsletter. I am indebted to Harold Heath, the association secretary for Eric's story.

"Several Army camps had set up speedway teams so it was not long before our club established one, which was called the Kabrit 'Eagles'. Then one or two other RAF camps formed teams, and a series of race meetings were planned to form a league. Without the use of machine tools, we converted the Norton 16H side valve engines into overhead valve by sawing off the valve chest, fitting push rods and a Matchless 350cc head, and filing pistons to allow the valves to come down. These performed quite well and the huge amount of work involved ensured that we did not suffer from boredom. Spares were mostly scrounged from Army guys at TEK, but batteries and inner tubes were the big problem. Luckily my Flight Commander joined the club and he gave approval for some to be picked up on a training flight to Nicosia, where it was possible to obtain new ones. Riding boots were also difficult to acquire, but once again our Army friends obliged and, as team captain I was sent in a small pick up to an Army camp, where I reported to an officer who gave me a sealed chest.

Back at camp we opened the chest to find it packed with despatch rider's boots and leather gauntlet gloves. Because of the high compression engines which we modified, we were forced to use the high octane petrol from aircraft to reduce detonation. This was obtained by filling cans from the drain taps in the bottom of fuel tanks of the Dakota .Our first attempt at building the race track required a supply of bags of cement. The task of obtaining this was delegated to a club rider who happened to be one of the station police. He would take the evening 'jankers' parade, and then detail a party to take a barrow to the civilian contractor's depot and fill it with bags of cement which were then safely packed into one of the guard room cells. We would then take the stuff to the starting gate position, mix it with desert sand and lay the starting grid. The big day came for the first race fixture of the home track, with the C.O in attendance. We had forgotten to consider the direction of the prevailing wind, and after the first few starts, the C.O, his wife and the other officers who were in the prime seats had turned into figures resembling the sandstone Nile monuments. After the prize-giving the C.O said some nice words, and then turned to the club chairman and said the next meeting would be held after the starting gate had been built on the other side of the track, so we had to go through the whole effort again.

Another set back concerning the track was when we asked the tank guys at Shalufa to come over with a bulldozer to level one of the corners. A Sherman tank arrived with a large scraper on the front, and after treating the driver to some NAAFI beer for his efforts, we showed him what was required. He said it was a doddle, got into the tank, lined up with the track, dropped the scraper and tore forward. The sand crust broke up, and the tank sank halfway into the sand. The next day another tank came over to rescue the first one, and we spent about three days filling the crater with shovels. Eventually we reduced the dust problem by emptying all the tanks of used engine oil from the aircraft onto the corners.

In 1973 I was helping to run the junior section of the Burnham-on-Crouch Rifle club, and on chatting to two brothers who had joined the club, found they were into schoolboy grass track racing, so I mentioned the Kabrit 'Eagles'. They immediately said it wasn't Eagles it was 'Ospreys', and they were sure because their dad had been a member. I went to see him and it transpired that he had been posted to Kabrit in the 50's and on nosing around the camp, had rubbed the sand off a window in our old building and to his delight saw a pile of bikes and equipment. He got the C.O's permission to sort it out and restarted the club .The birds painted on the canvass race bibs looked like Ospreys to him, and as all the previous club members had long since gone home, there was nobody who could correct him".

Arthur Holifield

Arthur was in the Home Guard and was a motorcycling enthusiast as the war was ending. Just after VJ day (September 1945), he was posted as a Lieutenant to Shalufa in the south of Egypt, but based in Suez. His son Chris takes up the story *"The story goes that his men had little to do and dad was told to keep them occupied and entertained. As he was a motorbike enthusiast he had the idea of building a speedway track in the desert and holding races. It's also said that accounts were written in magazines and newsletters of hair raising events involving burning bikes, which led to questions being asked about what this man doing with Army property"* Arthur was by profession a teacher and by a strange co-incidence many years later became Head teacher at a school in Norfolk. One of his early pupils was a certain Tony Davey who went on to ride for Ipswich and England. Chris explains *"My father believed in encouraging the pupil's ability and bought an old BSA Bantam motor cycle for the school. Tony amazed the whole school with his slalom riding skills on this bike through a row of cricket stumps where he showed amazing control and balance"*

Colonel Sam Roberts

Sam recalls at the age of 12 years old being flown out with his brother Mike, then aged 10 years from boarding school to visit his family during the summer holidays. His father Captain George Roberts was the Administrative Officer of 2 base workshops REME in Tel el Kabir and was involved in the running of speedway meetings. The picture shows Sam and younger brother Mike in the TEK pits. Both went on to distinguished Army careers with REME, reaching the rank of Colonel and Major respectively.

The Roberts boys 1947-48 at Tel el Kabir

Ron Walton

Ron served at RAF Kabrit between 1951-56 and became starter, track curator and all round factotum for the RAF speedway teams. One of his most unusual tasks was the painting of the Cobra team's race jackets. Ron, now a member of the Treorchy male voice choir, recalls with affection team members such as Al Alison, Johnny Johnston and Jock Duffy.

Tony Burgess

Tony was a Swindon speedway fan in the early 50's when his National service took him to Egypt and eventually Suez with the RAOC & REME. He was working in a motorcycle workshop in Faringdon near Swindon when his local cinema showed highlights of Army speedway from Tel el Kabir. Tony remembered the black and white Pathe News reel images on his arrival in Egypt, and set about tracing the circuit. It appears that TEK speedway had closed in 1953 due to reducing numbers of troops in the area, but he was keen to revive the sport but curiously could find no trace of the racing bikes. *"Either they were buried in the desert like so much other motorised equipment or the locals borrowed them for their own purposes"* remembers Tony *"I did ride my DR Matchless machine around the circuit but the bikes never did turn up and some where near Tel el Kabir I believe there are at least seven speedway machines just waiting to be discovered after over sixty years."*

John Bennett
John joined REME in October 1950 for his two years National service, carrying out his training at Blandford before being posted to 9th Central Workshops. *"In January 1952 I was posted to 2 Base Workshop Tel-el-Kabir which was a very large camp approximately 20 miles around the perimiter fence with large workshops reconditioning vehicles, guns and tanks. There were two cinemas, a swimming pool, football pitches and a speedway track on the site. There were two teams, the TEK 'Dons' and TEK 'Tigers' and we rode mostly Matchless machines although one had a Norton 16H bottom end and a Matchless head and barrel. Billy Bales who was in the RAF and rode for Yarmouth held the track record".*
Nicknamed 'Slip' Bennett, John is now involved in classic scrambles events whilst his son Paul is chairman of the Red Marley club which runs the world famous annual hill climb in Worcestershire.

GERMANY

The source of Nazism has its roots back in the early 1920's, with its power base growing progressively until 1933 when Adolf Hitler became Chancellor. The threat of German expansionism was apparent as early as 1936 and by 1938, Anschluss (Austria) and then Czechoslovakia were annexed before the invasion of Poland on September 1 1939, the action which drew Britain into war with Germany. Russia were initially Allies of the Germans until 1941 when Germany invaded the Soviet Union. Another war was raging in the Far East, Japan having been in dispute with China for several years and this combined with the European conflagration was to create a true world war spreading across the continents. For most of the period 1939-1943 German troops were on the offensive but gradually as 1944 panned out and the events of D-Day in June of that year unfolded, German troops were pushed back to their own country with an unconditional surrender to the Allies coming in Berlin on 30 April 1945. The horrors of concentration camps, murdering of the Jews and the brutality of the Gestapo under Hitler in the name of the Third Reich all marked the period as the most infamous in the history of Germany.

The post-war partitioning of Berlin into sectors controlled by the British, USA and Russia on the cessation of fighting would lead to further strife as the Soviet Union attempted to gain territory and spread Communism. To precipitate conflict, the Russians progressively introduced blockades to starve the Western sector into submission. This triggered off the Berlin airlift which involved the RAF, USAAF and civilian aircraft in continual supply flights day and night of all the necessities for normal life and prevented the Russians from taking control. The final Dakota aircraft with supplies flew into Berlin in September 1949 to break the siege of West Berlin. The 'Iron Curtain' as described by Winston Churchill had truly arrived and was to continue in place until the Berlin wall was brought down in 1989.

IN THE ZONE

Despite the affects of RAF bombing of the major German cities and destruction of much of the countries infrastructure, just months after the formal German surrender, speedway racing was being staged in Hanover by the

Squaddies in uniform enjoying the entertainment

Very early racing- Hanomag 1945

Royal Mechanical Engineers at the Hanomag stadium.The REME archives at Arborfield, Reading, have kindly supplied pictures of speedway racing in the summer of 1945, just months after the end of WWII.

The Potsdam conference held to divide the Allies territorial responsibilities in Germany in the immediate post-war era was held on July 28 1945, and that winter the ENSA speedway tour took place between November and February 1946 as part of a programme of entertainment for the troops in Germany. Lack of equipment and materials and the obvious loss of pre-war German riders in the war time fighting delayed Germany's racing development, with the British Army Occupying the Rhine (BAOR) reviving speedway interest in the North, whilst trotting tracks in Bavaria started to stage what was probably long track racing. By 1948 Stuttgart and other Southern German tracks measuring between 328yards -1,094 yards were opening up as equipment became available.The quaintly named St Hubert's speedway at Lubek was staging nine heat, three lap team events between Kiel and Lubek as early as May 1946, providing Hanover and Hamburg with a challenge for the title of the centre for forces speedway in Germany. By 1949, a little recorded Golden Helmet meeting held in the US sector of Berlin, sponsored by a Mr Hazel, the American sports director at the Garmison recreational centre marked the normalization of speedway racing in a largely destroyed country. Hazel was responsible for the staging of the first post-war meeting in Munich on the 400 metre athletics track at the Dante Stadion.A curious mix of forces and professional riders competed, including British Army soldiers 'Speed' Mcarthy and 'Oozalum' Fulljames who rode against German and Austrian riders including Fritz Dirtl and the Killmayer brothers.The stadium was in due course requisitioned by the Americans to accommodate their GIs.

A Combined Services championship was introduced for forces riders from 1948 at Hanover, with Corporal Paddy Pullen taking the first title beating Larry Lazarus who went on to ride professionally for Glasgow Ashfield. Ken Mckinlay who went onto a glorious professional career came equal sixth with 7 points in this inaugural championship meeting.This competition continued until the end of the 1951season, when it is believed the Hanomag stadium track closed.

TRACK INDEX: 1.Hamburg, 2.Hanover, 3.Ebstorf, 4.Brunswick, 5.Kiel, 6. Neumunster, 7.Munich (Dante), 8.Vilshofen, 9.Garmisch, 10.Lubek, 11.Schnde

'Waiting for their heroes'- Hanomag pits gate

I WAS THERE by Alan Clark

Signalman Clark, serial no 22349617, is well qualified to tell the story of the final (1951) season of Army speedway at Hanomag stadium in Hanover as he competed in both team and individual championship racing at this famous German circuit. Alan nicknamed 'Dart' Clark by ASM 'Whacker' Hurrel, the club secretary, was a member of the Birmingham 'Saints' team which won the club league championship of 1951. Although only a novice at the time, Alan rode several times for 'Birmingham' who won the league title in 1951 with 22pts from 'Wembley' 20pts, 'New Cross' 16pts and 'Odsal' with just 5 pts. Alan recalls that memorable last season, convinced he rode in the last ever meeting at Hanomag on September 29/30, when he competed in that years combined Services individual championship.

"In 1951 I was doing my National Service in the Army with the Royal Corps of Signals, stationed in Celle, Northern Germany. In the camp were two regular soldiers, Joe King and Warren Leather who talked about speedway. Being an avid fan I needed to know more and it transpired that these Signalmen belonged to the Hanomag 'Saints' speedway team and had been riding there for a couple of years. This was early in the year and the 1951 season was due to begin at the track in Hanover. I talked Joe into taking me to the first practice at the track to see what it was all about. At the time the organisers were getting all the stars, other riders and newcomers from both the services and civilians to form into four teams that were to be named after English clubs, namely Wembley Saints, New Cross Saints, Birmingham Saints and Odsal Saints. Four of the top riders were named as captains of the teams and were asked to pick riders they wanted for their team's. 'Zipp' Zammit had Wembley, George Broughton had New Cross, and 'Flyer' Jones had Birmingham whilst Joe 'Ace King' led Odsal. Each team had to include some of the German civilians as well as servicemen. In total there were some ninety six riders named for the four teams. I had a trial and was named amongst the Birmingham twenty four riders. As a first year novice I was just a name amongst the others

'Dart' Clark in Birmingham 'Saints' colours

After practice sessions, the first real meeting of the 1951 season was held on Sunday April 8th with the four captains picking a team of six riders for the match with two reserves named. Wembley Saints rode against New Cross Saints and won 38-16pts over nine heats. At the same meeting Birmingham beat Odsal 34-17pts. Besides the eighteen heats of the two matches there was another four heats for the reserves and non league riders in which the four winners went into the Knock Out cup competition final. The final race of the afternoon was for the Hanover Challenge Cup for the top riders with the first winner being ' Zipp' Zammit of Wembley. This made up a racing programme of twenty four races".

Meeting 2 -Sunday April 22nd. Wembley 36 Odsal 17pts. Birmingham 30 New Cross 23pts. 'Trailer' Smith of Wembley won the Challenge cup.

Meeting 3 - Sunday May 6th. Birmingham 33 Wembley 21pts. New Cross 33 Odsal 21pts. Zammit won the Challenge cup.

Meeting 4 - Whit Monday May 14th. Wembley 29 New Cross 24pts. Birmingham 37 Odsal 16pts. Zammit won the Challenge cup.

Meeting 5 - Sunday May 27th. The track was flooded and the meeting postponed until June 10th, but after four heats this meeting was also abandoned due to rain. I had talked my captain into naming me as reserve but didn't get a ride. The meeting eventually took place on Sunday June 17th Wembley beating Birmingham 34-19pts with New Cross beating Odsal 31-21pts. Zammit again won the Challenge cup and I had my first ride in the Knock out competition, taking a second place.

Meeting 6 - Sunday July 1st Wembley 27 Odsal 27pts. New Cross 28 Birmingham 26 pts. George Broughton of New Cross won the Challenge cup and as Birmingham reserve I won my heat in the Knock out and took third place in the final.

Meeting 7- Sunday July 15th was a wet weekend. Some of the Wembley riders had not turned up leaving 'Zipp' Zammit without a team. The reserves from the other teams were asked to ride for Wembley and I got a chance in their team. I paired with Zammit and we took the trophies for highest scoring pair with 13 from a possible 15pts. New Cross 33 Wembley 21pts. Birmingham 33 Odsal 20 pts. 'Smudger' Smith of Birmingham took the Challenge cup.

Meeting 8 - Sunday July 22nd . On the strength of my Wembley ride, my captain "Flyer" Jones put me in the Birmingham team and I scored a second place, a win and after falling in my third ride I scored 5 points. Birmingham 31 New Cross 21pts. Odsal 31 Wembley 22pts. George Boughton won the Challenge cup.

Meeting 9 -Sunday July 29th. I again rode for Birmingham taking three third places scoring 3 points but we lost 31-23pts to Wembley. New Cross 35 Odsal 19pts. Zammit again won the Challenge cup.

Meeting 10 – Sunday August 12th and I could not make it. Wembley 27 New Cross 25pts. Birmingham 30 Odsal 20pts. Zammit won the Challenge cup.

Meeting 11 – Sunday August 26th was the last league meeting of the season. Wembley 26 Odsal 26pts. New Cross 29 Birmingham 25 pts. I had three rides for Birmingham and scored just one point. Zammit again won the Challenge cup.

"The final meeting of the season was over two days of September 29th and 30th with the Combined Services 1951 championship and the German Club Riders championship. The Saturday meeting was for preliminaries for time elimination to select the sixteen finalists and the first eight heats of the championship. The Sunday was for the remaining twelve heats plus the eight heats of the championship and the last race for the Challenge cup".

After National service, Alan emigrated to New Zealand for some 25 years. During his years in the Rickety Isles Alan rode solo and sidecar speedway as well as reporting events for British magazine the *Speedway Star*. During his racing career in NZ, he won the countries sidecar title in 1965 and 1971 and he became the first rider to hold the New Zealand, North Island and Auckland sidecar titles at the same time. Until the closure of south London track Wimbledon in 2005 he held the post of track photographer at the luxurious venue.

Jimmy Gooch 1949 BAOR Combined Services Champion

LIONS CHASED ARMY TALENT

Captain Alec Jackson of the Royal Army Service Corps never forgot his civilian job as team manager of the famous Wembley 'Lions'. Barely was the war over in 1945 when he recognised the potential of the Army speedway activity in Germany and in preparation for the resumption of league racing in 1946, he invited aspiring serving despatch riders to write to him for a trial. A feature in the October edition of the *Picture Post* of 1945 highlighted his search for new blood to form the nucleus of the Lions 10 man squad. Following Jackson's appeal he received letters from all over the world, the only stipulation was that all applicants should be under 25 years old.

Many hopefuls had little experience but Jackson held the view, given an out of the way training track such as Rye House and the opportunities for concentrated practice, he could produce new stars in a much shorter period than the previously accepted two years. Over 350 hopefuls were put through their paces with all racing equipment provided. Jackson's opinion of soldiers who applied was that war service had toughened them up to such an extent that he could get them into 'first class' after just six months concentrated training. He found them able to take falls without injury and their physical fitness enabled them to practice for longer sustained periods than civilian applicants.

COMBINED SERVICES CHAMPIONSHIP

BAOR Championship rider parade 1950

By 1948, such was the standing and success of the Hanomag track in Hanover that the first of the annual BAOR forces championship meetings was stage there. The Saints club had been staging an annual individual meeting as early as October 1945, with Gordon McGregor being an early competitor. It was therefore no surprise that Hanomag stadium was selected to host the most prestigious meeting of the forces calendar. Evidence exists of Egyptian, Italian and Libyan forces championships being held in their particular warzones, but the Hanover circuit is the only forces wide championship. In reality the competition, was a full blown event with qualifying competitions for Army, Royal Navy and RAF personnel based in Germany and was considered by professional clubs in England as a good breeding ground for future riders.

Corporal 'Paddy' Pullen won the first event in 1948 scoring 14pts from five rides beating Larry Lazarus who went on to ride for Glasgow Ashfield. The championship ran from 1948 to 1951, with Ken McKinlay, Eric Boothroyd and Jimmy Gooch having their first speedway rides before progressing to league clubs in Britain.

COMBINED SERVICES CHAMPIONSHIP (1948-51)

1948

1st	Cpl 'Paddy' Pullen	14pts
2nd	'Jock' Lazarus	13pts
3rd	'Speed' McCarthy	12pts
4th	ASM 'Crash' Callaghan	11pts
	Sigmn 'Bronco' Hill	11pts
5th	'Lefty' Lancaster	9pts
	Cpl Harry Datridge	9pts
6th	Sgt 'Splash' Fountain	7pts
	Cpl 'Bill' Whatling	7pts
	Cpl 'Jock' McKinlay	7pts
7th	Sgt 'Oozlum' Fulljames	6pts
8th	Sgt 'Busty' Brindley	4pts
9th	Cfn 'Paddy' Scragg	3pts
	Pte 'Geoff' Moody	3pts
10th	Sgt 'Bill' Taylor	2pts
	'Tiny' Farr	2pts

1950

1st	ASM 'Crash' Callaghan	11pts
2nd	Fl Sgt 'Bas' Sheppard	10pts
3rd	Sigmn 'Ace' King	9pts
	Sgt 'Smudger' Smith	9pts
	Cpl 'Skid' Fookes	9pts
	Cfn Dennis McDermott	9pts
4th	Cpl 'Jimmie' Ireland	6pts
	Sigmn 'Warren' Leathe	6pts
5th	Cpl 'Flyer' Jones	5pts
	Fl Sgt 'Buck' Thomsett	5pts
6th	ACI 'Olly' Elliot	4pts
	Sigmn 'Dave' Thompson	4pts
7th	Sgt 'Splash' Fountain	3pts
8th	Cpl 'George' Boughton	2pts
	Cfn 'Nobby' Clark	2pts
9th	'Zipp' Zammit	1pt

Silver Helmets as trophies for BAOR Championship winners

1949

1st	Cpl Jimmy Gooch
2nd	Cpl 'Mickie' Meacher
3rd	Cpl 'Flyer' Jones
4th	Cpl Eric Boothroyd
5th	Cpl 'Des' Darwin
	Cpl 'Skid' Fookes
6th	ASM 'Crash" Callaghan
7th	Cpl 'Zipp' Zammit
	Sgt 'Kit' Yard
	Mr 'Jonnie' Wilkes
8th	Mr 'Trailer' Smith
	Drv 'Darkie' Bowden
9th	Sigmn 'Harry' Cook
	Cpl 'George' Boughton
	S.Sgt 'Splash' Fountain
10th	Sgt 'Oozlum' Fulljames

1951

1st	'Zipp' Zammit	12pts
2nd	'Mickie' Meacher	11pts
3rd	'Smudger' Smith	10pts
4th	'Ace' King	8pts
	"Splash" Fountain	8pts
5th	'Artie' Marsh	7pts
6th	'Ted' Sumner	6pts
	'Flyer' Jones	6pts
	'Warren' Leather	6pts
7th	'Slim' Evershed	4pts
	'George' Boughton	4pts
	'Skid' Fookes	4pts
8th	'Dart' Clark	3pts
	'Tim' Healy	3pts
9th	'Bill' Heffey	2pts
	'Yorky' Harness	2pts

MEMORABLE MATCH DAY

1949 Combined Services Championship

1ST Cpl Jimmy Gooch
2nd Cpl 'Mickie' Meacher
3rd Cpl 'Flyer' Jones

Jimmy (left)

Jimmy Gooch, who was destined for a professional speedway career in England at both club and country level, amazingly qualified for the 1949 BAOR Combined Services speedway championship with a Wembley contract already in his back pocket! On his previous leave back home in England Jimmy had applied for a trial at Wembley and Alec Jackson was so impressed with what he saw that he registered him as a Wembley asset. The BAOR championship was an annual event, held at the Hanomag track in Hanover, which was Jimmy's home track. Qualification was through a system of time trials with the 16 fastest riders going forward to the 16 heat, four ride championship. After his four programmed rides, Jimmy had tied on points with his fellow Hanomag 'Saint' Corporal 'Mickie' Meacher. He was victorious in a two man run-off against Meacher who had served in the Royal Navy before joining the Army, and so Jimmy was declared the champion. In fourth place was Cpl Boothroyd who was to join the Birmingham 'Brummies'and later became a successful promoter and a prominent member of the British Speedway Promoters Association.

That September day in 1949 was to end in tragedy for a German competitor riding in the four team German championship held after the main event. Herr Kuepper lost control of his machine and rode straight into a drain hole on the centre green, resulting in him having to have his leg amputated. A benefit meeting was held at the Schnde track to raise funds for his family and Colonel Dundas, President of the Hanomag club expressed the view that so keen was Kuepper on his speedway, that he didn't rule out him riding the following season with a wooden leg! The Colonel had to write to the British speedway press to assure the speedway world that the German rider hadn't in fact been killed in the incident.

MALTESE RIDER WON LAST BAOR FORCES CHAMPIONSHIP

Corporal George Zammit of 12 Heavy Base workshop REME , 'Zipp' to his legion of forces and civilian fans, made a clean sweep of the silverware in the last Combined Services championship meeting in 1951 , as racing ceased at the Hanomag stadium. George had served as an instrument mechanic with REME in Malta where he was born, before being transferred to German and discovering speedway. He had made gradual progress having competed in the 1949 and 1950 BAOR championships and captained the Wembley 'Saints'. The Hanover Challenge Cup, raced for at the end of each meeting at Hanomag almost became his personal property in 1951, winning the trophy eight times during the twelve meeting season. 'Zipp' had aspirations of riding professionally after leaving the Army and was quoted at the time as saying *"I've made many friends in Germany and England but what is most important of all, I have been able to get on the bottom rung of the speedway ladder"*. No evidence can be found to confirm 'Zipp' attempted to break into the professional scene in England.

'Zipp' Zamitt BAOR Champion 1951

ARMY TEAM KEPT THE FLAG FLYING

Whilst England were failing to win the speedway Ashes series back home in 1949 (the Australians won the rubber 3-2), the British Army team were upholding national pride in Germany. It was in September of 1949 that the Hanomag 'Saints' took on the full might of the ADAC (Allemagne Deutche Automobil Club) in a 25 heat team event in Hanover. A crowd of some 6,500 fans saw the Army defeat the Germans 99-51pts. Although the Army were using WD bikes modified for speedway by REME, times were fast. Corporal 'Flyer' Jones covered four laps of the 440 yards circuit in 86.5seconds which represented an average speed of 50 mph. The following season the meeting was repeated with a similar result, 95-36pts, even though the ADAC riders were by now competing on the more conventional JAP speedway machines. The Army team on this occasion received some assistance from the RAF with Fl Sgt Sheppard, AC Sidney Thomsett and John Ellis wearing Army colours.

TEAM RACING

Matches between Hanomag 'Saints' and German civilian teams as well as inter-unit team clashes involving REME, Royal Engineers, Royal Corps of Signals, Royal Army Ordnance Corps and Royal Army Service Corps were common in the late 40's. They were supplemented by 'International' matches against the 'Silver Streaks', the early return to a National German side which was of course politically sensitive at a time when the country was trying to forget the nationalistic days of the Nazi regime. Pre- season practice was always an exciting time as riders prepared for the new season and attempted to obtain team places. With so much interest there were some 76 registered riders for the 1950 season and some method of skill grading was required to ensure competitor safety and of course competitive racing for the 2,000 or so regular supporters. All riders were put through a time trial to decide their category for the season. Not unlike the Formula 1 qualifying system of today to determine grid position, four timed laps of the 440 yard Hanomag track being used to grade riders for the start of the season . To reach Main event standard needed a time of 92secs or less, Junior 92-98 secs and Novice 98 secs plus.

By the 1950's a new formula of team events was tried, with practical support in terms of race jackets and some equipment being given by the more enlightened professional British teams who could see the Army leagues as a good source of potential future stars. With the permission of the respective English promoters, four teams, namely Wembley, Odsal, New Cross and Birmingham 'Saints' started competing in a mini league. By 1951 some one hundred riders were registered with the Hanomag club, competing under the auspices of the MCRA, BAOR and ACU Speedway regulations.

'Crash' Callaghan BAOR champion 1950

ASM Callaghan, a founder member of the 'Saints' club retired from racing to become the club coach and steward, with Cpt Derby (RAOC) and Mr Jones (REME) often officiating at Hanover meetings. German riders had developed to such a standard that from 1949 their own individual championship meeting was staged alongside the Combined Services

event and it is believed the present day enthusiasm for speedway in Northern Germany stems from the memorable Sunday afternoon events at Hanomag! Records indicate that a gradual reduction in British forces personnel from the end of 1951 and the loss of key organisers, who left the Army, was to mark the end of racing at the Hanomag stadium.

George Broughton New Cross 'Saints' coaching a novice soldier

WARZONE MEMORIES

Mary Hodges

Mary was a Lance Corporal in the ATS in Germany 1945-46. *"I was stationed near Hanover just after the war and we sometimes went to the Hanomag speedway at the weekends. I remember we came back with dirty hands and faces from the cinder track. We really enjoyed our outings. Happy Times!"*

Nancy Richie Thompson

"I was an ATS girl with the RAOC at Wehnengen, outside Hanover, and many boys and girls in uniform would clamber aboard a 3 tonne truck on a Sunday afternoon to see the Hanomag 'Saints'. My name before I was married was Nancy Craven and I originated from Castle Douglas, later living in Thornhill in Dumfrieshire. I now have a son whose Christian name is Craven".

Ted White

Ted was with REME 1949-50 and remembers his time working on the track in Hanover. *"For six months I was the Hanomag track curator which I remember was located at the back of the 12 Heavy Base workshops in Hanover. Other than attending morning parade I spent my days grading and preparing the track for the fortnightly race meetings. I recall I had a German civilian who worked with me. Before the war the factory was a commercial vehicle manufacturing plant, but during the war it made type 88 guns for tanks. The REME lads were highly skilled at preparing WD bikes which they built from Army despatch motor cycles. One of the German lads had a proper speedway JAP but he couldn't get near the top Army riders. There was one memorable coach trip when the 'Saints' rode away at Hamburg against the "Lions". My lasting memory of Hamburg was the amount of bomb damage, it must have taken a real pasting from the RAF bombers".*

Phil Basey

Phil was attached to RASC between 1941-47 and spent most of his war in Europe. *"My love affair with the cinders game started at Norwich's Firs stadium in 1937 where I started as a pro-*

gramme seller. I rode after the war at High Beech but remained on the Norwich track staff until the track closed in 1964. I believe I was the longest serving staff member and think I am also the last person to ride at the Firs. It was the Sunday before the track demolition started in 1964, when I took my son along with our road bikes and had one last spin around the track".

In 1973, his motorcycling experience came in useful again when he doubled for actor John Le Messurier in a Dads Army episode called 'The Honourable Man'. Over 12 million viewers watched Phil on his faithful, restored Matchless G3L ride off into the distance playing Sgt Wilson.

Basil Sheppard

Fl Sgt 'Bas' Sheppard was something of an oddity at Hanomag as he was one of the few RAF personnel given permission to ride speedway by their commanding officers. *"One of my happiest and yet saddest memories of my time riding at Hanomag was the strong bond a local German boy formed with me when I was riding. When I arrived each week at the pits gate he was always there to carry my kit into the pits and we became close even though he couldn't speak English. I still remember my last meeting at Hanomag before returning home to England .The boy, I can't recall his name, understood I was going away and he wouldn't see me again. He stood outside the pits gate crying as I drove away for the last time and I often wonder what became of him".*

David Hurrell

As a young school boy in Germany after the war, David, son of ASM Frank Hurrell, Hanomag club secretary, was something of a local celebrity. *"I was still at school when dad became involved with the speedway and it was very exciting to mix with the riders. I was only nine or ten years old, and these men were local heroes but they treated me as very much part of the team. I was mascot for the 'Saints' team and I can still recall the after meeting parties held at our house when many of the team came round to drink and relax. I particularly remember 'Crash' Callaghan and 'Bas' Sheppard, but they were all great blokes and very kind to me"*

Captain Stubbs

As a war correspondent Cpt Stubbs was based in Northern Germany and got to know many of the Hanomag team of the late 40's.

"Staff Sergeant Edward 'Splash' Fountain was a regular soldier with REME, having joined the Army as a boy soldier in 1938. He was vice captain of the Wembley "Saints" team and the very backbone of the Hanomag club. During the war he fought in France and Germany before joining the Central Inspectorate of Vehicles where he had a fearsome reputation for speaking his mind if he found any maintenance work not up to the required standard. His wife and two daughters regularly watched him race. 'Splash' could always be depended upon to

'Splash' Fountain

share his mechanical and track craft skills with junior riders. He was the only rider to have competed in all four Combined Services championships held between 1948-1951".

***'Jimmie' Ireland** only joined the Army in 1950 as a Lance Corporal but he made sure he was based near Hanover as he had read about the Army speedway activities from articles in the Motor Cycle magazine. He was a one time pupil of Eric Chitty and Dicky Case and made the Harringay junior team before his National Service call up. He was always very complimentary of the engineering skills of the workshop engineers within REME, saying I give full marks to the backroom boys who pull the extra horse power out of what are practically standard motor. Our bikes are heavier than the average dirt JAP engine job, but they don't lack much in poke, and don't forget we run on standard fuel".*

***Corporal 'Mickie' Meacher** was something of an adventurer, he was in the Merchant Navy before joining the Royal Corps of Signals. His white helmet was his on track trade mark, and when off track he was an accomplished ice skater. A skilled Motor Transport fitter and a keen road racing exponent, Mickie was looking towards a professional speedway career when his stint in the army finished".*

***George Broughton** was a regular soldier, joining the Army in 1944 as a parachutist and served in India during the war. Corporal Boughton was an unconventional soldier in that he wrote poetry to relax. A mean footballer, he has aspirations to ride speedway professionally and had a trial with Les Marshall's Birmingham team".*

AUSTRIA

A Nazi invasion of Austria was inevitable as it had always been part of Hitler's grand plan to unite German speaking people and to develop Greater Germany. An Austrian by birth himself, Adolf Hitler gave the order in April 1938 to annex Austria by sending his armed forces across the border on the basis of "Establishing peace and to prevent bloodshed in Austria". The country was occupied more or less willingly until the end of the war losing 400,000 soldiers and 150,000 civilians during the near six years of conflict.

IN THE ZONE

Whilst not being a mainstream speedway nation prior to 1939, Leopold Dirtl was the pre-war National speedway champion, the arrival of British troops from Italy as the war was ending did much to kick start the post war racing scene. The Americans had entered Austria in May 1945, but by August of 1946 oval grass-speedway racing was being organised by the Styria club in conjunction with REME, RASC and the Royal Corps Signals at the Gossendorf racecourse in Graz. Currency problems made it almost impossible for Austrian riders to purchase equipment and so it was left to REME to cannibalize WD bikes for scrambles, time trials and speedway.

MEMORABLE MATCH DAY - August 5 1946

Generally regarded as the first motor cycle event in Austria since the cessation of hostilities, a grass-speedway meeting, was held on the centre of the Gossendorf horse race course near Graz. Under the auspices of the Styria District Motor Cycle Club and the 46th Infantry Division of the British Army, a meeting on what was described as the small circuit (119seconds to the lap) was staged. Records are understandably scarce but evidence of a seven team event, three riders to a team and points awarded on the traditional 3-2-1 point basis exists. Teams competing included 760 Base workshop (REME), 500 AOD, 519 Coy (RASC) and the 2nd Hampshire Regiment.

S.Sgt Jack Uglow well remembers this first meeting when serving with REME and recalls the events of the day.

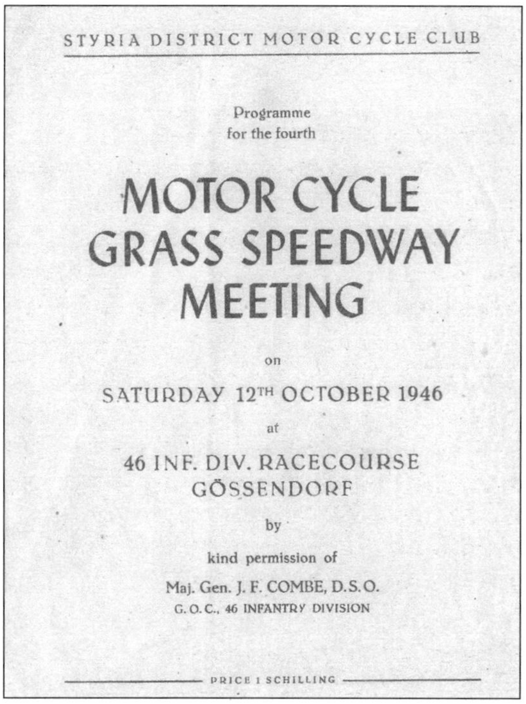

STYRIA DISTRICT MOTOR CYCLE CLUB

Programme
for the fourth

MOTOR CYCLE
GRASS SPEEDWAY
MEETING

on

SATURDAY 12TH OCTOBER 1946

at

46 INF. DIV. RACECOURSE
GÖSSENDORF

by

kind permission of

Maj. Gen. J. F. COMBE, D.S.O.
G. O. C., 46 INFANTRY DIVISION

PRICE 1 SCHILLING

Gossendorf programme

"In 1946, I was posted to 760 Base workshop REME, Thondon near Graz in Austria and competition motorcycles from Italy were moved to our new location, which allowed the continuation of motor cycle sport including some highly organised inter-services trials and grass track events. Motor Cycle grass-speedway was held at Gossendorf on August 5th and October 12th 1946. The track at Gossendorf was a large ' leg of mutton' shaped course with a hairpin bend at one end followed by a sweeping curve and a fast straight. I excelled, losing out only twice in a number of highly charged battles, and held the race record time. Here, without a doubt motor cycle sport was encouraged by the Army top brass particularly Lt Colonel Vaux who had moved up to Austria from Italy and who was himself a very able competitor. Because my machine ran so well, I was required to prepare engines for Cpt Ashley Wing and Cpt Perry who were in our team. I believe Cpt Perry came from the Bristol area and I often wondered if there was any family connection with Tig Perry who was involved in frame manufacturing in the 1980s. Photos of racing showed we raced in shirt sleeve order with helmet, breeches and knee boots, and I believe there was a barrel of cider in the pits for refreshments!

As well as grass track racing, trials motorcycle football, speedway, scrambles and hill climbs were held. I forget where the dirt track was located, but I have memories of racing in cold weather on a half mile dirt track with a terrifying outer fence of posts and rails! Another fun event was racing around a football pitch covered in deep snow towing someone on skis. I remember it was difficult to get moving, but once on the move the tension on the rope to the ski passenger tended to prevent over sliding on the bends."

First bend at Gossendorf racecourse

Cold weather didn't seem to deter practice during the winter months in Austria, as can be seen from this very rare picture of an unknown Sergeant practising a start at an unknown circuit riding a very early modified War Department 'dirt track' bike.

Unknown 'Dirt track sergeant' winter 1946

Martin Schneewies

POST WAR RIDER ROSTER

Fred/Fritz Dirtl, Rudolph Runtsch, Frank Aigner, Leopold Kilmayer, Joseph Chalupa, Raymond Voll, Frederick Lenny, Leonard Fassl, Ingemar Barder, Georgs Mach, Martin Schneeweis.

Footnote: Such was the standing of Schneewies in the Austrian post-war sporting heroes Hall of Fame that when he died he was given a tomb of honour in the centre of Vienna.

PALESTINE

After WW1, Palestine was administered by Britain under a Mandate from the League of Nations. Following WWII, Britain's position in Palestine progressively deteriorated, attacks by Irgan and Lehi factions on British officials, troops and installations caused damage to morale and encouraged a "bring the boys back home" campaign back in the UK. World opinion did not agree with the British policy of preventing Jewish Zionist holocaust survivors from returning to Palestine. Over 100,000 troops in Palestine were being funded at a time when the British economy was suffering a post-war depression. In 1947 the government announced the desire to terminate it's mandate and pass responsibility for Palestine to the United Nations. The UN introduced a partition plan with David Ben-Gurin, whilst the Arab committee ordered strikes on Jewish shops and households. These attacks led to widespread fighting between the Arabs and Jews, this civil war being the first phase of the 1948 Israel war of independence.

IN THE ZONE

The early issues of the Bar-None MCC monthly bulletins of 1945 confirms that a Palestinian branch of the club existed in Ein Shemer, with club meetings being held in No 2 Navigation class room at RAF Ein Shemer. Around 50 members, primarily RAF personnel were holding 'riding tests', described by the bulletin as a course which consisted of approximately three quarters of a mile of straight riding including two open bends, followed by two throttle control tests.

Veterans interviewed recall scrambles and trials in Palestine before the hurried evacuation of British troops to Egypt in 1947 onwards as the hand over to United Nations forces commenced. In 1947 an Infantry team, the 2nd Lincolns, accepted an invitation from El Ballah to bring a team of eight riders to ride against the 'Aces'. Led by Don Cuppleditch, who later rode for Edinburgh, the Lincoln's team was Cooper, Jolly, Hitchensen, Blowes, Ogden, Twine and Taylor. The match programme of the day explained *"Since the invite to ride here, the Lincolns have been to Palestine and have held a number of meetings there"* so implying that sand track trials(speedway) was staged in Palestine. RAF records show that eight operational airfields existed under the British Mandate arrangements which would have provided secure compounds, similar to an army garrison, which would have allowed the construction of oval circuits.

Further evidence comes from Scottish speedway historian Ian Moultray who found the picture featuring Lieutenant Don Cuppleditch in a late 1940's Edinburgh speedway programme. The caption accompanying this rare image does raise some intriguing issues.

Speedway Racing by the Dead Sea.

Lieutenant Don Cuppleditch riding for 2nd Lincolnshire Regiment

Evidence of 'speedway' in Palestine is extremely rare, and from a military strategy standpoint "Racing by the Dead Sea" (the lowest point on earth not covered by water or ice) would have been precarious. The sea measures 42 miles long and 11 miles wide, lying almost central between what is now Jordan and Israel and would have been a very hazardous location at the time of the Jewish-Arab conflict.

TRACK INDEX: Sarafand, Gaza

WARZONE MEMORIES

S/Sgt Gordon Miles

Gordon served with the Royal Army Service Corps attached to 800 COY, 16th Airborne Division. Based in Gaza 1964-47, recalls his motor cycling exploits in the Palestine warzone. *"A few of the lads wanted to go motorcycling so I asked if a supply of surplus WD bikes could be found for us. We were hoping for Matchless bikes but some weeks later six rather heavy BSA M20s arrived at the workshop on the back of an lorry" explains Gordon "When we weren't busy recovering or repairing Army transport of all shapes and sizes, we spent time practicing on our at bikes at Gaza and I believe Sarafand. The equipment was basic but we made progress and we even rode in a challenge match at Tel el Kabir in Egypt. The TEK speedway guys absolutely thrashed us, but I can still recall the journey under military escort across the Sinai desert. The journey took days across some hostile country".*

Sgt Gordon Miles (far left) riding for RASC in Palestine

After the war, Gordon was heavily involved in grass track racing and was the starter at Minety Vale meetings. Gordon's Army mechanical skills were put to good use when he built a starting gate for meetings at Long Newnton and the gate was so successful that it was used at National Championship meetings.

Len Wood

Len served with the Lincolnshire Regiment in Palestine (1946-48), and one of his most enduring memories of his time in one of the most dangerous of warzones, was the bombing by terrorists of the King David Hotel in Jerusalem where British Army officers were based.

"My recollections of the Lincoln's speedway team surrounds how they 'acquired' the bikes which they rode" explains Len "There was a fire in one of the stores where all the transport, cars, bikes, lorries were parked and everyone who could drive or ride became involved in the rescue of these vehicles from the fire. Some seven brand new Despatch riders bikes somehow were never returned! and were modified by the REME unit for the team to race. The big name rider I remember is one Jack Kitchener but I have no idea what happened to him".

Ray Freeman

Ray from Worcester was in 2 Air Support Signals as a DR and recalls the Royal Corps Signals speedway team which he rode briefly for, including a match against the Lincolns in Palestine. *"The 2nd Lincolnshire Regiment challenged 2 ASSU to a speedway match on the sand. They had a team organised by Lieutenant Cuppleditch who I believe had ridden professionally. We were disadvantaged from the start when our C.O. only agreed to us competing on the condition that if we stripped down our motorcycles for racing, they had to be put back in*

A1 condition in time for the next inspection. The 2nd Lincolns had their own REME unit who had built up bikes out of scrap motorcycles just for racing. We had no track to practice on and were not allowed a practice lap on their track before racing started. They beat us easily but we had an enjoyable afternoon on the shores of the Dead Sea. I was demobbed shortly afterwards and I was home in time to watch myself racing on a newsreel at the local Gaumont Cinema".

Frank Gale

Frank served with the Lincolnshire Regiment in an Intelligence unit at Sarafand in Palestine *"I recall the Mechanical Transport Officer was a keen motorcyclist and he arranged a speedway match on the sand at Sarafand. I volunteered to help in the organisation and with a corporal ended up running the 'bookies' table which enabled troops to bet on the four men in each race"*

Frank Gale ,cigarette in mouth, at the bookies table at a Sarafand speedway meeting

"My only other memory of those events of 60 years ago, was the metal steel shoes the riders wore. One rider had made a 12" x 8"mini metal ski which he wore on his left foot. It was crude but very effective and acted like a snow ski, enabling the rider to skate around the corners without his foot digging into the sand and slowing him down".

On demob, Frank found that in 1948 his home town Coventry entered professional speedway as the 'Bees'. Frank became a supporter, with Vic Emms becoming his favourite rider.

Don Cuppleditch

Don served in Palestine between 1945-47 and is seen by many Army veterans as the father of forces speedway in this most dangerous of warzones.

Speaking from his home in Adelaide, Australia Don remembers *"I was transport officer for the battalion and organised a trials event amongst the sand dunes. At the presentation event, Brigadier Davis asked if I could organise an event which would provide entertainment for the troops as all bars, clubs, cinemas etc were out of bounds to forces personnel because of the terrorist threat. He offered me six Matchless G3L motorbikes which were much more suitable 'sand trials' (speedway) than our heavy BSA machines. The only condition was that we had to be able to rebuild them to full WD specification after stripping them for racing. I recall arranging two speedway events in Palestine by the Dead Sea located between Jericho and the Bitter Lake. We also travelled to Egypt and rode 'away' meetings at Fayid and Cairo. To ensure tight security for both riders and spectators, the two Palestine meetings were only advertised in military newspapers and travelling supporters and the competing riders were given a military escort to the track"*

Don, now 84 years old, still has fond memories of his professional career, in particular riding against an Overseas team comprising of Australians and New Zealanders. A meeting at Wembley in front of an enormous post- war crowd and his 1953 season when he was second highest top scorer in the UK that year are other highlights which still remain with him to this day.

Busetta 1949

Located just outside Tripoli, Busetta was primarily a racecourse where horse racing was the regular attraction. Early meeting were not publicised but once the locals became involved, crowds of 2,000 were common!

Seaview Speedway 1950

Located on the seafront at Tripoli, this rare picture circa 1950 shows a packed stand, floodlights and all the facilities which would have not been out of place back in Britain in the post war boom!

LIBYA

Italy conquered the Libyan capital of Tripoli during the Turkish-Italian war of 1911-12, and by the Treaty of Ouchy which ended the war, Turkey granted Tripoli and Northern Libya autonomy. By 1914 Italy occupied much of the country, although they were forced to undertake a series of wars of pacification until Libya was made an integral part of Italy in 1939, Libya became one of the main battle grounds of North Africa after Italy entered WWII in June 1940. Contrary to expectations the British, under General Wavell, made the first moves in desert fighting by ordering General O'Connor to form a Western desert force to attack Italian frontier positions in Libya. After the Allied victory over the Axis powers in 1943, Libya was placed under an Anglo-French military government. Great Britain, France, United States and the USSR failed to reach agreement about the future of Libya as stipulated in the 1947 peace treaty with Italy. The United Nations was given jurisdiction and decided that Libya should become independent which it achieved on Christmas Eve 1951.

IN THE ZONE

Brigades of Guards, particularly the Coldstream, and Grenadiers, were deployed to the Tripoli area during the period of British administration prior to independence. Many had been evacuated from Palestine in 1948, with Gaol and Prinn barracks becoming home for their time in North Africa. Despatch rider bikes were rescued and loaded for the trip to Libya, and so it was that these rather basic damaged bikes provided the raw material for what was to become for a brief period at least, a golden period for Army speedway.

Busetta Racecourse speedway -1949

Two tracks are recorded in the coastal city of Tripoli, namely Busetta and Seaview. Busetta was the local horse racecourse which, with a fully equipped grandstand on the home straight provided ideal seated cover for crowds of up to 2,000. The first recorded meeting here has been traced to Boxing Day 1948, when the Grenadier Guards team the 'Hellcats' defeated the Irish Guards 77-45 points. These early meetings were not officially open to the public, but gradually a number of teams were formed, with the Royal Corps Signals 'Meteors' team becoming the 'Hellcats' greatest rivals. Some 2,000 spectators attended the first Busetta meeting open to the public in April 1949. Well tuned bikes, professional track preparation and even team race jackets made by serviceman Dougie Ashfield all added to a professional show and proved great entertainment for the troops. Such was the interest in Tripoli for speedway racing that during the winter of 1949, £1,000 from the Army Welfare fund was used to construct a quarter mile track on a disused sea plane landing strip in front of the famous Tripoli promenade which faced the sea. The track aptly named 'Seaview' was a true cinder, rather than sand track, and remarkably had full seating on one side and even floodlights installed by M troop. Meetings were originally held on Sunday evenings but proved so popular that Wednesday night meetings were added to cope with the local interest. At its peak some 12 teams were competing against each other, including an Italian team called the 'Black Devils'

TEAM LIST 1950

Coldstream Guards -'Whirlwinds'
6th Field Regiment - 'Outlaws'
RAOC - 'Pirates'
Grenadier Guards - 'Hellcats'
RCS - 'Meteors'
Coldstream Guards - 'Wombats'
Command Workshop - 'Tornadoes'
RASC - 'Cobras'
Guards Brigade - 'Bulldogs'
'Rascals', 'Camerons' (Unknown)

Track index: 1. Busetta (Tripoli) 2. Seaview (Tripoli)

Seaview Tripoli 1950

MEMORABLE MATCH DAY

Grenadier Guards 'Hellcats' v Tripoli MCC April 1949

The first ever public speedway meeting at the Busetta racecourse track on the outskirts of Tripoli, previous meetings had been closed to the public, saw the Grenadiers defeat the Italian Circolo Motociclistico de Tripoli club in a 16 heat team match. It was however the Italians who gained revenge by winning 5-1 in a motorcycle football match staged after the racing. The historic meeting was covered by the local Tripoli newspaper that had a staff reporter present to record what was the real start of Libyan forces speedway.

1st Battalion Grenadier Guards 'Hellcats'

"Hellcats" Gain Narrow Victory Over Italian Team

(By a Staff Reporter)

WE were promised thrills—we had more than enough; we were promised spills—we had those too; in fact Tripoli's first public Speedway meeting at Buscetta on Sunday last was all that was promised and generally considered a success from start to finish.

Close on 2,000 spectators watched the 16 heats and saw the « Hellcats » (1st. Bn. Grenadier Guards) emerge the victors over Circolo Motociclistico di Tripoli, by the narrow margin of seven points.

On the other hand, fastest track time was recorded by Sig. M. Barbera, Italian team manager and crack rider. He clocked 65.222 kms. p.h.—three kilometres faster than his nearest rival, « Flash » Walker, captain of the « Hellcats ».

It was every bit as impressive as Stamford Bridge or Wembley as the teams rode abreast onto the sand track which was fenced off with esparto grass, to make their debute.

Relayed gramophone music gave us the stirring strains of « The entry of the Gladiators ».

Bouquets of carnations were exchanged by the team captains and the racing began in earnest. Excitement ran high as, towards the end of the meeting, the Italians crept up almost to level points.

TOUCH AND GO.

The last heat provided one of the finest finishes of the meeting. « Crash » Jackson lived up to his name—and crashed. It was left to « Dusty » Smith, whom, I learn, is just out of hospital, to gain a valuable two points with second place.

Then « Flash » Walker and « Crash » Jackson (making amends) clinched matters by carrying off first and third places respectively in the re-run of heat 11, a heat that

Team Managers: Sgt. « Smokey » Last and Sig. B. Barbera.

Track Officials: Starter: Gdsn. G. Green; Timekeepers: Sgt. J. Baker, Sig. Modena, Comm. Viganò; Announcer: Sgt. J. Last; Judges: Sgt. Allen, Cpl. Ball, L/Cpl. Thomas, Sgn. Morrison, Sig. Pappalardo, Sig. Paganelli, Sig. Chiarelli and Sig. Brandani.

Pit Attendants: Gdsn. T. D. C. Blowers, Gdsn. W. Hills, Sig. Agodi, Sig. Scarso, Sig. Casesi and Sig. Bagni.

'biting the dust' and the fourth going inside the tape.

A brief interval and we were treated to ten minutes each way of Motor Cycle Football. No one actually managed to 'take off', but there were spills in plenty. Score: Tripoli Motor Cycle Club 5, « Hellcats » 1.

Lieut.-Colonel E.D. Good, C.B., Royal Signals, presented the cups at the close of a very successful meeting.

TEAMS

« Hellcats »: Sgt. « Skid » Chance; Sgt. « Slide » Taylor; Cpl. « Flash » Walker; Cpl. « Thrasher » Cook; Gdsn. « Crash » Jackson; Gdsn. « Slogger » Holmes; Gdsn. « Tot » Townsend and Gdsn. « Dusty » Smith (1st. reserve).

Circolo Motociclistico di Tripoli: Sig. Mantovani; Sig. Mazzoni; Sig. Barva; Sig. Busetta; Sig. Barbera and Sig. Bonaccorso.

Match report from the Sunday Ghibli

I WAS THERE by Tom 'Brassy' Taylor

Sgt Tom Taylor, now living in France with his wife Beryl, recalls well his time in the 1st battalion Grenadier Guards when it was decided to build a speedway track as a sporting recreation for servicemen in Tripoli.

Explaining the building process of 1949 Tom explains *"We found a fairly flat area of desert near the Busetta racecourse suitable for a track. I removed the body off an Averion 15 cwt truck which had a steel body. We then removed the tail board to make a scoop, like a digger bucket, then attached two jeeps to either side and pulled it around the oval to mark out the track. As it was towed around we shovelled the excess sand to the outside to form the track perimeter."*

Tom, nicknamed 'Brassy' continues *"After the mornings work, we went back to the barracks for lunch. When we returned to pick up the body we had removed from the truck earlier in the day, to our surprise it was not there. The Arabs had stolen it! The mystery was there were no footprints and as they didn't have a helicopter we just didn't know how they did it. I was put on a charge for losing it".*

Tom remembers the rivalry between the 'Hellcats' and the 'Meteors'. Early in 1949 the 'Meteors' gained revenge for previous challenge match defeats between the by winning 46-44points. The Hellcats team that day nearly 60 years ago was: Sgt Chance, Sgt 'Brassy' Taylor, Cpl 'Hookey' Walker, Cpl Ray Cook, Gdsmn Jackson, Gdsmn Holmes, Gdsmn Townsend and Gdsmn Smith.

WARZONE MEMORIES

Signals Corps 'Meteors' celebrate a successful seasons racing

Dusty Miller.
"I joined the Royal Corps Signals 'Meteors' speedway team in 1949 on arrival at 1 Div Signals in Tripoli. I had travelled with several of the White Helmet motorcycle display team which had been appearing in the Royal Tournament. As I remember it, the team was made up of myself, Sgt Ken Allen (captain), S.Sgt Brierley, Sgt Taffy Burgess, L.Cpl Tillotson, the other lads being national servicemen. The photo was taken after we had won the 'Hookey' Walker memorial trophy (the full story of Walker's death is featured later). The Tripoli track was I recall on the sea front (Seaview) and crowds of around 5,000 attended. As I recall the Italians had three teams, the Arabs two more with REME, the Guards and ourselves. On my return to the UK I had a trial at Wimbledon arranged by Ronnie Greene but like most soldiers could not afford a machine of my own so that was that!"

Christopher Wallace
Chris, who served in Libya between 1948-51, was the adopted brother of Mrs Farrant of Gloucester. The family had a tradition as a forces family with her father being buried in Singapore after being killed whilst serving with the Army. Chris rode for the 'Pirates' at Seaview before his demob back to England. His love of motor cycles was to lead to his sad death .Whilst returning home from work one day, his motor cycle was in collision with a dust cart and he was killed.

Alex Peters
Alex saw service with the Queens Own Highlanders in Libya, Egypt and Germany as a despatch rider and a piper in the battalion band. *"It is over 60 years ago but I can distinctly remember being based at Prinn barracks outside Tripoli and it was suggested we should try to build a speedway track inside the perimeter of the camp. The sand sadly was too fine and deep to enable broad- siding on our heavy DR bikes. Still they were happy days".*

Jimmy 'Mitzi' Green
"I was never a rider but was proud to play my part as the starting marshal and machine examiner at the Busetta speedway events. Living in Gloucester I used to watch speedway at Swindon before joining the Guards and I really liked being involved with the 'Hellcats'. Being in the speedway team gave you some real status amongst the lads and we used to reckon it was worth a stripe if you made the team".

Jimmy Green (white coat) pictured with the 'Hellcats'

The Sunday Ghilbi was a well read newspaper in Tripoli in the late 1940's, regularly carrying match reports of the racing. A reader Mr H Wood was so impressed with the entertainment at Busetta that he wrote to the sports editor suggesting that league racing be introduced. Mr Wood's letter read *"At Busetta on Saturday last, I, amongst a large gathering of people witnessed a thrilling speedway meeting between 1st Inf, Div Signal 'Meteors' and the 1st Coldstream Guards 'Hellcats'. The good impression left upon all around me by this much belated arrival on Tripoli's short list of amenities were considerable, as also was the enthusiasm radiated by both teams. Such a sport as speedway, that gives so much enjoyment to so many, is deserving of the help from the Army authorities. Help, if forthcoming, would enable other units to raise teams, and then enable the formation of a Tripoli speedway league. The inauguration of a speedway league would bring with it more pleasant Saturday afternoons for riders and spectators alike, valuable technical experience and last but not least, a more profound esprit de corps amongst units of the Army based in Tripoli."*

Captain E J Woolnough
Military observer Cpt Woolnough kept the speedway fans back in the UK abreast of speedway racing in Tripoli in the early 50's by reporting on events in the British press. *"News of yet another desert star. He is Sgt Douglas Burgess of Pontypridd. In blue jerkin and white crash helmet a familiar figure to soldier and civilian speedway fans at week end meetings in Tripoli where he is stationed. 27 year old Sgt Burgess is a member of the 'Meteors' speedway team of the 1st Infantry Division. Arabs, Italians and American servicemen swell the enthusiastic crowds of British soldiers and families who thrill to his skill and nerve in exciting competitions between*

seven Army teams of the Tripoli club. In fact he was racing against the Italians own 'Black Devils' when he recently captured the Club's track record covering the three laps in 60.2 seconds. Sgt Burgess was employed as a transport driver until he joined the Army seven years ago (1944), and learned to ride in his early youth. One of the pioneers of the 'Meteors' team when it was formed early last year (1950), he built up his own machine in the unit workshops out of odd parts from the scrap heap. Speedway riding, I love it "said Burgess" *I intend to find a job as a vehicle mechanic in Pontypridd when I leave the Army and then I hope to join a speedway club".*

Corporal Fern Parker

"I well remember riding for the Signals speedway team on the Seaview track in Tripoli. The track surface consisted of clinker from a local power station, regularly dampened down with waste diesel oil. We used to rush out each Sunday morning to buy the Sunday Ghibli newspaper which carried match reports of the previous weeks meeting. We were not a professional side but it is nice to be remembered in the Warzone Speedway book".

Pre meeting parade at Busetta 1949

Maurice Jackson

Maurice's memories of riding in the Grenadier guards 'Hellcats' team are remarkably on public view just yards from Buckingham Palace. It is doubtful if many modern day speedway fans are aware of a unique piece of speedway history residing just down the road from the Palace in Birdcage Walk. The Guards museum houses much memorabilia including a 'Hellcats' race jacket, photographs and press cuttings in the sports section of the museum. Maurice passed away in 2002, but his personal records were donated to the museum for posterity.

Bernard Crossland

Based in Tripoli as a Guardsman in the 1st Battalion Coldstream Guards - 1st Guards Brigade, Bernard often went to the Tripolitania Speedway racing club events at Seaview speedway which was based on the foreshore, on the East side of Tripoli Harbour. Bernard's memories of Sea view are not restricted to racing however, the site being used on June 8 1950 for the annual Kings Birthday Parade. The parade, pictured below, involved the Grenadier, Coldstream and Queen's Own Cameron Highlanders in a march past in front of Brigadier W L Steele OBE. The parade also saw the trooping of the Regimental colour of the 1st Battalion Cold stream Guards on the occasion of the Tercentenary of the raising of the Regiment.

Seaview - Venue for Kings Birthday Parade

OTHER COUNTRIES

Europe, along with the Middle and Far East, were the major theatres of conflict during WWII. It was late in 1944 before armed forces speedway was possible in Italy and later Egypt as the war reached its conclusion. Periods of British occupation post-war in Austria, Germany, Libya and later Malaya gave troops further opportunities to become involved with racing. Racing was however totally impossible for many countries with pre-war speedway tradition, as their country was at the heart of a major warzone and even the re-introduction of speedway post-war was a real challenge. For completeness of the warzone story of those mainly European countries affected, and to reflect the racing story in post war warzones such as Hungary, Ireland, Rhodesia and Israel amongst others, this 'Other countries' category and the history of their post-war revival is appropriate.

Two of the biggest protagonists of WWII, namely Japan and Russia would you might think have no place in this chapter. However with a combined death toll of almost 28 million armed forces and civilian in the six year conflict and with speedway in Japan as early as 1950 and Russia some what later in 1958, you begin to understand their inclusion.

JAPAN

Japan's involvement in WWII goes back to at least 1937 when the Chinese-Japanese conflict followed the move by Japan into Chinese territory. By September 1939, Japan was in control of much of coastal China and although at this time there was no military link with Germany's invasion of Europe plans, by 1940 they had become Allies. The attack on the US fleet at Pearl Harbor in 1941 was the catalyst which effectively brought the Japanese and the United States into WWII. East Asia, the Pacific, India, New Guinea, Burma, Singapore, the Philippines and Hawaii all became targets for Japan's ambitions. After much bloody fighting the war in Europe ceased in May 1945, but Japan's determination saw the war in the Far East continue throughout the summer. Despite continual bombardment from the air, Japan refused to surrender and so it was that on August 6 the first atomic bomb was dropped of Hiroshima. This was followed by a second on Nagasaki on August 9. The following morning the Japanese sued for surrender.

IN THE ZONE

I am indebted to Australian speedway journalist Peter White for use of his research which has uncovered evidence of oval dirt track racing in Japan as early as 1950. Junich 'Jimmy' Ogisu, Takeo Sato and lady rider Nanae Ahmoto emerged as the best known rider of that era with four tracks operating at a club level. Further evidence came in 1957 when South African rider- promoter Buddy Fuller made public his plans in conjunction with Japanese promoter Mr Hogasaki to take a touring team to Mauritius and then main land Japan.

'Jimmy' Ogisu left his homeland in 1962 to ride for Australian promoter Aub Lawson at his Westmead track in Sydney and he eventually came to Britain to compete in the 1970 Wills Internationale meeting at Wimbledon. The real story of Japanese speedway came when in 1968, the government banned speedway racing on loose dirt as it considered it 'too dangerous' and ordered that all tracks had a tarmac surface laid. This led to a fundamental re-organisation of the sport with betting on racing introduced and riders using a range of Japanese manufactured bikes including Eicoh, Toyo, Megura, and Kyohuto machines. Kawaguchis speedway in Tokyo became the centre of the new sport and effectively killed all possibilities of conventional speedway gaining a foot hold in the Far East.

RUSSIA

With the postponement of Operation 'Sealion' (Germany's invasion of Britain), Germany's attention was turned to an offensive against Russia. Under the code name Operation 'Barbarossa', this campaign was launched on June 22 1941 and whilst not supported by all of Hitler's Generals, it had the effect of breaking the Nazi-Soviet pact. Bad winter weather and a fierce resistance from the Soviet forces saw 'Barbarossa' grind to a halt in December 1941, but a full blown war on the Russian front commenced. Bloody battles in Leningrad and Stalingrad ensued, with the latter being considered by many as the most significant battle of the war in Europe. By January 1945 with the Germans in retreat, the Russians launched a massive offensive from the East whilst the Allies carried out a similar push on Berlin from the West. There was a race to capture Berlin, and Russian leader Stalin felt his Red Army should have that honour. The taking of Berlin cost Russia 80,000 dead and 280,000 wounded.

Partitioning of Germany and Berlin itself was to lead to the Berlin Air Lift crisis and eventually East (Communist) and West Berlin being separated by the famous wall. The 'Iron Curtain' and Cold War was the outcome and relations with Russia and the West were very tense for many years.

IN THE ZONE

The USSR first showed interest in speedway racing in 1958 after success in the sport of Moto-Cross. It was at the Ufa club, an Army sponsored club, where Igor Plechanov, Boris Samorodov, Olejnev, Drobysko and Szajnirov first trained for speedway. Their near neighbours Poland, now of course under Soviet influence as part of the Eastern Bloc, passed on their speedway experience by acting as trainers to their Soviet master's. By 1961 international tours by the Russians to Poland and 1962 to Sweden were possible with a three test series of England being arranged in 1964. Plechanov was to prove the best of the first tranche of Russian riders, twice earning runner up spot in the World Championships of 1964 & 1965.

As with most Eastern bloc countries at this time, the Ufa club had strong Army funding which effectively gave its members professional status as full time riders. Similar arrangements existed in Czechoslovakia with Red Star Prague having strong Army links whilst in Poland the Gwardia (Police & Army) supported clubs such as Bydgoscz , and Gdansk was a Navy funded club.

MALTA

Being just 60 miles from Sicily and on the direct route to Italy's North African empire of Tripolitania, the island of Malta between 1940-43 played a key role in the struggle for the North African Warzone. Just 17 miles long and 19 miles wide with a population then of approximately 250,000, Malta's strategic naval position between Force H at Gibraltar and the Mediterranean fleet at Alexandria cannot be under estimated. The island and its habitants were bombarded daily by the Italians and the German Luftwaffe, with at one stage just ten RAF fighters available to challenge this air power.

By 1942 Malta was suffering ten air raids a day and by the end of that year 14,000 tonnes of bombs had been dropped on the island. King George VI recognised the Maltese contribution to the war effort by awarding the country the George Cross which symbol has since been amalgamated into the countries flag design. The King described the honour as "to bear witness to a heroism and dedication that will be famous in history". Britain's submarines and destroyers operated out of Valetta and it is estimated that Rommel's supply lines through shipping was reduced by over 30% such was the effectiveness of the efforts of the island based British forces. The island which acquired the nickname of 'Britain's unsinkable aircraft carrier' was the venue of British and American talks before the Yalta conference which influenced the political shape of the post-war world.

IN THE ZONE

For a country to produce a World speedway champion yet have no facilities for the sport would have been unusual, if not unique. That however looked to be the position that Mark Loram, the 2000 champion found himself. In fact Mark's country of birth, Malta (his father was in the Army on the island when Mark was born), did stage the sport under the forces banner in the early 50s. Even during WWII, the island had tenuous links with the sport. 'Buck' Whitby, an Australian joined Edinburgh in 1939 before three years RAF service on the beleaguered Malta and 'Zipp' Zamitt a Maltese rider joined the British Army and starred in the REME organised Hanomag meetings in Hanover.

Buck Whitby

Racing on the island began at Christmas time 1950 when a group of Royal Navy, Army and RAF personnel along with four unknown Maltese locals competed in meetings at the Schreiber Sports stadium in Paola. Telegraphist Ron Cawdell of HM submarine 'Teredo' competed and broke the news of racing to readers of the *Speedway Gazette* magazine. The track was just ten foot wide and only had room for two riders per race, but on stripped down WD road machines they raced for £1 per point on a sandstone composition surface. With crowds of under 500 the promoter (an English businessman) negotiated a percentage of the gate money as payment for the riders and crowds improved to 700 weekly. By February of 1951, a new promotion had been formed with racing moving to the grandly named Empire stadium in Sliema just up the coast where the British Fleet moored in Valetta harbour. With a conventional cinder track and with width for four riders, the standard of racing resembled much closer the British version of speedway with crowds peaking at 1,000. The venue was a key football stadium and saw Stanley Matthews play and coach local football teams there when he moved to Malta following his retirement from British football. Records show that Army officers rode at Sliema, the last meeting recorded meeting being April 2 1951.

'Dusty' Miller recalls a short spell in Malta after his time riding with the RCS 'Meteors' in Libya. "*We took the bikes to Malta but I went home to England after just two weeks but S. Sgt Ken Allen, S.Sgt Taffy Burgess and Ken Bonner would no doubt have been involved in the racing*". Ron Cawdell explained in his reports from Malta that the promoters were still losing money and plans for Army organised racing in Marsa was considered as a possible venue. The Marsa recreation grounds was a British forces sports facility which was only handed back to the Maltese in 1979 when British Forces withdrew from the island, so whilst no records of speedway racing have come to light the fact, this fact would support the high probability of the use of this venue for racing.

AUSTRALIA

In September 1939, Australian Prime Minister Robert Gordon Menzies declared war on Germany in support of Britain and the Commonwealth. Aussie troops saw action in the Middle East and North Africa as well as near to home when Japan threatened to invade Australia from the North. When the Japanese bombed Pearl Harbor on December 8 1941, Australia declared war on Japan as the fighting came closer to their shores. A Japanese attack on New Guinea, off the North East coast of Australia, really brought the war home to the Australian population. In 1942 the Japanese bombed Darwin in the Northern Territory having overrun Malaya and the Australian territory of Rabaul. Darwin was the major port of Northern Australia and the main supply base for ABDACOM (American, British, Dutch, and Australian Command). With negligible opposition the Japanese sank five vessels and damaged three others. The port itself was badly damaged with 240 people killed and 150 wounded. Japanese forces attempted to take Port Moresby in New Guinea which led to significant battles with Australian forces. Records show that Australia mobilised 68,000 troops, suffering 34,000 deaths.

IN THE ZONE

Records indicate there was no racing 'down under' between 1940-45 with most riders away on war duties. Bluey Wilkinson, the 1938 world champion returned home from England intent on joining the Royal Australian Air Force but was tragically killed in a motor cycle accident on a road bike. Many riders joined up, with Lionel Van Praag, the 1936 World champion, becoming a decorated Australian in the armed forces of WWII, when he awarded the George Medal for his exploits in saving his crew as a pilot with the RAAF. Vic Duggan, Max Grosskreutz and Englishman Cliff Parkinson worked in the De Havilland aircraft factory where it is reported Duggan learnt his famed skills in frame making, utilising light aircraft tubing which would prove so invaluable immediate post-war when he returned to English racing with his 'special' speedway frames.

The Sydney Showground, Brisbane Exhibition grounds and Melbourne's Olympic Park were all still under military control as war ended, and so it was that the Sydney Sports Ground became the first track to stage post-war speedway in Australia. It was a rider consortium called International Speedway Club led by Lionel Van Praag which secured the racing rights and staged their opening meeting on September 1 1945. The consortium consisted of Van Praag, the Duggan brothers, Max Grosskreutz, Frank Dolan and Cliff Parkinson with racing run under this banner until the end of the 1947-48 season. During that first season 1945-46, Frank Dolan won the first post-war Australian solo title. Aub Lawson, featured in the 'Khaki Professionals' chapter later in this book, was reputed to have appeared in the early Sydney Sports ground meetings whilst recovering from his war injuries and bouts of malaria. Jim Shepherd, author of *A History of Australian Speedway* describes how Lawson rode under the name of 'Martin' and was smuggled in and out of the local hospital to race in the Sydney meetings with the co-operation of medical staff!

With passages to England by ship still very limited and passports also difficult to obtain in 1946, Lionel Van Praag approached the Australian Disposal Commission with a view to purchasing an ex WWII Australian Air Force plane. Van Praag was of course a fully qualified pilot and he planned to fly an Australian test team to England for the 1947 season. Travel restrictions did however improve in 1947, with the Aussie top liners returning to English league teams. An interesting 'speedway promoter' entered the Australian scene around this time when the Returned Soldiers Club (the equivalent to the British Legion), financed the opening of the Windsor Speedway on the outskirts of Sydney. The recommencement of racing at the Sydney Showground, Claremont (Perth), Adelaide (South) Australia) and Bathurst (NSW) followed and by the summer of 1947 a 5-0 whitewash of an English team took place on Australian soil.

TRACK INDEX: Sydney (Sports Ground), Sydney (Showground), Brisbane Exhibition Ground, Perth (Claremont), Newcastle (Broad Meadow), Melbourne (Kinjo), Adelaide (Kilburn).

POST WAR RIDERS:
Vic Duggan, Lionel Van Praag, Ray Duggan, Cliff Parkinson, Frank Dolan, Aub Lawson and Max Grosskreutz.

A visit from a New Zealand team of riders in 1946-47 boosted competition although machines and spares were still in desperately short supply. The emergence of new names, Ken Le Breton, Jack Arnfield, Eddie Bracknell, Jack Biggs, and later Graham Warren were to be the grass roots of the next generation of Australian stars.

FRANCE

Just as in WW1, the Allied Generals expected a German offensive into France via Holland and Belgium and this is exactly what happened in the spring of 1940. In just six weeks, May 10-June 25, German troops advanced through the Low Countries to take Paris by way of Antwerp, Brussels and Calais. They pushed the Allies back to the beaches of Dunkirk and so followed the biggest evacuation of troops in modern history. The evacuation to England of 220,000 British and 120,000 French and Belgian troops by the flotilla of small boats under the code name of Operation 'Dynamo' was to be one of the most humiliating events of WWII. Some four years later in June 1944, Operation 'Overlord' was to see the D-Day landings in Normandy and mark the turning point of WWII.

IN THE ZONE

The occupation of France by the Germans made any speedway impossible for some six years. As early as 1927, Victor Boston senior, after seeing speedway in Australia, introduced the sport to St Ouen. By 1930 racing at the Buffalo stadium in Paris attracted stars such as Frank Arthur, Billy Lamont, and Arthur Westwood. Charles Belisent and Fernad Meynier proved the top French riders, Meynier winning the French championship in 1929-31. He also won two 'European' championships in 1932-44, even laying claim to the first unofficial 'World Championship' in 1933. Post-war Ron Johnson, Eric French, and Les Wotton reignited speedway interest in France with promoter Boston running meetings at Lyon, Brest, Nantes, Rheims and Lille. French promoter Boston imported more British based riders in 1948 including ex RAF pilot 'Tubby' Flash to supplement local riders, a policy which was to continue throughout the 1950's.

TRACK INDEX: Paris (Buffalo), Lyons, Brest, Nantes, Rheims, Lille.

POST WAR RIDER ROSTER: Charles Belisent, Pierre Belisent, A. Dimanich, Jean Roger, Jean Berhet.

HONG KONG

Located in what was a key strategic military location, Hong Kong was a British Colony at the time, situated near Southern China and was defended in the early 1940's by battalions of Indian and Scottish troops. An invasion of Hong Kong via Kowloon was anticipated as part of the Japanese expansionism programme and it came on December 8 1941, curiously the same day as they attacked the American fleet at Pearl Harbor. Ten days of aerial bombardment drove the Allied defenders, led by Major-General Charles Maltby back to Hong Kong Island where they fought bravely alongside some 800 Canadians. The Allied garrison finally surrendered to the Japanese forces on Christmas Day 1941. Many prisoners were murdered in one of the most infamous incidents of WWII. 7,000 prisoners of war were held in Shampui Po barracks, many dying of untreated diseases. Following the dropping of the atomic bomb on Hiroshima, the Japanese finally surrendered on August 16 1945 to effectively signal the end of WWII.

IN THE ZONE

The only recorded evidence of speedway racing in this country known more for it's passion for horse racing at 'Happy Valley' than any interest in motor cycle racing, appeared in the August 1947 issue of *Soldier* the British Army monthly magazine. Correspondent Archie Quick wrote a feature on the prospect of Army despatch riders dominating the sport of speedway in 1948. *"Forces tracks overseas still flourish (1947) and many a speedway bike has been ingeniously run up from salvage. There are tracks as far a field as Germany, Italy and Hong Kong where soldiers are practising and waiting for the day they can exchange their puttees for racing leather".* No records have been found to date but the author would be pleased to receive any details of racing from this era.

IRAQ

Despite Britain giving Iraq it's sovereignty in 1930, when WWII broke out the Iraq Prime Minister Rashid Ali, who was pro-Nazi, threatened a coup in the country. On April 3 1940 Ali seized power and vital air links between India and Egypt were threatened. The British government took swift action, ordering troops to march on Baghdad and they reached Habbaniya in just three weeks. Despite Iraqi resistance the force reached Baghdad by May 30 1941. To avoid bloodshed the British fooled Ali into thinking they had much larger numbers than in reality. He panicked and fled the country with the pro British Regent regaining the throne.

IN THE ZONE

Speedway in Iraq sounds impossible in this modern day cauldron of death and destruction. Almost 70 years ago however REME were involved in competitive motor cycling in this dangerous location and even formed themselves into a club. A leading light in the formation and construction of a desert speedway track was one Howard Chipman. The track, believed to have been located at Shaibah, a garrison near Basra in the South of Iraq gave Howard the opportunity to hone his broad-siding skills. On demob he bought a second hand speedway bike and gained second half rides at his local track Tamworth, where he progressed to making occasional rides for the 'Hounds'.

TRACK INDEX: Shaibah

HOLLAND

Holland was invaded by Germany in May 1940, despite a meeting between Ribbentrop, the German Foreign Minister, and the Dutch & Belgian envoys. At this meeting Ribbentrop convinced the envoys that the German Army only crossed the border to protect the Dutch neutrality, as an attack from the French and English was imminent. Queen Wilhelmina sought an armistice, but the Germans occupied The Hague. By the end of May she ordered the Dutch fleet to be placed at the disposal of the British to ensure the countries gold reserves and the vast diamond treasures in Amsterdam could be put aboard British warships before she and her family travelled to England to continue the fight. In the autumn of 1944 the Allies attempted to cross the Maas, Waal and Lower Rhive rivers. It was a joint airborne operation called 'Market Garden'. After five years of German occupation, the Allies captured Arnhem in April 1945 and the remaining German forces by May 4 the same year.

IN THE ZONE

Like other European countries devastated by WWII, it took some time before organised speedway was possible post-war. In 1947 some 10,000 fans crowded into the Rijswijk stadium for one of the earliest of post-war meeting, with racing also being staged in Amsterdam, Lisse and Alkmaar. Healthy crowds everywhere led to plans for racing to be introduced at Eindhoven, Hilversum, Rotterdam, Nijmegen, Hengelo and Geleen. By 1948 an embryonic Dutch league had been formed with the 'Windmills', 'Flying Dutchmen' and the Dutch 'Lions' competing in Sunday afternoon matches. Howdy Byford (West Ham), Buddy King (West Ham) and Jimmy Grant (Harringay) were amongst British riders who supplemented their British racing earnings by riding for Dutch teams.

Henk Stemen, who was to captain the Dutch league champions of 1949, competed in the Olympiad tournament at West Ham to celebrate the staging of the first post-war Olympic Games in London. By the end of the 1948 season, eight professional speedways with floodlights and tracks ranging in size between 438-638 yards had been constructed, with Rotterdam being the most successful attracting crowds of up to 60,000.

TRACK INDEX: Amsterdam, Rotterdam, Lisse, Alkmaaar, Rijswijk, Deventer.

POST WAR RIDER ROSTER: Henk Stemen, Tinus Metzelaar, Arend Hartman, ???Bosman, ???Janssons, T Bissschops, Dammers, Van Rijswijk, Van Doornik, Nick Van Dorcum, Van Aartsen.

NORWAY

Germany's early invasion of Norway (April 1940) had much to do with the vital iron ore supplies in the country. They did have another reason for the occupation, the reason being traced back to WW1. In that war Britain had a barrage of mines supported by warships patrolling the North Sea which kept the Kaiser 'bottled up'. This time around the Germans planned to have bases in Norway where she could sweep down on British shipping. When the Norwegian forces in Northern Norway capitulated in June 1940 after two months of fighting, the King, Prime Minister and other Government officials were evacuated to Britain. The exiled Norwegian Navy operated 118 vessels and the Air Force consisted of four squadrons. More than 1,000 Norwegian merchant ships and 27,000 sailors sailed in the convoys and a small Army operated in exile, mostly based in Britain.

IN THE ZONE

Lief 'Basse' Hveem had been the top Norwegian pre-war rider, winning the national speedway title on a regular basis. He however missed out on the first post-war title (1946) due to an ice racing accident staged at the Bislet stadium, now famous as an international athletics stadium. Fifteen meetings were staged in 1946, including the Scandanavian title meeting at the Bjerke trotting track where Hveem saw off stiff competition from Sweden and Denmark. Short track (speedway) on tracks up to 440 yards and long track over 1,000 yards to the lap, combined to provide Norwegian fans with a mixed oval racing scene, a tradition that continues to the present day. By 1950 the 'Phantoms' were entertaining a variety of International touring teams.

TRACK INDEX: Oslo, Tronheim, Bergen, Stavanger, Larvik, Horten and Daelenengn.

POST WAR RIDER ROSTER: Leif 'Basse' Hveem, Thorleif Andreasen, Henry Andersen, H W Hansen, Leif Samsing and Edvin Fredriksen.

Mechanical Mayhem

MATCHLESS BY NAME - MATCHLESS BY NATURE

Back in 1928, some eleven years before WWII was declared, the Matchless name appeared on the pioneer dirt tracks, when the curiously named F H Blackpool rode in sidecar races on a Matchless 495cc combination at Stamford Bridge. Like other manufacturers the marque disappeared quickly from the dirt track scene as the company preferred road racing and trials to promote their brand. In this companion book to *Speedway Flyers*, it is appropriate to record the exploits of Captain 'Mad' Jack Woodehouse of the Royal Flying Corps. At a famous 1920 meeting at Brooklands, Jack agreed to a match race against a car driven by Malcolm Campbell (later to go on to land speed record fame) on a Matchless motor cycle. Campbell proved an easy winner of the match race but 'Mad' Jack reached 73mph on a track with which he was not familiar.

Now fast forward 19 years to the out break of WWII. Ask any self respecting Despatch rider who served in that conflict what bike he preferred and the chances are his answer would be a Matchless G3/L. Whilst appreciating the sturdiness, reliability and engine performance of the Norton 16H, Triumph or BSA M20, the Matchless 350cc overall performance just had the edge.

Over 80,000 Matchless units were supplied to the War Department between 1939-45, all manufactured at the Matchless factory in Plumstead South London, just across the road from the famous Royal Arsenal. The origins of Matchless can be traced back to 1878 when HH Collier began manufacturing Penny Farthing safety bicycles. His son's Harry and Charlie commenced the early motor cycle production in 1899 by putting engines on to the front wheel of bicycles. H H trained as an engineer at the Royal Arsenal factory, considered at the time to be the world centre for engineering excellence. His two sons had obviously inherited their father's skills and by riding the bikes at Canning Town, Crystal Palace and Brooklands tracks, developed the Matchless engines reputation. It was also not unknown for a Matchless prototype to be tested on the tank proving grounds on Bagshot Heath.

The first real breakthrough came when Charlie was successful in the first Isle of Man TT races in 1907 on a Matchless powered by a single cylinder over head valve JAP, the same Tottenham company which would much later dominate the speedway engine market. Later the Matchless also became the first motor cycle to cover 50 miles in an hour and eventually the marque took the world one mile record at over 90mph, a tremendous speed at the time. By 1912 the first Matchless engine was born, a single cylinder $3\frac{1}{2}$ bhp similar to the previously used JAP versions. As an aside the 'Matchless' name, a truly priceless name for a motor cycle had been acquired by H H Collier from another bicycle manufacturer, George Singer of Coventry who let the trade name lapse.

The company, like most motor cycle companies dabbled with the new craze of flying and in 1909 built a mono plane to enter the Daily Mail £10,000 cross channel race. Unfortunately the prototype was written off after a crash in trials at the Brooklands circuit

During 1914-18, the factory was turned over to war work, being contracted by the Ministry of Munitions. Some motor cycles were made but only 136 were used on the battlefield. Car manufacturing was tried in 1923, but fierce competition from Austin, Ford and Morris drove Matchless out of this activity, although some 1,200 motor cycles were manufactured in the same year. Acquisition of other bike manufacturers namely AJS and Sunbeam, expanded the factories production and in 1938 the Associated Motorcycle Company (AMC) name appeared to reflect the breadth and range of the companies models.

During 1939-45 the factory was again turned over to war work. The AJS model ceased production and the whole of the Matchless output was turned over to war work with motor cycle production being concentrated on just one model, the Matchless G3 and later G3L which were produced for the Army in their thousands in olive green colour. The military version included a lower compression engine, provision for masked lighting, a rear carrier rack for pannier bags (essential for despatch rider work) and a re-inforced side stand. Originally with girder forks, from 1941 the G3L was equipped with 'Teldraulic' front forks for a smoother ride and became the most popular WD motor cycle model available. With a top speed of 70 mph and a very suitable 'speedway' gear ratio, the G3 and G3L were to form the base machine used by REME for modification as a warzone speedway machine. That some 80,000 machines were produced in a factory, located next door to the strategic German bombing target of the Royal Arsenal factory yet suffered no appreciable bomb damage is one of the miracles of the war. At one time the Plumstead factory was in fact the only motor cycle factory to be in full production.

Post-war restrictions on exports, whilst battling against imports into the UK made trade very difficult for Matchless, especially as many working people were for the first time able to purchase small, economical cars.

SPEEDWAY ENGINE IS BORN

During the warzone speedway period, the Matchless proved the main stay of the modified 'speedway bikes' produced by the Army workshops. It was however curious that some 20 years later, in 1965, the Matchless name was to hit the professional speedway headlines. Rumours abounded in the speedway pits of Britain that a well known road bike manufacturer was developing a speedway model. Nigel Boocock (Coventry) and Norman Hunter (West Ham) were selected to test the Matchless G85 CS in second halves and Malcolm Simmons used one on the grass tracks. The G85 was developed from the successful 'Grandstand Trophy' scrambles machine ridden by Chris Horsfield. The engine was designed to fit into any standard speedway or grass track frame and production commenced in October 1965. Speaking at the launch of the engine Mr W J Smith, joint Managing Director of Matchless motorcycles (AMC) said "*The G85 CS will be available at a highly competitive price and of great importance, spares will be available in ample supply. Speedway is enjoying renewed following in Britain and is becoming increasingly popular abroad. We have already had enquiries from the United States and Germany".*

The engine was alloy and had been developed by the Associated Motor Cycle Company in conjunction with Jack Emmot, a technical expert specialising in the preparation of speedway machines. Sadly the Matchless engine was launched in Britain at a similar time to the Czechoslovakian JAWA which ended the JAP era, so the G85 did not gain a big enough foot hold with speedway riders to survive.

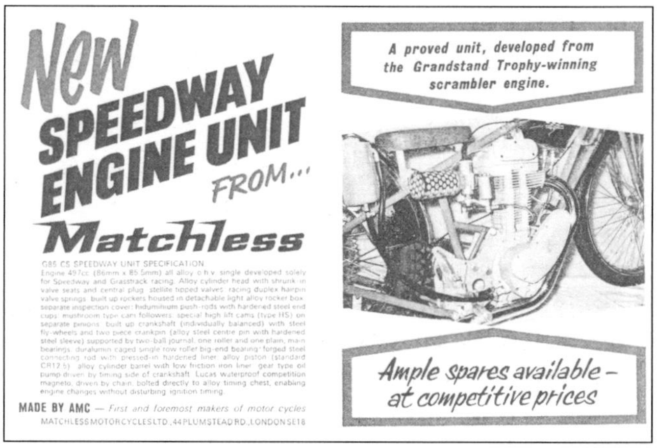

AMC trade advert- 1965

THE EXPERIMENTERS

"Make do and mend" and "Innovation is the mother of invention", both WWII mottos, were very applicable to the events surrounding the racing exploits in the warzones. REME, (Rough Engineering Made Easy) according to Jim Phillips who served in Egypt, played a leading role in bike building, cannibalisation, and the tuning of 'speedway' engines. There was considerable rivalry between Regiment teams and particularly Army and RAF so any technical advantage was seized upon if it meant success on the track. This competitive spirit led to many experiments to gain extra speed, performance and a racing edge over the opposition.

Jim Griffiths - Start Marshall (Tel el Kabir, Egypt)
"A very active speedway league existed in 1947-48, the major teams being TEK, Suez and Fayid. If the bikes stayed upright TEK always won. Various REME types got together in the workshops (12 Shed) and sandwiched a 600cc Norton side valve barrel on top of a 350cc Matchless crankcase, topped over all with a Matchless head. Suitable slots having been laboriously carved in the side valve barrel enabled the ohv to be suitably prodded which gave us a 250cc advantage over the opposition. It was also said that the cams had been breathed on by one of the German POW's who had been involved with the BMW racing team pre-war."

Re-printed courtesy of Vintage Motor Cycle Club magazine

W G Herbert - RAF Kabrit 1949

"The speedway bikes we used were modified Norton 16H machines comprising of a frame and the bottom end of the engine. These were quite tough but had a long stroke and side valves. With a bit of begging at RAF El Firdan, Matchless over head valve heads arrived at Kabrit to enable modifications to the engines. Valve seats had a layer of Stellite welded on, a process which required a lot of skill to avoid air holes and then overheating of the valve. Push rods were manufactured for the replacement heads and valves were ground to give the correct angle seat. I think it was at this time we learnt that Tel el Kabir workshops had also looked into this, which gave us the push to complete the modifications. The fuel used was special 100 octane petrol".

Jim Phillips - Royal Electrical Mechanical Engineers
Some twenty years before nitro (a special fuel additive) was introduced to professional speedway by Norwegian Leif Hveem, special cocktails of racing fuel were being mixed by the Army workshops. Jim Phillips recalls one special formula. *"A 'Brasso' type cleaning fluid came in five gallon drums which was distilled in the baking sun of the desert, before being separated and then sieved through RAF supplied chamois leather. The wood alcohol residue liquid was then added to high octane fuel and a little castor oil obtained from the medics was added to provide a potent mixture"*

Henry 'Dickie' Bird - Military Policeman El Ballah 1946

Henry was a military motorcyclist in his role as a military policeman when he rode at El Ballah speedway and discovered the ideal gearing configuration for the Matchless G3 motor cycle.

"I worked out that the 3rd gear on the G3 model, fitted into the Matchless G3L which I rode on the speedway. This gave me three very close ratio gears which was ideal for the needs of getting away from the straights yet retaining a good top speed down the straights".

Sgt 'Dickie' Bird in action Egypt 1946

Vic Orange in action

Vic Orange - Egypt 1947
Vic's runner up spot in the 1947 All-Egyptian individual championship behind REME Sergeant Harry Mappin was the highlight of his Army racing career, but there was a whole chunk of Vic's involvement in the warzone speedway story which has largely been forgotten. Based at Fayid near the Suez Canal, Vic played a lead role in the track construction and bike development of Army speedway in Egypt. Writing in the late 40's his influence is there for all to see.

"Take the track for example. No it wasn't cinders-it was sand. For months we searched the area for a suitable piece of ground-one that was flat enough, firm enough and near enough to the camp. Eventually a site was decided upon, although it was far from ideal. And then we were unable to obtain the authority to have it improved, and in the end we did the work ourselves, marking out, levelling, watering and so on. Our main trouble was that the track was situated in the middle of the desert, and thus we could not erect barriers, stands etc. We did once try to install a fence but it disappeared overnight, no doubt for some vital part of a desert Arab's prefab. Nor could we keep passers by off our little piece of ground, and on many occasions we worked for hours smoothing and levelling, only to return the next day to find the track cut to pieces . It seems that passing DRs, not to mention drivers of jeeps and even Bren gun carriers found the temptation just that bit too strong.

Speedway Irons (bikes) were at a premium, and hours were spent discussing how best to use parts of standard WD machines to obtain the desired result. The result on the whole was pretty good. Frames were cut, shortened, lowered and drastically lightened. An engine was evolved which eventually became virtually standard in Egyptian speedway. This was an over head valve engine of 460cc running on part Pool, part Aviation fuel and incorporating parts of many types of machines and some which were home made. I don't know what the manufacturers thought of our hybrids but we were very proud of their 30 brake horsepower, and reliability. The gear box was retained and usually two gears were employed".

Lt Colonel Penfold
Both Lt Colonel Penfold and Eric Brown have similar recollections of the introduction of a very unusual form of fuel tanks for speedway machines in the warzones. As part of the efforts to streamline the still quite bulky standard despatch rider bikes, the fuel tanks were replaced by small portable hand (Pyrene) fire extinguishers. These fire fighting devices were standard on all Army vehicles and were therefore in plentiful supply. They were hollowed out and were just the right size and volume capacity to hold enough fuel for the four lap races.

THE HANOMAG STANDARDISATION

In 1949, the Technical Director of the 'Saints' REME speedway club, Major Gershon was tasked to develop and introduce common standards for racing machines used on the Hanover track. Eventually all cannibalised WD machines which had served the club so well between 1946-48 were withdrawn, being replaced by sixteen new machines to the newly agreed specification with sixteen learner machines being based on the traditional Matchless model. The *Craftsman* magazine, the voice of REME to this day, recorded in its January 1950 issue the challenges that this standardisation programme presented.

A standardised bike flashes over the line at Hanomag

"In previous years the general tendency had been to develop various engines composed of WD parts, run on alcohol fuel and although admitting this was the most orthodox method of tuning, development on these lines was decided against, in conformity with the BAOR, MCRA ruling that standard MT fuel only would be permitted for speedway racing. All machines were withdrawn from individual riders care, collected together, and points of interest noted. There was a motley collection, some bad, some quite sound, but no single machine possessed all the desirable features necessary for the projected standard machine. During a visit by the Wembley 'Lions' team last season some very useful information had been given about frame design, and most riders were now agreed on this. In fact, three frames, ex-Triumph, had already been constructed and were accepted without further modification as the pattern to be utilised. In this, as in every other step, the riders had the final word. A countershaft to replace the normal gearbox had also been constructed and was considered suitable for adoption. It consisted of a steel sleeve, machined from solid, housing two ball races and a shortened BSA main shaft and clutch, this being the strongest unit. Large sprockets for rear wheels were made of scrap plate and Matchless wheels were adopted.

The engine itself proved more difficult. It was decided that 500 cc was necessary, and this meant that no WD engine could be used as it stood. All WD 500's are side valve engines and overhead valves are essential for the type of engine needed. Engines previously used were generally based on side valve engines and the original barrel was usually a Norton or BSA with sawn off parts. No attempt had been made to produce a really efficient unit, irrespective of the parts employed; the general drift seemed to be "get by" with the largest capacity and the highest possible compression ratio and to ignore other factors. This did not work out too badly on a cool running dope engine, but it made quite another story when such a hybrid unit was detuned for petrol. Little or nothing had been done to cylinder heads, carburettors or cams and any exceptions to this were crude and pointless. Considerable progress had however been made in the cylinder barrels and some examples machined from special steels were in existence".

Consideration had to be given now to each component in order to produce a short list of standardisation, bearing in mind; a. Utility b. Spares availability. The following specification was eventually arrived at:

Crankcases and Flywheels- Matchless or Norton
Cylinder head - Matchless or Triumph
Barrel -Manufactured
Piston - Norton

These assemblies, in any combination could be built up and the spares supply was good. The Matchless crankcase was unaltered; its lightness and reasonable cam box compensating for the rather flimsy mainshafts. The flywheels lent themselves to drastic machining, and the conrods were sufficiently robust to withstand the extra capacity. Flywheels were lightened by approximately 4 lbs and re-balanced with Norton pistons to 60% of reciprocating weight. The barrels were machined from a chrome steel and were given extra oil-ways at the rear of the piston. The pistons were cut away to allow for valve overlap, cylinder head ports were ground out and polished, the inlet being opened from 25mm to 28mm in the process. Heads were spigoted to barrels, carburettors were bored out to 27mm, a safe maximum, and air slides were removed. Timing cases were modified to bring the magneto down 2 inches, in order to allow the carburettor to be fitted direct to the head, dispensing with the Matchless distance pieces.

Continuing his explanation Major Gershon said *"The first trouble was that the standard valve springs, though re-enforced, were not strong enough and every piston bore valve marks and some bent valves. This was overcome by fitting springs considerably stronger, supplied by Matchless. During this period a number of heads, as an experiment, had been given larger valve throats and were fitted with shortened Humber valves. The engines, though faster, were not reliable, as the valves were too small in stem diameter and fractured at the cotters in spite of four different cotter designs, and the Humber idea was abandoned.*

The next problem was more permanent and still is (1950). The engines were prone to detonation and to cure this, the compression ratio was altered to 7 $\frac{1}{2}$, after having been tried at 7. Not one word has yet been said here about cams and in this direction it was considered that the generous Matchless cams, together with 'opened' ports would be sufficient to cope with the extra capacity. We were however mistaken, for the last and most successful experiment concluded prior to the end of the season was the grafting of Norton cams onto Matchless cam wheels, with a resulting increase of valve dwell. This considerably increased the top speed".

The final result of all the technical development was that for the 1950 season the Hanomag club and its riders had at their disposal sixteen 500cc fully spec'd speedway machines and a mixed assortment of sixteen 500cc machines based on the standard Matchless.

I am indebted to the REME archives for use of this story, originally printed in the January 1950 edition of the *Craftsman* magazine.

REME THE WORKSHOP WONDERS

Prior to 1942, the year in which the Royal Electrical and Mechanical Engineers (REME) was formed, the recovery and repair of military vehicles was mainly the responsibility of the Royal Ordnance Corps (RAOC) and Royal Army Service Corps (RASC),

REME Workshop Chilwell

The new REME Corps organised its maintenance and repair on an echelon system from the first line to base. Light Aid Detachments (LADs) and attached tradesman operated with forward teeth arm units, while second and third line repairs were affected by REME Workshops. Base and Advanced Base Workshops, often employing local civilian labour, carried out major overhauls and rebuild programmes. Although only formed on October 1st 1942, REME won its spurs early on in the Western Desert at the battle of El Alemain. Back in the UK, Chilwell in Nottinghamshire, was a large Static Workshop, whose role included the repair and rebuild of various brands of motorcycles.

This and many similar Workshops carried out the base overhaul of the full range of military vehicles and equipment, from tanks to communications and instruments. Skilled tradesman, many of who , both male and female were recruited from civilian life, joined those trained within the Army, to carry out the mechanical and electrical work associated with an ever increasing range of mechanical, electrical and electronic tasks. A repair or replacement policy ensured that fit vehicles and equipment were constantly available to the front line. In addition REME Workshops carried out tyre and battery repair together with electro-plating and deposition, in order to make best use of components and parts.

From a motor cycling perspective, much equipment was lost at Dunkirk, (it is estimated some 100,000 motor cycles were lost in the evacuation of France in 1940). This led to a major shortfall in available machines which suppliers could not immediately replace, hence the need for a quality repair service from REME. The skill and ingenuity of the craftsman to cannibalise different models (typical was fitting of Matchless Teledraulic forks to a BSA M20), was later to be used by the same REME workshops in building Army 'speedway' bikes from damaged machines officially classified as BER (Beyond Economic Repair).

REME Craftsman were fighting soldiers as well as tradesman, this collective centre of excellence for repair playing an increasingly important role as the war progressed. A "make do and mend" policy was crucial to promote technical advantage, with Light Aid Detachments providing true front line recovery and repair facilities.

No 21 Advanced Base Workshop

Young girl mechanic working on a Matchless G3L

RULES & REGULATIONS

In the very early days of forces speedway (1944-45), racing equipment was rescued from Military transport dumps, most bikes being ex-despatch or motor cycle escort machinery. Suitable racing apparel i.e. helmets, gauntlets, boots, goggles and riding breeches were also on the shopping list from the local Quartermaster stores.

The need for some form of regulatory control became apparent when in July 1946 in Egypt, Signalman A. Jackson was killed whilst competing in a motorcycle event (not speedway). The Bar-None Motor Cycle Club had led the way from it's earliest days, with machine examiners, Clerk of Courses, Medical officers, Judges and Flag Marshalls all being standard officials on duty at all its events as the Army 'top brass' insisted on some official structure to meetings. These officials and an element of officialdom did much to negate the concerns of some Commanding officers in a period when racing was taking part in what were still officially war theatres! A broken leg sustained whilst racing, could have been considered as a 'self inflicted wound' and liable to a Court Marshal charge!

Demonstrating how seriously events were managed, some of the racing regulations under which racing took place are detailed below:

> Before commencing racing a competitor had to be in possession of an Army form AFG 3518 which was signed and endorsed as TRAINING.
>
> M/Cycles will always be a standard type, stripping to a limit was permitted, but any unauthorised parts or cutting or damage to WD property will not be entertained. This rule was gradually relaxed as can be seen from the Pits Side Specials feature in this chapter.
>
> After meetings riders must be prepared to remove, or have removed by a competent REME fitter, the head of the machine they have been using, to ensure the machine conforms to the cubic capacity of the training in which they have been taking part.
>
> In the event of a rider injury which necessitates professional medical attention, a member of the organising committee must be prepared to accompany the injured person to hospital to ascertain the extent of the injuries (preferably a member of the CMP accident branch or the RAF).
>
> Crash helmets will be worn by all riders unless excused on medical grounds, proof of which must be given in writing.

Early meeting programmes give only the minimum guidance of rider racing apparel, with an obligatory helmet having to be worn along with riders 'suitably'dressed. The only instruction was that all competitors were to ride with their sleeves rolled down!

Specialist clothing, such as leathers were very rare indeed, but the ingenious squaddies begged or borrowed protective wear through the surplus stores system. The despatch rider WWII standard issued equipment, progressed dramatically from 1940 when the British Expeditionary Forces DR was not even issued with a helmet, the khaki coloured flying helmet being supplied as head protection. Tear drop shaped goggles barely changed throughout the war and photographic evidence exists of these being used on Army speedways. By 1941, the first 'pudding basin' shaped pulp helmets had been introduced for despatch riders and Military Police motor cyclists. The new protective head gear, whilst better than the flying helmet, was only made of pulped paper and rag. It was not unknown for motor cyclists to ride in their 'Brodie' pattern tin helmets, but even with an oval padding built into the helmet to protect the wearer, this form of safety gear was quickly outlawed because of the dangers it brought to the rider.

Tank crews wore specially designed helmets with all round protection, similar to a modern day full face helmet, with later versions having built in ear pieces for communication purposes. There is evidence of their use on the German tracks in late 1945, as some of the earliest competitors found them the only option available. By D-Day 1944 DR gear had improved still further with breeches and specially designed knee length boots, with ankle protection replacing the standard issue battle dress trousers and boots. Pictures do exist of soldiers using their short blouse tops with insignia and stripes clearly visible. Throughout the war, leather gauntlets were commonly worn and by 1945 much improved safety helmets became available for racing use.

A corporal in uniform demonstrates the dangers of an ill fitting helmet

Troops and civilians watching racing from improvised stands made from Army trucks

PITSIDE SPECIALS

We know from research that the roots of the forces speedway motorcycles lies within the standard War Department issued models, primarily but not exclusively Matchless, Triumph, Norton, Royal Enfield and Ariel. The ingenuity of the Army engineering workshops knew no boundaries in those far off days of the late 1940s. Tracing with exact accuracy the machine specifications of these machines is impossible. However, through the kind loan of prints from veterans, many variations of machines have surfaced. Where precise details are not available, the rider, country where ridden or year of photograph has been used as a reference point.

Frame - 350cc Royal Enfield
Front forks/Wheels - Triumph
Gear box/Clutch - Royal Enfield
Engine/Crank Case - Norton
Cylinder Head - Norton
Piston - Norton 16H
Carburettor - Delloite Inlet/Exhaust valves (MAC) American truck!

Bari 'Bitsa' - Italy 1946

Early modified BSA - Egypt 1946

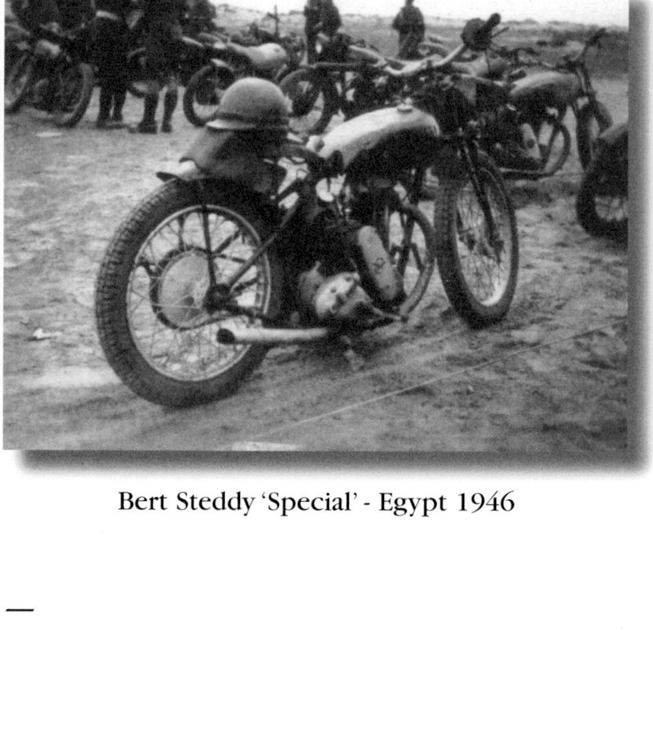

Bert Steddy 'Special' - Egypt 1946

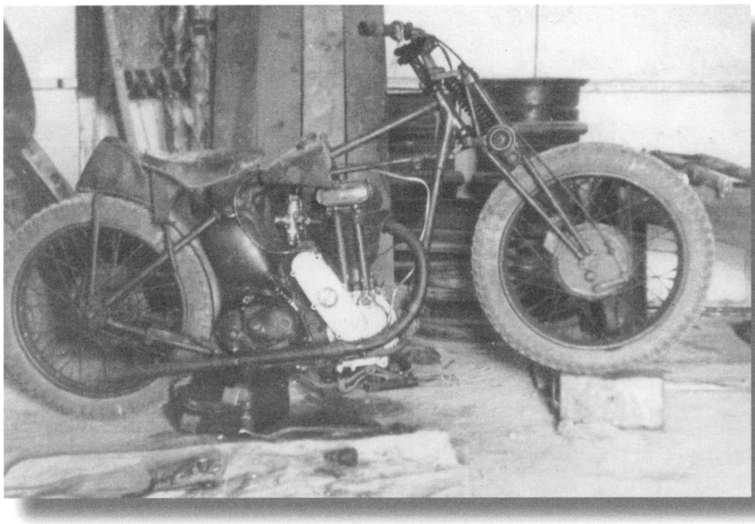

Matchless 350cc

Waterman 'Special' - Italy 1945/46

Triumph with front forks reversed Egypt 1946

BSA M20 500cc

Stripped down despatch rider bike 'Ready to race'

German POW's with modified Matchless 1947

Tiger Hart 'Special' - Germany 1947

Don Francis 'Special' - Fayid 1949

Tel el Kabir team bike - Egypt 1949

Matchless - Egypt 1950

RAOC team bikes - Tripoli 1950

Hanomag 'Standard' - Germany 1950

Roy Davies 'Special' - RAF Kabrit 1950

Matchless/BSA - Egypt 1951

Ariel 350cc - Egypt 1949

Ariel 350cc - Egypt 1949

'Clutchman Special' 1951-52

'Clutchman Special' 1951 - 52

Deep in the depths of Cornwall, not a million miles from the spiritual home of Cornish speedway, St Austell, lies a unique example of mechanical history from the Warzone era. The late Claude Bennet, who died in 2003 aged 74, had served in the Royal Engineers and experienced at first hand armed forces speedway racing in Egypt. Claude was not only an accomplished motorcyclist, he was also a fine engineer whose reputation spread far and wide. Claude who had worked for Rolls Royce for a time, returned to family life in Cornwall and was a regular on the grass track scene of the Duchy. Son Chris who rode for the St Austell speedway team 1997 - 98 takes up a remarkable story. *"Dad was a remarkable engineer, he could build a car from the ground up, and it was when I started racing speedway his thoughts returned to his Army speedway days. He decided to build from scratch and memory a replica of the AJS/Matchless machine he rode out in Egypt. He manufactured a hand built frame, fuel tank and other parts and finished it off in Royal Engineer colours."*

Claude who served in the Royal Engineers with famous clarinetist Akker Bilk, took many hours to build the machine. Some license must be given for the modern 'forks' and front wheel. However the bike does provide a fascinating link with Royal Engineers 'races' of 1947!

Carrying the Royal Engineers Colours

Claude's historical legacy

Despatched to Ride

The mechanisation of warfare prior to WW1 saw the first use of motorcycles on the battlefields of France. Communication technologies were also improving at this time, with semaphore flag signals gradually being replaced by improving mobile telegraphy and radio, whilst Morse code was well established within the armed forces.

The strategic importance of good, accurate intelligence in war was not lost on the military planners. The Royal Corps of Signals formed in the 1920s was playing an increasingly important role in battle planning. The RCS use of despatch riders (DRs) for carrying urgent communications can be traced back to WW1, when difficult terrain made the benefits of two wheels rather than four advantageous, and so grew the need for experienced motor cyclists.

Jim Gegory DR- Cairo 1947

Members of the RCS will argue that only their Corps of riders, wearing the blue and white armlet could truly use the name 'despatch rider'. Putting this argument to one side, the first recorded Army despatch rider, a Captain Longley of the Royal Engineers, went to Mons in 1914 to take charge of a company of DRs.

The definition of a despatch rider as opposed to a motor cycle orderly does require some investigation. What is not in dispute however is that the motorcycling skills both DRs and motor cycle orderlies developed did provide the raw material for the formation of many Army speedway teams.

At the outbreak of WWII, the need for experienced motorcyclists was grasped by the trade magazines, namely *Motorcycle* and *Motorcycling*, which were both published throughout the hostilities. Both launched recruitment campaigns through their pages. As early as October 1939, the *Motorcycle* printed registration forms seeking DRs for the Royal Corps Signals. Readers not in reserved occupations between the ages of 22 years to 35 years were urged to submit applications for the fifty a month quota the Signals were seeking. Pay allowances for a Signalman ranged from 2s 3d to 3s 3d per day dependant on experience and qualifications. Similarly *Motorcycling*, edited by Graham Walker, father of Formula 1 commentator Murray, printed an Army registration form for DRs to join the RCS, RASC and the Homeguard. Once recruited a motor cyclist was expected to develop his riding skills via courses, usually run by pre-war scramble or trials factory works riders. To become a fully fledged despatch rider would require a recruit to undertake a 12 week course at locations such as Barnard Castle near Catterick, which had suitable moorland terrains nearby. Lectures on a range of subjects, including motorcycle theory, Army structures and organisation, Highway Code, map reading, machine maintenance and the work of a Signals lineman all supplemented the basic training of a soldier.

A typical despatch rider squad in training

The prime role of a DR was carrying messages and communications that it would have been unwise from a security or time standpoint to send by other methods. Various forms of messages were graded into firstly operational orders and maps, sketches of the battle areas. A second grade of communication would have been unit orders and fighting strength returns. Some despatch riders were given SDR status (Special) and only they were authorised in carrying messages from the GOC and senior staff office. Less important documents would wait for the DRLS (Despatch Rider Letter Service) which was in effect a secure postal service between Army units. It was a requirement for a DR when on duty, to be ready for the road within 10 minutes of being summoned. A DR was also expected to have a practical understanding of RCS lineman duties and undertake trade testing throughout his period of service. By undertaking a Class III trade test a DR could improve his weekly pay by 6d per day which meant for a married signalmen a weekly wage of fourteen shillings.

The debate of a DR versus a motorcycle orderly still rages amongst Signals veterans who claim they alone were true despatch riders. That aside, motorcyclists were involved in convoy control which required them to control a fleet of moving military vehicles. Ensuring that a convoy, which was not allowed to exceed 20mph, remained intact, with any stragglers or breakdowns being managed, made the motor cycle out rider a crucial player in the movement of armoured vehicles. The skills in 'Shepherding' a convoy of perhaps 200 vehicles were not inconsiderable. The process was formally known as 'Motor Marching' and was developed using a mathematical formula which took account of speed, cruising speed, density of the convoy and the use of strategically positioned traffic control posts.

A key factor in the calculation was that the spacing of 5 to 10 vtm would probably prevent air observation, 10 vtm did not offer a good bombing target with 30-40 vtm being suitable for night time convoys. (VTM- vehicles to mile).

The despatch rider (messenger) was but one facet of the Royal Corps Signals, there being three 'Companies' with differing roles:

> Construction- Responsible for the construction and maintenance of the communication line.
>
> Operation - Responsible for running the network via line cable, wireless or messenger.
>
> Artillery - A Signals section for Corps units.

Each unit had a signals office, which was the terminal for all communications in and out of the formation; in charge was the Signals master, who was directly responsible to the Commanding officer for the efficient handling of Signals personnel. The duty was normally performed by a junior officer in the wireless, operating or line section. A phonetic alphabet was used for standard messages, with messages produced in plain language, cypher or code dependant on sensitivity. Communications were classified according to its content, with a hierarchy of officer sign off

A despatch rider receiving his brief

as appropriate. Interestingly a category 'By Safe Hand' existed, indicating the delivery was to be carried out by a trusted messenger, which demonstrates the trust and status afforded to a despatch rider.

All Signals ranks on duty were required to wear a blue & white arm band to signify their role.

Many speedway riders were recruited to the ranks of DRs, either with the military or various civilian bodies such as the National Fire Service, Air Raid Precaution, Home Guard, Civil Defence and others emergency organisations. Prime examples included Geoff Pymar (Norwich) Harwood Pike (Wombwell), Bob Oakley (Southampton), Ron Clark (Eastbourne), George Craig (Bristol), Aub Lawson (West Ham), and Gerry Hussey (West Ham) amongst others.

To complete the sporting link with this hazardous forces activity, Tom Cooper a Liverpool FC defender, who was killed whilst on motor cycle duties as a Military Policeman. It was following this accident that the instruction that all DRs were required to wear a hard hat, rather than the soft leather flying helmets was introduced.

THE MAKING OF A DESPATCH RIDER

Many motor cyclists who enlisted as despatch riders with the Royal Corps Signals considered themselves competent motorcyclists. That was until their enrolment in the extensive three month DR course required to gain their proudly worn arm band. To illustrate the significance of the training, the late Colin V Morgan of the 51 DR squad who rode in the El Ballah speedway team, details his memories of his despatch rider training.

Colin V Morgan

"Following my completion of basic training, individuals were classified and transferred to other relevant training courses within the Royal Corps Signals. Most DRs, if not all, were trained at Catterick. There we underwent further fitness training and military training including marching drill and the like. In addition to developing our riding skills on the local moors, general motorcycle knowledge and maintenance, which included motorcycle workshop duties was essential, this entailing full engine strips, decoking the engine and the grinding or fitting of new valves. Full clutch stripping and re-lining and rebuilding was involved, as well as spring loaded kick start and foot change mechanism. Battery and lighting also played a major role as many of our duties took place in the hours of darkness, so stripping and replacing lighting harnesses and re-wiring dynamos and lighting switches all formed part of the course.

Although REME were responsible for undertaking much of this work, our DR careers and further training prepared us for wider ranging and more comprehensive mechanical work in order that our machines would always be ready for use and service. Some entrants, of course, were already able to carry out this skilled work, but for others there was always someone to help when needed. Much of the daily maintenance would be done under covered outdoor areas, with more advanced and technical work being carried out in a fully equipped workshop under supervision and instruction. An important aspect of the training was our contact with A.B.C.A -the Army Bureau of Current Affairs, which comprised of up to date lectures on how the war was progressing, as well as participation in a certain amount of religious studies. Training, in short was intense and comprehensive to prepare us for any eventuality".

To put into context the scale of a DRs work load the following statistics not only make interesting reading but pay their own tribute to the work of the Air Formation Signals which Colin served with in Egypt. AFS DRs carried over half a million despatches every month, 6 million between D-Day and VE Day covering the equivalent of 240 times around the globe without any recorded loss of a despatch!

Colin during training as a DR -1943

Few records exist of the way the Army trained its motor cyclists, but a military training pamphlet, number 24, gives an insight into the skills which would enable the despatch rider to quickly transfer his riding skills to the warzone speedways. Advice on travelling at speed on sand was particularly relevant. It said "*Speed combined with power at the back wheel is the only way of retaining stability and a technique of driving through a bend with the throttle open to ensure continued forward movement"* which describes the art of broadsiding on a loose surface precisely.

Young school boys growing up in the 1940s dreamt of becoming Spitfire pilots, train drivers and despatch riders, such was the exciting image that surrounded these 'occupations'. To many 10 year olds of the time, a DR was the equivalent of the Pony Express in the Wild West, and many comics and books of the time were filled with stories of their exploits. What was the reality? Through the stories of four despatch riders, three of whom went on in peacetime to professional speedway careers. You decide.

Jim Gregory - Royal Corps Signals
"When I joined the RCS in 1945, I thought little, of undertaking the 12 week DR at Catterick as I knew I could ride a motor cycle or so I thought! After three months of intensive technical and practical training in all sorts of conditions on the moors around the camp, I realised that perhaps I wasn't as clever as I thought. I remember travelling through France before transferring to Alexandria and a posting in Cairo attached as a despatch rider with GHQ. Most of my time was spent carrying despatches on my trusty Matchless armed with a .38 revolver for protection. They were dangerous times, and one time I fell off my bike after a dog ran in front of me. I was knocked unconscious, but luckily the locals didn't steal my revolver. I was still given 14 days for damaging the bike".

Ron Clark - Royal Corps Signals
Few soldiers of any rank can possibly have been quite so close to the centre of WWII history than RCS despatch rider Ron Clark. In 1940, Ron, who after the war rode in the 1947 Eastbourne team which won the 3rd Division title, was given the duty of transporting Prime Minister Winston Churchill's despatch boxes from his country retreat to his London underground war planning bunker. Ron, who was introduced to speedway at Wembley by his father when a small boy before the war, saw DR action from Normandy to Hungary before being demobbed in 1946.

Ron Clark (Eastbourne)

Alan Johnson - Royal Corps Signals

Alan, one of the founding members of the Bar-None M.C.C, which was fundamental to the introduction of Sand Track Trials (speedway) to the Middle East, is still an active motorcyclist with the Vintage Motor Cycle Club. He well recalls his time as a despatch rider in the desert with 3GHQ Signals near Cairo. Riding a Norton 16H, Alan was part of a six man DR squad under an NCO.

Describing a typical working day Alan remembers "*On leaving camp we had to call at the guard room to draw our revolvers and ammunition, then ride in convoy to GHQ. There we sorted the bags of official mail and made up our own runs, the equivalent of a postman's round. Many of our calls were within the base itself, although others were in remote locations out in the desert. At this time the Signals were issued with 16H Norton's and BSA M20 motor cycles, and we really envied the RASC with their lighter Matchless G3s with girder forks. The Royal Army Service Corps boys were never given the title of DRs, this was reserved for the Royal Corps Signals, but they did convoy work which none of us envied. To see them work shepherding long strings of sometimes not too expertly driven trucks, overtaking one truck after another to indicate a route change, leapfrogging all the while, made one realise they really did know how to handle those G3 Matchless.*"

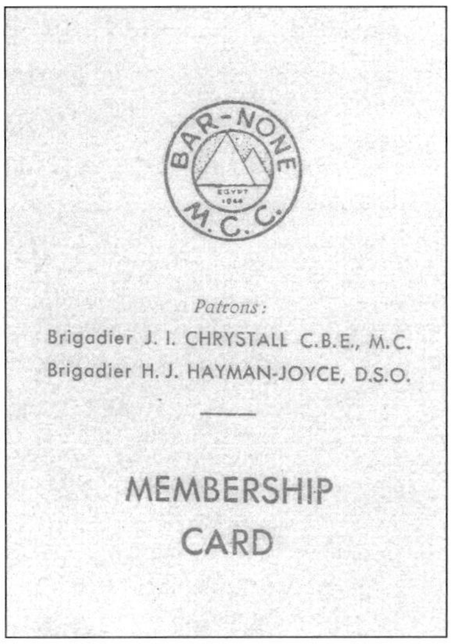
BAR-NONE
M.C.C.

Patrons:
Brigadier J. I. CHRYSTALL C.B.E., M.C.
Brigadier H. J. HAYMAN-JOYCE, D.S.O.

MEMBERSHIP
CARD

WHITE HELMETS DISPLAY TEAM ATTRACTED RACERS

Brian Craven also a member of the "White Helmets" display team

History can trace the formation of the Royal Signals motor cycle display team back to the late 1920's which was then supplemented by a team of horseman. As early as 1920, despatch riders from the RCS gave shows of their riding skills at Maresfield Park (Sussex) and Tidworth tattoo in Wiltshire. Appearances at the Royal Tournament and a host of county and agricultural shows around the country added to the teams growing reputation. During WWII team members reverted to despatch rider duties and when the team reformed post-war, it attracted the attention of Cyril Maidment. Having joined the Signals on National Service duty, Cyril was so keen to join the team that he approached his CO asking for a trial. Admiring his enthusiasm the CO arrange a seven day trial which Cyril successfully passed, joining the 'White Helmets' as the team was called, for the 1949 season. One venue for a display was the Johnnie Hoskins Glasgow Ashfield speedway stadium. Always on the lookout for talent, Hoskins offered the whole display team a speedway trial, but the team authorities refused permission for fear of injuries. Cyril was however to have a ride at a speedway stadium again later in the year, when the 'White Helmets' appeared as the interval attraction at the World Speedway Final held at Wembley stadium in September. Other speedway riders who made the grade as a 'White Helmet' include Vic Emms (Coventry), Brian Craven (Newcastle) and speedway's own 007 James Bond!

James Bond in 'White Helmets' team action

Bond who rode cycle speedway in his youth for Sutton Coldfield 'Stars' was one of the last National Service intake in 1960 when he joined the RCS. *"I did my despatch rider training at Rippon where Rick France who rode for Middlesbrough and Coventry was my instructor. I decided to try out for the display team and as luck had it they were looking for some smaller riders so I was delighted to be selected"*. Jimmy rode all over the UK with the team and also went to New York to perform in Madison Square Gardens. *"My particular skill was that I could ride a bike backwards and often did the 'Reverse Jimmy' (see picture above). One night at the Aldershot tattoo and with Louis Mountbatten in the crowd, I fell off after being dazzled by the lights. Lord Louis sent a messenger down to the pits area to check I was OK!"* James now lives near Taunton where he is an accomplished bell ringer and motor cycle restorer.

DESPATCH RIDERS ON THE SILVER SCREEN

Dirk Bogarde as 'Bill Fox'

A feature film "Once a Jolly Swagman" released by Wessex films in 1948, but set in a pre-war era re-enforced the links between speedway and the despatch riding roles. Produced by Ian Dalrymple, the film starred a budding actor Dirk Bogarde in what was only his 5th film role of what was to become an illustrious film career. Bogarde played Bill Fox, a factory worker who progresses to become a speedway star before joining the Army as a despatch rider. During the film Bill Fox and Duggie Lewis (Cyril Cusack) are coached in riding a DR bike as part of their training. Fox is able to demonstrate his brilliant broad-siding skills on the machine much to the annoyance of the Sergeant instructor. The film which also featured Bill Owen (Last of the Summer Wine), Thora Hird and Moira Lister was a box office hit, with some 10 million speedway fans paying to see it. Racing scenes were filmed at New Cross stadium with ex RAF man Frank Arnold from Rayleigh speedway and Jack Cooley, a West Ham rider acting as technical advisors to the director.

Wartime Personalities

ALICE HART

Alice Hart, right in conversation with Jack Parker at Belle Vue

Fay Taylour the lady rider of the late 1920's could lay claim to the title of speedway's 'First Lady' on track, but off track Belle Vue's Alice Hart has no contenders. Her career in speedway administration started in 1933-34, when the Aces manager of the time E.O Spence of Camberley club fame, advertised for a secretary. Alice was jobless at the time and admitted at her interview that she was not really interested in speedway racing. She was promptly offered the job as Spence admitted later he wanted a secretary who wouldn't be distracted by the glamour of the riders. By 1941, with war raging and war time meetings at the Zoological Gardens track already underway, Spence was made managing director of the whole Belle Vue complex, which at the time was England's equivalent of Alton Towers. He immediately appointed Miss Hart as his speedway manager and she was to run all speedway matters at Belle Vue throughout the war period and beyond. So successful was she that she eventually joined the Belle Vue board herself. One of her biggest innovations was the introduction of novice races which discovered riders such as Dent Oliver, Louis Lawson, Ken Sharples and Peter Craven. At one stage as well as running Belle Vue she was involved as promoter at Sheffield in 1950 and was also a director at other clubs.

MAJOR C D 'PAT' LITTLEWORTH

Pat was a professional soldier serving in the British Army from 1939-62, but his links with speedway can be traced back to 1928 when, whilst living in Fulham, he attended the very early meetings at Stamford Bridge, where he recalls with fondness the exploits of 'Sprouts' Elder and Billy Lamont. When he was posted to Fayid (Egypt) as Deputy Director of Mechanical Engineers, golf, sailing and fishing were already established as sporting activities for troops with time on their hands. Along with a Major from the Royal Engineers, he contacted the Olympia athletics stadium authorities in Fayid and reached an agreement to lay a speedway track. Prior to the Olympia venue, racing had taken place on an improvised track in the desert, but with covered stands, pits and public facilities which would not have been out of place in the newly formed English Third Division, Olympia quickly caught on, with crowds of 3,000 common place. Pat's responsibilities included managing track preparation, publicity, producing the programme and he also hosted a 20 minute radio programme called 'Speedway Corner' on British Forces network radio every Friday night. He even rode for Fayid at Tel El Kabir, but was badly injured and so decided to stay on the safe side of the racing fence.

'Cliff' Clifford ,right, pictured with 'Ginger' Wilde

F J 'CLIFF' CLIFFORD

Cliff was posted to Egypt in the Middle East with the Royal Air Force Volunteer Reserve in June 1945 and quickly became involved with the activities of the Bar-None MCC. He inherited the motorcycle of the club's secretary Sgt Scotson and this enabled him to support Corporal 'Ginger' Wilde of REME in the organisation of trials, hill climbs and eventually sand track racing (speedway). One of Cliff's regular tasks was to hire transport, arrange personnel to act as track marshals, 'girder boys' (track graders) and other officials, primarily from the RAF. His role grew and he had to attend meetings with the Patron of speedway racing in Egypt, Brigadier H L Hayman-Joyce DSO along with 'Ginger' Wilde. Further administrative duties included editing match programmes along with Bert Steddy, who had a column in the match day programmes under the name of 'Gripper', gaining publicity for events via the Egyptian Gazette newspaper and feeding the Forces broadcaster Gus Soderbergh with speedway news, to ensure healthy attendances at his local track of El Ballah.

Racing continued full throttle until mid 1947 which is when most of the 147 DR section, 18th Air Formation Signals left for home. On the day before Cliff's departure for England, his Norton 16H motorcycle was stolen. As the machine had been borrowed from Sgt Scotson and was not 'on record' the thief could have had some awkward questions to answer if he had been found.

Track preperation in the desert

ALFRED COLE

Alfred Cole

The National Fire Service (NFS), earnt many plaudits for their work during the dark days of the Blitz in London. In fact the NFS was an invaluable service throughout the capital and Southern England as they tackled the impact of German bombing raids. The arrival in 1944 of Self Propelled Explosive Missiles (V rockets) made the service even more crucial and the use of motor cycle despatch riders to provide quick communication was an integral part of the NFS.

The man responsible for this vital motorised element was non other than Divisional Officer Alf Cole, who pre-war was in charge of the New Cross speedway workshops, keeping the team machines ready to race in the white hot National League of that time. During the war Alf arranged courses at the BSA factory in Birmingham, when men and women DRs from the National Fire Service spent a week learning bike maintenance and improving their riding skills on a specially constructed obstacle course. The NFS despatch riding service became one of the largest organisations of its kind in the world with a riding strength of 1,137 riders and 1,250 machines painted in their all grey livery. Alf recruited riders from motor cycle clubs and numerous speedway riders also entered this very dangerous service. Training of recruits, under Alf's watchful eye took place in the New Cross stadium car park, with the speedway workshops given over to the maintenance of bikes. Post-war Alf, who entered speedway as the mechanic to New Cross and England star Tommy Farndon, moved from the workshops to take on the role of team manager for New Cross. Alf was not alone in his sterling war work, New Cross promoter Fred Mockford being awarded the George Medal for bravery in the Blitz.

ALLAN JEFFERIES

The Jefferies motorcycling dynasty can be traced back to father Joseph who combined motor and motorcycle trading with working as a chauffeur in the late 1800s. Allan left school at the age of sixteen joining the family firm with a full driving licence, which he acquired at the age of just 13 years old under the wartime Defence of the Realm Act during WWI. He was a pre-war works rider for Triumph and Scott motorcycles and represented Britain in the International Six Day Trials Team, as well as trying his hand at speedway with Belle Vue in the early 1930s. Alan's main link with speedway was as mechanic to Northern star rider Frank Varey, who he accompanied to Buenos Airies on a winter riding tour of South America and on occasions he was also called upon to ride. Allan became a civilian instructor to service despatch riders before entering the services himself.

Cpt. Allan Jefferies -REME

Allan had a remarkable war as a captain with REME when he became involved in the liberation of the Belsen concentration camp. He was responsible for managing the reconnection of the water supply to the camp, and the memory of the day lived with him for ever. I am indebted to John Whittaker, the ex- speedway referee from Shirley in Yorkshire for permission to print Allan's letter to John's mother, his sister, regarding the horrendous experience.

Letter from Captain Allan Jefferies from his hospital bed to sister Elsie April 21 1945

Dear Elsie,

Your letter with the query re Goering's car I had answered before getting the query. (Allan had acquired Herman Goering's actual staff car after the war). *Much has happened since then. I had a lot of rushing about to do in my jeep acting as liaison officer for the Corps. One day I did 360 miles in one day on rotten roads. We liberated a concentration camp and I got the job of laying water to the camp, which had been waterless for 157 days. This I did with a series of fire pumps and fire hoses from a small river ½ mile away.*

You will be interested, though shocked, with the details of the camp. This isn't a case of hearsay but what I saw with my own eyes. Five hundred were dying daily. There were 50,000 people in the camp. The bodies had not been buried for ages so that there were literally thousands of naked bodies all over the place. In the huts, in the roads in carts and trailers. There was a place for burning them but it was out of order. Half the inmates were walking skeletons and it was common to see one drop dead. There was an area twice as big as a football pitch covered with bodies.

When I got the water going, they fought for it until I could get several points going. As soon as they had drunk their fill the women and men stripped off in the open and washed their bodies as well as they could without soap. The sewers were hopelessly inadequate and had choked up through lack of water. Those that had not got typhus had got dysentery, so the stench was unbelievable. This is a horrible letter to write but I want to tell as many people as possible, what kind of animal a German is. I was in the Jewish camp, which of course was easily the worst. I spoke to many of the men and women. I got several offers from people to work for me for life without pay because I had got water for them. Dysentery became worse when they had drunk the river water and it was alarming at first to be talking to a beautiful Jewess when she would suddenly get down and relieve nature.

The S.S and German Army had stayed on to hand over the camp. The prisoners said the Army had not been bad, but the S.S had been too horrible for words. We locked the Commandant up in the refrigerator in his undies and by 'accident' turned the current on. The S.S men didn't like it because some of the bodies had been dead a long time and fell to pieces. A lot of kicking and bayoneting had to be resorted to, to keep them at work. Two committed suicide the first night so we made S.S women carry them through the camp and bury them. Another tried to run away and everyone emptied their guns into him. I'll bet he had the world's record number of bullets in him.

I see now that what we would have had to put up with in England if we had gone down and its heaven help any Conchy (conscientious objector) or Peace Pledge Union man if I meet him. So now I am in hospital as I got no food or sleep for three days and just collapsed with dysentery myself. I shan't be long before I am out again, adding my quota to the German punishment. In case you think this is awful, let me tell you I haven't been able to tell you all. You can't imagine how horrible it was.

Best love Allan Excuse pencil, I can't write so well in bed.

Allan Jefferies died in 1978 leaving a remarkable motor cycling and business legacy. His sales showroom was the first officially appointed BMW dealership in the UK, Allan himself becoming vice president of the Auto Cycle Union and chairman of the ACU's Benevolent Fund whilst son's Nick and Tony rode in the trials and road racing scene respectively, with distinction.

RON 'JOCK' POPE

There can't be many servicemen who can claim to have experienced three D-Days, but that is the claim of Ron Pope from Bournemouth. Ron was a budding grass track rider before the war, riding at Cannfield, Ringwood and Oldstock speedway (Salisbury) until war duty called. 'Jock' as he became known, wanted to join the RAF, after experiencing flying at a Sir Alan Cobham Flying Circus event. The authorities saw things differently however and his motor cycling and driving skills were directed towards the Corps of Military Police as a Lance Corporal. In this role he was to see action across Europe, Sicily and the Middle East.

Jock , left on bike, with General Dempsey's staff car

Ron's war was to take a dramatic turn, when in 1943, whilst in Sicily with the 13th Corps of MPs, he was ordered to report to General Miles Dempsey for duty as a motorcycle outrider. It was a proud day when Ron was handed the chequered flag which he was allowed to attach to his motor cycle, giving him absolute priority wherever he went. Ron was to experience the invasions in Sicily, Italy and Normandy as an out rider for General Dempsey. Writing in his biography *To War on Two Wheels* he describes the time he met Prime Minister Winston Churchill. *"About a week after D-Day in France, an ADC asked me to help get Mr Churchill out of the way for a while! He wishes to see some Germans, do your best was my instruction, you know where to go"* said the ADC. Ron successfully escorted the jeep carrying Churchill to give Winston his desired sighting of the enemy.

'Jock' pictured with General Dempsey's car was demobbed in March 1946 and after a period as a chauffeur to a Poole businessman he returned to his pre-war job as a photographer on the beaches of Swanage and Sandbanks.

'Jock' was to return to grass track racing and also tried his hand at solo and midget car racing on the speedways. Second half racing at Poole saw him sustain a very bad injury which kept him out of racing for sixteen weeks. Whilst injured, a Maltese engineer based in Bournemouth approached him to manage a speedway track he proposed to open in his home country of Malta. Sadly Ron had to decline and the project was not progressed. On his return, the steady income of photography was to steer Ron away from racing but he became the track photographer at Poole's Wimborne road stadium, so allowing him to combine his two passions.

FRANK 'BUSTER' BUCKLAND

An accomplished rugby union player, speedway rider, businessman, electrician and speedway promoter come tour manager, Frank had a remarkable appetite for work. As early as 1929, Frank became involved with the infant sport of dirt track racing at Exeter. He was at that time working for the Southern Electrical Engineering Company and he was tasked to install floodlights for the soon to be introduced sport of speedway to the town's County Ground rugby stadium. 'Buster' rode in these early Devon meetings, combining this with his rugby playing activities.

Some 16 years later, just as WWII was ending, Frank's all round organisational skills were called upon to assist with the re-introduction of impromptu speedway to celebrate VE day with a meeting called 'European Victory'. This meeting was staged at Exwick Field as the County Ground was still at the time in the hands of the military. A single meeting was possible before the site was ploughed up for food production on the instruction of the Ministry of Agriculture.

Barely six months after that Whit Monday revival meeting Frank, along with Eric Chitty of West Ham fame was masterminding the first ever ENSA speedway tour of Europe to entertain the troops in Europe waiting for demobilisation. Over twenty meetings were staged between November 1945 and late February 1946. A second mini tour of Belgium in the winter of 1946 saw Frank carrying out almost every role imaginable from referee, track builder, start marshal as well as printing programmes and drumming up publicity for the meetings. By 1948 Frank had decided to emigrate to Australia where it is believed he became a farmer.

ARTHUR 'WESTY' WESTWOOD

Arthur was something of an entrepreneur from his early days and during 1929 he rode in and promoted meetings at Wolverhampton. A riding career saw him wear the colours of Sheffield, Birmingham (Hall Green), West Ham, Wimbledon, Southampton and Clapton. In 1931 'Westy' as rider - promoter staged racing at the Buffalo stadium in Paris. Known at one time as the 'Woolworths of speedway', he was running four tracks at the same time in 1938, namely Leeds, Sheffield, Birmingham and Nottingham. A larger than life character, Arthur was involved in entertainment for the troops in France in WWII. Following the Dunkirk evacuation he was tasked with producing a radio programme called 'Private Smith Entertains' for Southern Command. It proved to be one of the most popular radio programmes of the war.

ARTHUR SIMCOCK

Australian by birth, E A (Arthur) Simcock left his homeland in 1927 following a successful oval racing career on the one third of a mile banked Melbourne Motodrome. Simcock travelled from Down Under to compete in the Isle of Man TT races, initially riding AJS machinery and later Sunbeam and OK Supreme. In 1931 he was part of a team, Alan Bruce and Phil Irvin were his partners, which built a 996cc Brough Superior - JAP to make an attempt on the motor cycle land speed record.

Wolverhampton 'Wasps'. Arthur Simcock in suit.

Wembley speedway quickly recognised his experience and appointed him as Clerk of the Course at the Empire stadium. The experience of working with Arthur Elvin in running professional, slickly presented speedway meetings, would prove crucial in the war years when he played a leading role in the organisation of forces speedway in Italy. At the opening meeting at Bari July 15 1945, Major Simcock as he was by then, officiated as ACU steward and Clerk of the Course and his efforts were recognised in the programme notes. *"We extend our thanks to Major A E Simcock RASC, the ACU representative whose untiring efforts and organisational abilities have done much towards making today meeting possible. It is regrettable that circumstances are such that he can no longer offer his services".*

Such was Arthur's growing reputation that he was appointed selector and team manager for the Australian team and was their representative on the British Speedway Control Board. In 1951, he took over as promoter of the Wolverhampton team which entered the National League Division 3.

MAJOR W W 'BILL' FEARNLEY

League speedway racing resumed in Britain in 1946 after a series of open meetings and challenges in 1945. The 1946 season saw a two league structure, National League (Division 1) and Northern League (Division 2) drawing enormous crowds as the general public clamoured for entertainment after the dour war years. Such was the potential boom that loomed for 1947, that the incumbent manager at the Control Board Dick Southouse resigned to become a promoter himself.

Looking for a new manager, the job was given to Major WW Fearnley, who had officiated as judge and timekeeper at Belle Vue and White City Manchester and became a respected steward in the 1930s. Bill, as he was affectionately known, was a soldier as early as 1914, when he enlisted as a trumpeter in the Royal Artillery, aged just 15 years old. His other Army duties were as a horseman when he was required to 'Break in' horses needed to haul guns and other artillery to the front line in France. In 1939, he re-joined the Royal Artillery as a 2nd Lieutenant, being eventually promoted to Major with the Cairo Artillery training school. Post-war he joined the Chloride battery company in their public relations department before moving to the Control Board in Pall Mall, London. There he joined Lt-Col R C Vernon Brooke (Chairman) and Captain J G Procter M.C who was responsible for track construction and safety maintenance, to form a powerful Army trio charged with steering the sport.

The boom season of 1947 was almost ruined as the government were not keen on mid-week racing, which they believed would affect the countries factory productivity. Many of the new 3rd Division tracks wanted mid-week racing and the Control Board led by Vernon Brooke and Fearnley eventually convinced the Home Secretary Chuter Eade of the need for these tracks. As the tapes rose for the 1947 season some eight new tracks formed the new 3rd Division to herald a golden period for speedway with attendances challenging and on occasions beating those of football.

FRED EVANS

1939, was set to be a big year for Fred Lindop Evans! The one time greyhound trainer, official and later speedway manager at tracks as far afield as Birmingham, Nottingham, Sheffield and lastly Hackney Wick (London) was set to open his own track at Ramsgate. Fred's plan was to enter a team in a proposed Third Division speedway league at the Newington stadium in Ramsgate, but with war clouds gathering his investment looked under threat. Ever the thinker, and not wishing to loose his financial stake in the Ramsgate project, Fred wrote to the War Office suggesting the venue would be an ideal location for an Army speedway unit. As you can see from the response letter from the War Office recruitment director, the Army didn't quite share Fred's vision, but were keen to recruit speedway riders and mechanics as motorcyclists and mechanical engineers.

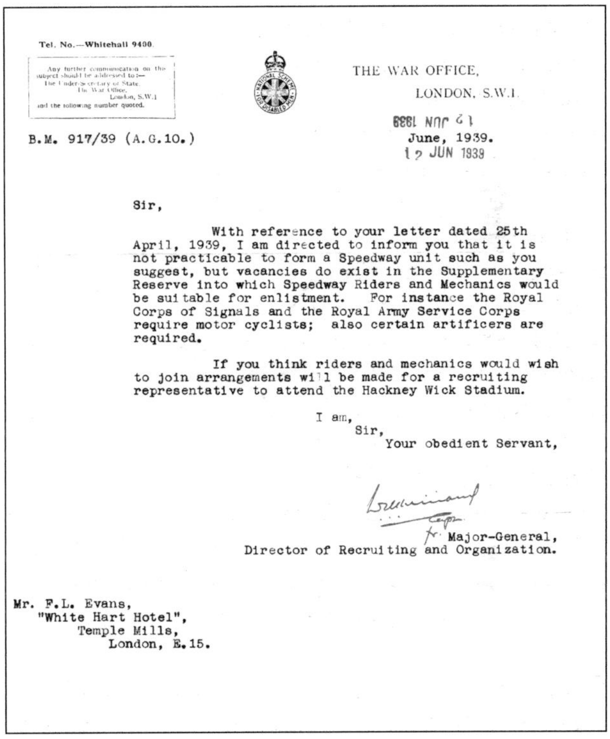

Tel. No.—Whitehall 9400.

Any further communication on this subject should be addressed to:— The Under-Secretary of State, The War Office, London, S.W.1 and the following number quoted.

THE WAR OFFICE,
LONDON, S.W.1.

B.M. 917/39 (A.G.10.)

12 JUN 1939
June, 1939.
12 JUN 1939

Sir,

With reference to your letter dated 25th April, 1939, I am directed to inform you that it is not practicable to form a Speedway unit such as you suggest, but vacancies do exist in the Supplementary Reserve into which Speedway Riders and Mechanics would be suitable for enlistment. For instance the Royal Corps of Signals and the Royal Army Service Corps require motor cyclists; also certain artificers are required.

If you think riders and mechanics would wish to join arrangements will be made for a recruiting representative to attend the Hackney Wick Stadium.

I am,
Sir,
Your obedient Servant,

for Major-General,
Director of Recruiting and Organization.

Mr. F.L. Evans,
"White Hart Hotel",
Temple Mills,
London, E.15.

The War Office Response

By August 1939, Fred knew the project was dead, and although aged 38 years he joined up with the Army in the Territorial Reserves as a Lieutenant in the Royal Army Service Corps. The Times newspaper of August 26, recorded Fred's enlistment and his links with speedway were brought to a temporary close. Fred, who was always something of a mystery man, lived in hotels and golf clubs for most of the 1930's, did however appear at a war time Belle Vue race meeting dressed in a Captain's uniform apparently, in charge of a Barrage balloon group. It was to be 1950 before Fred surfaced again, when now known as Major Fred Evans he was appointed as team manager of the Norwich team. The real mystery surrounding Fred is that almost 60 years later, a battered suitcase was bought in a Greenwich junk shop for a few pounds. The case contained Fred's pre-war passport, personal papers, cheque book and scrap books covering his speedway career. Where had the case been all that time? Why didn't Fred collect it after the war? What secrets did the contents hold?

I am indebted to Mr Chris Illman for his help in compiling this piece on Fred. Until the mystery is solved the case remains in the custodianship of Chris!

FRANK V HURRELL

Frank Hurrell seated centre front row

Frank Hurrell, a professional soldier with the Royal Electrical Mechanical Engineers was a leading light in the Hanomag 'Saints' speedway club based in Hanover began his involvement around 1947. He began as joint judge (referee) before taking over the role on his own in 1948. A period as race starter in 1949, combined with club secretary led to the whole Hurrell family becoming involved in the organisation of the regular Sunday meetings. Son David became club mascot and led the weekly parade of riders before the start of every meeting on a machine especially constructed by the nearby workshops. During the winter of 1949, under the direction of Colonel Dundas, the Saints club President, Frank was asked with raising funds for the club. Similarly to Johnnie Hoskins at Wembley in the early 1930's, he suggested a supporters club with badges, pennants and other club favours earning valuable revenue to ensure the continuity of racing with strict Army regulations limiting the use of public funds.

Reaching the rank of Armt. Warrant Officer, Frank became Meeting Controller in 1950 and was very proud to explain, when interviewed, the clubs aims and objectives:

1. *To keep the lads occupied either with riding themselves, maintaining machines, increasing their technical knowledge, or just watching a good afternoons sport.*

2. *To try impress on the German public that speedway, as run under ACU regulations, is in fact the cleanest and most sporting of any sport, brings out the real essential of sportsmanship and comradeship within the riders, thereby making the foundation of a very happy club.*

3. *To give those riders who wish to take up speedway racing as a living on leaving the forces, the basic training and riding rules required of them, especially as a team or a partner.*

David 'Lightning' Hurrel -Hanomag 'Saints' mascot

WHO WAS CAPTAIN PEACOCKE?

Charles Ochiltree
Coventry manager
1948

Twenty years before that famous Coventry promoter Charles Ochiltree, who served as a Warrant Officer in the Royal Army Service Corps, arrived at the Brandon stadium, there was another Army military man at the helm of the long running Midlands club.

Ask any speedway aficionado where and when the first England v Australia speedway test match was held and the chances are they will give Wimbledon 1930 as their answer. Research has however revealed that a little known Ashes 'test match' was staged at Coventry as full nine months earlier than the famed London event. Captain L G L Peacocke, a WW1 Army officer, was the original Clerk of the Course at Coventry when they first opened for racing on September 29 1928.The Captain, in addition to running public meetings, organised mid-week training schools for aspiring local dirt track riders. It was also his idea to stage a test match between England and Australia which was staged on September 9 1929 before an enormous crowd of 25,000 spectators.The meeting was run as a series of match races (one against one) rather than the traditional four man in a race formula, and it is therefore not accredited as an official fixture in the record books. England ran out winners $9\frac{1}{2}$ points to Australia's $6\frac{1}{2}$ with England being represented by Jack Parker, Wilmot Evans, Syd Jackson and Arthur Jervis. Australia fielded Frank Arthur, Max Grosskreutz, Col Stewart and 'Cyclone' Billy Lamont.

Little else is known of Capt. Peacocke who disappeared from the speedway scene in 1931, so if any reader has any further knowledge of his background, the author would be delighted to hear from you. Safe to say, this story emphasises yet again the major influence that armed forces personnel have had on speedway throughout the years!

FRED MOCKFORD (George Medal)

When war was declared and his New Cross team became a victim of the decision to abandon league speedway in September 1939, pre-war promoter Freddie (Crystal Palace 1928-33 and New Cross 1934-39), joined the Air Raid Precaution Service as his part of the war effort. It was a dangerous role as an Incident Officer in the ARP in the London Blitz, but Freddie ignored the personal dangers and was consequently awarded the George Medal for saving numerous lives in air raids.

The London Gazette recorded no less than nine separate incidents between September 1940 and May 1941, when Frederick Eric Mockford, put his own life on the line to save the lives of bomb victims. Freddie was involved in rescues at the South Eastern hospital, New Cross Gate railway station and the tram depot, all within walking distance of his New Cross, Old Kent road speedway stadium.

The George Medal was initiated on September 24 1940 as the second highest civilian award possible and was the civilian equivalent of the Victoria Cross for armed forces personnel. Freddie's name appeared in the London Gazette of August 1941, where all honours and awards were announced.The Gazette, the longest continuously published newspaper in Britain was first printed in November 1665 and is where all service and civilians who were 'mentioned in despatches' appeared. Several curious speedway links surround the George Medal, with Pilot Officer J H F (Morian) Hansen RAFVR who rode for West Ham, Hackney, Bristol and Wembley before the war becoming the first recipient of an 'Honorary' George Medal on December 18 1940. Lionel Van Praag, the 1936 Australian World Champion was also honoured with a GM for his exploits as a pilot in the Royal Australian Air Force. In more modern times, Ronnie Russell, who promoted at Rye House and Arena Essex was similarly awarded the George Medal for the part he played in an incident in the Mall in 1974 when HRH Princess Anne was attacked by a gunman who tried to kidnap her.

RONNIE GREENE M.B.E

Professional ballroom dancer, chemist, boot manufacturer and speedway promoter. All roles that the versatile Ronnie Greene had undertaken before the out break of WWII. Greene had re-opened Bristol speedway in 1936, before returning to London one year later as promoter at the luxurious Wimbledon, Plough Lane stadium. Like many speedway officials, Ronnie turned his skills to the war effort, joining the National Fire Service, reaching the rank of Assistant Commander. The NFS had been formed in 1941 to coordinate and supplement the Auxiliary Fire Services and regular Fire brigades, which came under the umbrella of the local authorities. The NFS was a 350,000 strong force of men and women which remained in operation until 1947 and played a leading part in fire fighting following the German bombing raids and later V rocket attacks on the capital. Greene encouraged speedway supporters to join the service and was awarded the M.B.E. Ironically in 1943, a stray German bomb badly damaged the Plough Lane home of his beloved Wimbledon 'Dons' team, completely destroying the main grandstand and causing major disruption to the venues electrical wiring system. When the war ended, Greene was keen to re-enter the 'Dons' in the 1946 National League but the Ministry of Works initially deemed the repairs he wished to make not a necessity. He was advised by a friend to write directly to the King for help! Amazingly within days a permit for work to start was issued. Racing restarted on April 19 1946 in a daylight match against Bradford Odsal with the floodlights being fully operational the following week.

Forces Favourite

ROY 'DODGER' DAVIES

Now living in retirement in New Zealand, Roy Davies' time spent with the RAF speedway team the 'Eagles' is still remembered by many forces veterans who served in Egypt after the war for his exploits on a gloriously sunny Sunday in September 1949.

After joining the RAF in 1947 as a flight mechanic at the age of 18, he served for over two years with 114 Squadron maintaining Dakotas in the Canal Zone of Egypt. Roy initially rode a BSA M20 around the airfield, before discovering the activities of the 'Eagles' speedway team based at Kabrit. Roy quickly adapted his road riding skills to the sand surfaced speedway track, which had been constructed within the base and he qualified for what was one of the most prestigious forces meetings at the time, namely the Canal Zone Championship.A crowd of 1,500 spectators gathered that September afternoon to see 32 riders, including Roy, compete for the title.'Dodger' progressed through the early rounds to reach the final, where he lined up against Hesketh (Diamonds), Greenway (Tel el Kabir) and Bollington (Argosy). Roy won the final in a time of 1mins 38 secs ahead of Hesketh to take the honours.

The locally sponsored Grand Hotel challenge trophy was presented to Roy by a Mr Popodopolus and he was carried shoulder high from the track by his RAF supporters.

LES MULLINS

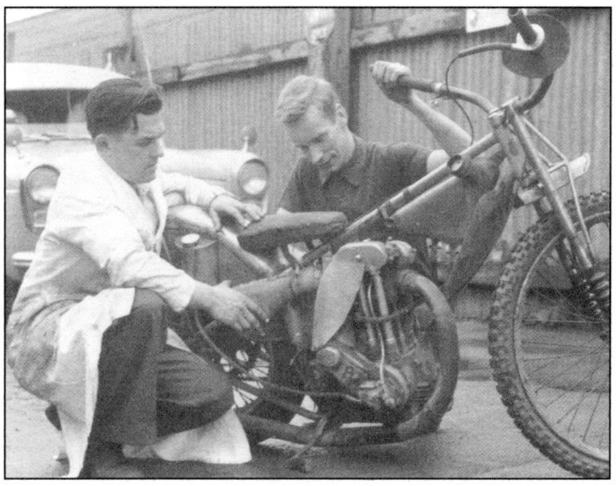

Les, in white coat, pictured with Ove Fundin

The name will ring a bell with all post-war Norwich fans, but it was as 'Mad' Mullins of the TEK 'Dons' who raced at 2 Base workshop sand speedway track that Les first came to prominence in the speedway sense. Les was involved in logistics and transport with the Royal Army Ordnance Corps between 1945-48, when he became established as an Army speedway rider, his highlight, that of coming third behind great friend Harry Mappin in the 1947 Egyptian championship. His father, on hearing of his success in the Middle East, showed photographs of his son's win to the Norwich speedway management. It was 1948, and after a trial, Les was loaned out to the Yarmouth 'Bloaters' team just along the coast.A racing accident was to prevent Les progressing as a rider and he re-joined Norwich as a team mechanic. Billy Bales was a rising star at Yarmouth and he also served in Egypt with the RAF. Les and Billy became great friends, Les was Billy's best man at his wedding, and they still live as neighbours in the same road in Norwich after over fifty years. Les became Ove Fundin's mechanic in 1955 when the Swede joined Norwich, and was in the pits with the Swedish star for all his five World Individual Championship successes (1956, 1960, 1961, 1963 and 1967). The no nonsense riding style of Ove often upset opposing fans and it was not unheard of that Ove, accompanied by Les, required a police escort from some away tracks.

Cpl A.L. 'BERT' STEDDY

'Bert' volunteered for the Army in 1943 and after Primary, Infantry and basic training at Prestatyn in North Wales, he undertook the 12 week Despatch riders course at Catterick. Bert's story has been well recorded by the Air Formation Signals Regiment Association that still has 400 members to this day! Below, in his own words is the story of arguably the most prolific Army speedway rider in Egypt of the immediate post-war era.

"Following our entry into Europe on D-Day June 6th 1944 and our eventual arrival into Germany, together with VE Day, most of the younger element of 15th Air Formation Signals were posted into the 18th AFS. This was the fate of 147 DR Section as a whole, being re-enforced by younger members of 145 DR section to bring 147 DR up to full strength. This resulted in the return of the Regiment from Germany to the UK in July 1945 with the prospect of the invasion of Japan as the next project! Most of the Regiment was despatched for 28 days embarkation leave before Japan. Victory in Japan on August 15 did not stop the process as many of us had thought and so we found ourselves at Southampton docks in December bound for all points East, although it turned out we were off loaded at Port Said just before Christmas. I first recall my involvement with the Bar-None MCC in January 1946 when the news went around that their was some motor cycling hill climbs at a place near Cairo called Gaza or Meena. This was my indoctrination to the Bar-None and as such I was determined to take part in these events, as were others of my comrades in 147 DR Section.

In the meantime we in 18th Air Formation Signals had moved to Maadi and 147 DR section had joined up with the Cairo branch of the Bar-None. They had staged a few events at Qadima along with the RAF called 'Sand Track Trials', though this to me was speedway racing on sand and the equivalent to a cinder track back in the UK. It was here that I met up with Bert King and we both shared a passion for this kind of event. He was due for demob at any time, and he was the best by far of any of the speedway lads. He had a machine that was as near to proper speedway machine standards as you could get with the use of surplus W D parts. We had access to many spare parts from an Army dump at a place called Helwan. We were in another world rooting around all sorts of disused military transport not only British but, German, and Italian as well. Bert's bike was past on to me when he left for the UK and it served me well as my scores will show. Bert wound up riding for Middlesbrough speedway in 1947 and I met up with him one night at West Ham after I was demobbed."

Apart from riding Bert (under the name of Gripper), was responsible for the compilation of programmes at El Ballah during the 1946-47 season. The offer of a trial with Harringay was received from Frank Whitehead but finances being tight, he was unable to fund a bike. Later in the 1950's, Bert did appear at the Green Lanes track when he competed in some of the early stock car meetings held at the North London stadium.

TERRY SMALL

A regular points scorer for TEK 'Dons' in the Egyptian 1948 season, Terry Small almost sprung a surprise in the Egyptian Speedway Championship of that year. Described in the meeting programme thus "*When in the mood he can make the fastest skate and how. On paper he may not have the same chance of winning as some others, but don't be surprised if he pulls something out of the bag*". How prophetic those words were as Small finished runner up to the eventual champion Corporal Bob Oakley with 14 points, dropping his only points in five rides to champion Oakley in his opening ride.

On demob, his forces speedway and grass track experience earnt him a team place with the Poole 'Pirates' of 1949. He was awarded the 'Freshmans Tankard' award for the most improved novice and went on to ride for Poole until 1956. He was a key rider in the South coast team's back to back league championship wins of 1951(Division 3) and 1952 (Division 2).

CYRIL 'HOOKEY' WALKER

'Hookey' Walker's military funeral

Sgt Cyril Walker, the captain of the Libya based Grenadier Guards speedway team the 'Hellcats' was given a full military funeral in 1950 after his shock death in the British Military hospital in Tripoli following an operation. Just 25 years old 'Hookey' from Mansfield had been a leading rider since forces speedway had been introduced 9 months earlier. Barely three weeks before his death, Walker had led the 'Hellcats' to a victory over their greatest rivals, the Royal Corps Signals 'Meteors' team. The funeral cortege had a guard of honour and the service was conducted by Reverend H C Sell, the Guards chaplain. Many serving soldiers and a large representation from the local speedway community attended the funeral. Sgt Walker was buried in the British Military cemetery and amongst the wreaths laid was one from the Italian speedway team the 'Black Devils' who were regular opponents of the 'Hellcats'.

HAROLD 'NOBBY' STOCK

Born Harold William Stock, was a milkman before the war and was nicknamed 'Nobby' after the horse which pulled his float. He had his first rides on the speedway cinders at Arthur Warwick's training school at Dagenham when he was 19 years old. That was in 1937 and by 1938, he had made so much progress that he signed for Second Division Hackney 'Wolves' helping the East End club to the league title. 'Nobby' saw action with the Royal Army Service Corps in North Africa, France and eventually Italy, where he played a leading role late in 1944, by assisting Major Simcock with the construction of the Trani track, where he also rode. His pre-war professional experience quickly saw him make a name for himself, winning the South Eastern Italian championship and claimed a host of tack records including the Bari four lap clutch start 92.2 secs, two lap rolling start 46.0 secs and the one lap flying start 21.6 secs. On demob 'Nobby' was signed by first division Harringay before he was loaned out to Bristol to help the 'Bulldogs' win the Second Division title in 1948.

BILL KEMP

Bill, born in Rainham, Essex in 1921, he too had been a milkman before the war and only became interested in speedway when the Bari, Italy forces speedway was built in 1945 near the San Spirito camp. A driver with REME, Kemp at one stage was almost unbeatable on Italian tracks in spite of quality opposition such as Geoff Bennett, 'Nobby' Stock, Bill Carruthers and of course 'Split' Waterman. At his peak, 'Driver' Kemp as he became known, broke a leg whilst riding at Bari which prevented him from taking up a professional career with Wembley until 1947 alongside his Army comrade 'Split' Waterman. After Wembley he was to ride for Midland clubs Cradley Heath and then Oxford.

Bill Kemp in Cradley Heath colours

HARRY MAPPIN

Sgt Harry Mappin service number 14857671 served with REME between 1944-48, but had never seen a speedway meeting, when an Irish Corporal Kelloway under the auspices of the Bar-None club introduced the sport to the Tel el Kabir garrison where Harry was based.

Remembering those days of sixty years ago Harry says "*I learnt to ride a motor cycle whilst I was in 610 Command Vehicle group. I was put in charge of no 9 workshop which was responsible for the maintenance of all WD motor bikes on the garrison. I remember having a dozen POW's in the workshop, including a German called Otto Pries who had worked in the BMW factory before the war. I recall Otto always ensured that mine and the other TEK 'Dons' machines were always in tip top order. The track was built as part of the Army's effort to provide troops with entertainment and sporting facilities, after many of the lads, who were expecting demob were delayed in going home.*"

A great friend of Les Mullins, Harry's most memorable speedway day was November 9 1947, when he won the 1947 Egyptian Speedway Riders Championship. The event consisting of riders from Suez 'Lions', TEK 'Dons' and Fayid 'Dicers' was held on the Tel el Kabir track. Harry won the meeting with 14pts from Vic Orange 13pts and Les Mullins 11pts. On returning to civilian life, a trial with Norwich didn't develop, so Harry used road racing as his motorcycling outlet. He managed a motor cycle shop in Pickering and rode a 250cc Rudge in competitions across the north of England. After 60 years Harry is still in touch with Les Mullins and also German POW Otto Pries, just to prove that an Army buddy is a friend for life.

DON FRANCIS

A 23 year RAF career (1943-66) had many memorable moments for Don Francis who served abroad in Italy, Burma and Egypt as an MT specialist. Few however could match his forces speedway career which spanned 1949-51, a period in which he led the RAF team to victory over the Army and saw him win the Canal Zone Match race championship on a regular basis. The Zone match race championship was raced on a one against one basis each meeting, with a new challenger being found each week. Francis became the Jack Parker of Egypt by rarely being beaten in the best of three series of races.

Don remembers well one particular challenge *"One memorable challenge was against Chuck Hesketh of REME. He told me on the Thursday I wouldn't stand a chance on Sunday as he had some new gear. We were always pulling each other's leg about something. Come Sunday he had a very thin front wheel. It will hold my line around the corners"* he said *"and won't create as much resistance as a wide tyre. I had the inside line, Chuck's front wheel was about halfway alongside mine. I held the lead and won that race, the second race was immediately after the interval. Chuck was on the inside, but I made a better start and was just in front of him when we got back to the start line. That carried on until we were getting to the bottom corner for the last time and I realised I didn't know where he was. Is he trying to get through on the inside, or is he going round the outside ?. Not watching where I was going, I went on a patch of sand that always gave problems and ended up going flat out into the safety fence. My engine was still going, but no sign of Chuck, so I pulled the bike away from the fence, the front forks were badly twisted, but I rode it slowly to the finish. Chuck's narrow front wheel had collapsed and he had been thrown off and suffered a hard fall but we were both OK"*

LEN 'DOUGHY' BAKER

Warrant Officer Len Baker served with REME for 24 years (1940-73) as a professional soldier. 'Doughy', as he was known, spent almost four years at Tel el Kabir garrison whilst involved with the REME Vehicle Inspectorate duties. In his spare time he rode for the famous TEK 'Dons' alongside team mates Duqenine, Free, Lancaster and Greenwood. At one time in charge of 2 Base Workshop, he was able to ensure the TEK speedway bikes were always in top condition and ready to race. The camp blacksmith was also commissioned to make the teams individually tailored steel shoes from left boots supplied by each team member. Len remembers that ambulance bodies were removed from their chassis to make workshops and pits areas for the bikes, whilst the inside line was made from old fire hoses. Now living in Somerset, Len secured a trial with Bristol 'Bulldogs' in 1953, but decided on an Army career.

Much later in his Inspectorate career he had to visit a site in Shrivenham near Swindon. Len was tempted to have a spin on a repaired motor cycle and broadsided outside the workshop on the loose gravel. Barracked by some of the mechanics he suggested they should show him how it was done. It turned out that one of the watching crowd was Dick Bradley the Bristol and England international rider who duly gave a superb broad-siding demonstration to the dismay of 'Doughy'.

JOE BOWKIS

Joe was born in Chigwell in 1923 and was barely 20 years old when he joined the Army with the Royal Army Service Corps. He spent his war years in France before reaching Hamburg as the war was ending. He rode on the WD modified bikes at the Hamburg Army speedway before being demobbed in 1947. Harringay 'Racers' had spotted his progress in Germany and his potential was confirmed when he won the Rye House track championship. In 1948 he was appointed captain of the newly opened Poole team in Dorset. He was forced to retire from racing through ill health after a period with Leicester, but later took up midget car racing.

HERBERT 'HERBY' KING

Corporal King of the Royal Corps Signals was being talked about in forces speedway as early as October 1945 when he rode in the second ever meeting at Bari in Eastern Italy. Signalman King, known as Bert in his Army days, captained a team called "The Rest" to a $41\frac{1}{2}$ pts - $23\frac{1}{2}$ pts victory over 'London'. Within nine months he was posted to Egypt and was again marking himself out as a name to watch scoring 11pts in the first Army v RAF clash at camp Qadima near Cairo. Bert used his tuning knowledge to build and tune an ultra fast machine which was inherited by his big chum Bert Steddy. Demob saw a trial with Wembley but a contract with Middlesbrough followed. Herby scored 201 points in 1947 and 245 points in 1948. When Middlesbrough closed he joined another North East club Newcastle and was believed to travel north each week on the train from his Ascot home to Brough Park. In 1951 he joined Oxford, also in the Second Division, thus reducing significantly his travelling time.

THE GRATUITY GAMBLE

Having sampled forces speedway many soldiers, sailors and airmen used their demobilisation gratuity to attend the Tiger Stevenson or Rye House speedway training schools in the hope that a league club would spot them and sign them on. In 1947 the newly formed Third Division was on the look out for raw new talent and experience on forces tracks was seen by promoters as a good recommendation. Some eight new tracks had opened and it was estimated that some 300 riders were competing for team places. Many armed forces personnel left the force with a small gratuity but with £150 as a good estimate for a racing machine, leathers, helmet and a vehicle to get to some far flung track, many just gave up through lack of funds. It was not surprising that many would try however, as with pay rates for the top men meaning with start money, points money and crowd bonuses £70 per week was not impossible to earn. This at the time when a league footballer was still earning £10 - £12 a week.

Khaki Professionals

At the conclusion of WWII, tens of thousands of soldiers, sailors and airmen were being demobilised and preparing to return to civilian life. Most expected to return to their pre-war occupations, although with many factories and work places now operated by women who filled the gaps during the war years, it would be a very different work place to which they would return. Many who had lived through the dangers of the last six years had lived life on the edge and the thought of going back to a 9-5 existence was not a happy prospect.

A professional speedway racing career, with a league team, appealed to many and their warzone speedway experience was recognised by promoters as a source of new talent for the newly formed 3rd Division of 1947. The first chart below endeavours to log armed forces personnel who progressed from warzone speedway to league clubs, whilst the second details those who had worn uniform for King and country but without any previous experience made the grade on the professional scene. The lists are not intended to be complete but represent a cross-section of serving soldiers.

		WARZONE CLUB	PROFESSIONAL CLUB
Jimmy Coy	-	Bari	Eastbourne
Bill Dalton	-	Hanover	Glasgow White City
Nobby Downham	-	Bari	Fleetwood
Joe Bowkis	-	Hamburg	Poole
Dan English	-	Egypt	Hastings
Bob Fletcher	-	Hamburg	Coventry
Vic Gent	-	Hamburg/Kiel	Exeter
Al Alison	-	Hanover	Halifax
Terry Small	-	Egypt	Poole
Bunny Burrows	-	Hanover	Halifax
Herby King	-	Bari/El Ballah	Middlesbrough
Gordon McGregor	-	Hanover	Glasgow
Nobby Stock	-	Bari/Naples	Harringay
Howard Chipman	-	Iraq	Tamworth
John Hancox	-	Naples	Exeter
Don Hardy	-	Naples	Exeter
Harold Sharp	-	Germany	Glasgow White City
Arthur Bush	-	Kiel	Yarmouth
Geoff Bennett	-	Bari	Birmingham
Bill Kemp	-	Bari	Wembley
Nelson Wilson	-	Bari	Wembley
Split Waterman	-	Naples	Wembley
Jimmy Gooch	-	Hanover	Wembley
Angus McGuire	-	Hanover	Glasgow
Larry Lazarus	-	Hanover	Glasgow
Eric Boothroyd	-	Hanover	Birmingham

	PROFESSIONAL CLUB
Gerry Hussey	West Ham
Harry Edwards	Walthamstow
Bob Lovell	Birmingham
Wally Mawdsley	Rayleigh
Johnny Myson	Exeter
Bob Baker	New Cross
Ken Smith	Hastings
Jimmy Squibb	Southampton
George Butler	Poole
Ron Clark	Eastbourne
George Craig	Bristol
Bob Wells	Wembley
Vic Emms	Coventry
Dave Anderson	Stoke
Bill Thatcher	Plymouth
Jack Bibby	Bristol
Harwood Pike	Wombwell
Paddy Hammond	Norwich
Aub Lawson	West Ham
Billy Newell	Plymouth
Wally Green	West Ham
Cliff Watson	West Ham
Jack Freeman	Norwich
Reg Duval	Liverpool
Len Read	Plymouth
Bob Mark	Edinburgh

Bill Carruthers	-	Italy	Yarmouth	Howdy Byford	West Ham
Ken McKinlay	-	Hamburg	Glasgow	Leif Hveem	West Ham
Sid Hipperson	-	Hanover	Yarmouth	Les Hewitt	Coventry
Jack Hadley	-	Hamburg	Harringay	Cyril Page	Tamworth
Bob Oakley	-	Egypt	Southampton	Ken Adams	Stoke
Jim Seagar	-	Germany	Wombwell	George Bason	Southampton
Ernie Rawlins	-	Bari	Southampton	Ken Le Breton	Glasgow W.City
Don Cuppleditch	-	Palestine	Edinburgh	Bill Darque	Wombwell
Rod Laudrum	-	Lubek/Bari	Ipswich	Harry Bastable	Cradley Heath

It is recognised by the author that riders had more than one professional club.The team shown is considered to be the most significant during the rider's career. It also mustn't be forgotten that many post-war riders in the 1950s undertook two years National service which they had to combine with a riding career!

KEN ADAMS Royal Tank Corps
Riding Career: Stoke (Hanley) 1948-53, Southampton 1954,Weymouth 1955, Wembley 1955-56, Ipswich 1956, Rayleigh 1957, Poole 1958, Oxford 1959-60, Stoke 1960-63, Long Eaton 1964-65, Kings Lynn 1966.

Born in February 1924, Ken joined the Army in 1943, after applying a year earlier as a 17 year old whilst working as an office clerk in a brewery. Ken's duties in the forces were varied, including a gunner-wireless operator in the Tank Corp, which involved him in ferrying tanks across the English Channel to France. His motor cycle interests were exploited by the Army when he served as a Despatch rider instructor in Britain, Burma, and he undertook DR duties himself in Rangoon. Demobbed in 1947 Ken attended the Tiger Stevenson speedway school which was designed to find new riders.This led to him signing a contract for Hanley and in 1949 he led the 'Potters' as captain to the Division 3 league championship title. Ken sampled ice racing in Sweden during the early 50s and this almost cost him his shale speedway career. During an ice meeting his foot was badly spiked by the 2 inch razor sharp spikes protruding from the ice bike's tyres which were used to keep the riders upright on the ice. Ken who was rarely seen without a pipe, retired from racing in 1967 after riding for a variety of clubs including the famous Wembley 'Lions'. His final involvement with speedway being when he was invited to team manage the Crewe 'Kings' in the newly formed Second Division of 1968.

GEOFF BENNETT Royal Corps Signals
Riding Career: Birmingham & Cradley Heath 1947, Birmingham 1948-50/52

Born in 1924, Geoff was a despatch rider serving in North Africa and Italy.A road racing fan Geoff discovered speedway when he and future professional riders Herby King and 'Nobby' Stock rode on the Italian forces tracks.A broken collarbone was to delay Geoff's on track progress, but he was to become the East Italian champion in 1946, hold the track record at Bari speedway and become one of the very few riders to beat 'Split' Waterman around the Vomero track in Naples.'Nobby' Stock suggested Geoff was good enough to turn professional back in England and Stock recommended Geoff to Wembley manager Alec Jackson.The 'Lions' had no gaps at the time and so it was that Birmingham promoter Les Marshall contacted Geoff who was despatched to Bristol's Knowle track to attend the Tiger Stevenson school.*"I remember I had yellow jaundice at the time but I went anyway"* says Geoff *"I only had boots, but they supplied a bike and leathers and after three wins I was taken on by Birmingham"*. After second halves on the Perry Barr track, Geoff earnt a team place with sister club Cradley Heath for the 1947 season, before securing a contract with First Division Birmingham.

Geoff has many happy memories of his war time in Italy, not least his marriage to Italian opera singer Vittoria Steffano who he met when she was working as a translator. For many years the Bennett family ran a restaurant in Minorca before returning home to live in Worcestershire. His wife's musical skills spread throughout the Bennett family and led by Geoff who is an accomplished violinist, the whole family raised money for Midland charities. A bad injury sustained whilst racing in Ireland in 1951 caused Geoff to miss the whole of that season, but he came back in 1952 to captain the 'Brummies' after a serious injury to Graham Warren. Geoff's racing career finished one night at New Cross when riding for Birmingham. He was replaced from a race by team manager Vic Scales, totally unfairly in Geoff's opinion, so he loaded up his bike never to ride again.

ERIC BOOTHROYD Royal Corps Signals
6th Airborne Signals Division
16th Independent Parachute Brigade
Riding Career: Tamworth 1950, Cradley Heath 1950, Birmingham 1951-57, Oxford 1958, Leicester 1959, Oxford 1960, Middlesbrough 1961-63, Long Eaton 1964, Halifax 1965-68.

Born in Halifax in 1927, Yorkshire man Eric served in Egypt and Palestine as a regular soldier before joining the 16th Independent Parachute Brigade with a posting to Northern Germany. One of is earliest of postings saw him billeted in the Tower of London handling War Office signals in the capital. It was on his posting in Germany that Eric discovered the Hanomag speedway scene and inherited the bike ridden by Larry Lazarus who had returned home to Scotland. He quickly progressed to top grade status, qualifying for the 1949 Combined Services Championship where he came 4th. Eric's speedway potential was obvious to all but with several years Army service left to do, it looked as though speedway racing would have to wait. His mother came to the rescue by offering to pay the £70 Eric needed to buy his way out of the Army and so his professional speedway career was up and running. Les Marshall the Birmingham promoter had strong links with Hanomag 'Saints' and so it was that Eric attended the Brummies training school. Stan Dell, a Birmingham rider was running the school and he spotted Eric's potential and he recommended to Marshall that he signed the Yorkshireman. A team place with Tamworth (Third Division), Cradley (Second Division) and then Birmingham (First Division) saw Boothroyd reach the top echelons of speedway in a little under two years. By 1956 he qualified for his first World Championship final, scoring 7 pts, and then undertook a riding tour of South Africa with team mate and friend Alan Hunt. This tour was surrounded by controversy and on the teams return to the UK all participants were fined £50 and banned for a month by the Speedway Control Board as it was deemed that the tracks they rode on were unofficial or 'black'. The tour was also marred by the tragic death of Alan Hunt due to a racing accident and many believe this tour and its problems led to the closure of the Birmingham track.

Cpl Boothroyd meets royalty whilst serving Germany

Eric rode for some 18 seasons before entering the sphere of speedway promotion, running Middlesbrough, Bradford and his home town team of Halifax, alongside a string of greengrocer shops. For almost three years he was Chairman of the British Speedway Promoters Association and also took on the role of track inspector before retiring from the sport.

KEN LE BRETON Australian Infantry Force

Riding Career: New Cross 1947, Newcastle 1947-48, Glasgow Ashfield 1949-50.

Born in Sydney, Australia in 1925 Ken's spectacular, but all too brief racing career started in May 1946 when, after initially being turned down for a riding trial, his persistence earnt him rides at Sydney Royale speedway. To ensure he looked different from the other young novices vying for rides, he painted his bike and leathers brilliant white and introduced himself as the 'White Ghost', a nickname that was to stick with him throughout his racing years. Ken endured a difficult war, having enlisted in the AIF in 1942 as a gunner and served in New Guinea where the Japanese were building up their forces for a possible invasion of Australia. Conditions were horrendous with high temperatures and torrential rain leading to serious illness amongst the Australian troops. A combination of swamp fever, malaria and battle fatigue saw him evacuated to a military hospital, where he saw out the war before being demobbed in November 1945.

Ken sailed to England in early 1947 in search of an English racing career and he signed for New Cross. The standard of the English First Division was a little high for Ken and he transferred to Newcastle who raced in the Second Division. By 1949 a move to Glasgow saw his career really take off, and he was to ride for his country against England in test matches. In 1950, he remarkably beat the reigning world champion Tommy Price in a match race at Wembley, breaking the track record in the process. He attracted interest from First Division clubs who wanted to sign him, but Glasgow put a price of £4,000 as a transfer fee to put off suitors. With the speedway world at his feet, Ken was, in January 1951, sadly killed in a test match in Sydney whilst riding for his country against England. In a race featuring himself, fellow countryman Jack Gates and English pairing Eddie Rigg and Bob Fletcher, Ken hit Rigg's back wheel and was thrown over the handlebars and collided with the wooden safety fence. Le Breton never regained consciousness and died 24 hours later with a fractured skull and punctured lung.

DON CUPPLEDITCH Infantry Regiment

Riding Career: Edinburgh 1948-54, Belle Vue 1954-55.

Donald Dearnley Cuppleditch, born a Yorkshireman in Leeds in 1923, joined the Army and reached the rank of Lieutenant with the 2nd Lincoln regiment before, settling in Edinburgh after the war with his new wife Elsa. He initially became a draughtsman but retained the motor cycling bug he acquired in Palestine with the Bar-None club by becoming a member of Edinburgh St George motor cycle club. When the Edinburgh 'Monarchs' speedway team was launched in 1948, Don attended the Monday night trials where he was quickly spotted as a potential future prospect by the club. Second half and guest appearances for Bristol, Fleetwood, Sheffield and Middlesbrough who all arrived a man short for matches at Old Meadowbank, led to a full Edinburgh contract for Don in September of 1948. By 1950 Don was an established team member scoring 187 league points in a team which included future world champion Jack Young. The early 50s saw the post-war speedway boom fade and the introduction of television encouraged Don to seek business interests to supplement his speedway earnings. He bought a high class sweet shop, gaining him the nickname of the 'Candy Kid' and later he became a hotelier and also owned a motor cycle agency. In 1953 a match average of over 10pts per meeting saw Don with the second highest average in the Second Division, behind Tommy Miller. Edinburgh closed in the middle of the 1954 season, with Don joining Belle Vue, but he retired in 1955 after only 5 matches.

FRANCIS 'HOWDY' BYFORD

Riding Career: West Ham 1947-55, Oxford 1956-61, Exeter 1961-64, Hackney 1965, Kings Lynn 1966.

Born Rainham, Essex 1919, 'Howdy's' war experiences could fill this complete chapter and make a superb film! Howdy, real name Francis Howard, actually signed up for the Royal Navy as he wanted to see the world, but he was eventually posted into the Army. He volunteered for the Independent Corps which was later to become the Commandoes. This saw him train in demolition, hand to hand fighting, driving a Bren gun carrier and motor cycle despatch riding.

Howdy's sporting prowess, he was offered a football trial with Fulham before war broke out, earnt him the Essex Regiment welter weight boxing title of 1940 and with it promotion to corporal. A road accident involving a Bren gun carrier broke the scaphoid in his arm, so life with the Commandoes was put on hold. He was transferred to the Suffolk Regiment and sailed with them to Nova Scotia, Iceland and Greenland supporting the convoy patrols. Howdy's war then took him to Cuba, Trinidad, Cape town and finally to Bombay, the warzone that was to play such a significant part in his time with the Army. With his arm now fully recovered, he rejoined General Wingate's Army and headed to Singapore and the Far East with some trepidation as the Japanese had made such strategic progress since Pearl Harbor. Little did he know that on the last few miles on foot to Singapore, his capture by the Japanese along with twenty seven comrades would shape his war for the next three years.

Howdy in jungle gear

Moved to a compound at the infamous Changi gaol, the captured British POW's were initially put to work burying the dead and were then tasked to build a shrine for the traditional Japanese Shinto rites ceremony. Later thousands of prisoners, Howdy amongst them, were transported through Thailand to a site near Bangkok where, they along with many others, were forced to build what became known as the 'Railway of Death'. The plan was to build a 400 kilometre track through largely virgin jungle, the rail road being required to transport the Japanese army for the invasion of India. Hunger drove Howdy to eat snake and suffer a regular diet of grasshoppers, silkworms and rice when available, just to stay alive. Cholera was a common disease in the prison camps and Howdy himself contracted malaria. When the Atomic bomb was dropped on Hiroshima and Nagasaki (which could be heard in the camp where Howdy 'lived'), his nightmare came to an end. Interviewed in 1992 about his experiences in the POW camps, Howdy recalled his horrific experiences. *"After the Americans dropped the second bomb, the Japs knew they had lost the war, but we suspected they were going to get rid of us any way. Whilst they were having a meeting, ten of us crept up to their hut. Me and this other fellow bashed in the door, I grabbed a Samurai sword and slashed at the figure at the head of the table. His head slumped down and fell to one side!"*

Howdy was transported home aboard the liner Queen Elizabeth, returning home some six stone lighter than when he left his Essex home. Howdy's interest in speedway can be traced to early morning chats with his milkman, 'Nobby' Stock, of Italian Army track fame, who encouraged Howdy to try his hand in the Dagenham amateur meetings. When fully recovered from his war time experience he tried his hand at junior events at Rye House before securing a West Ham contract whilst working at the Hammers Custom House stadium in his trade as plumber. As a 'Hammer' he progressed to international standard, riding for his country in England, Australia and South Africa.

Riding for England in South Africa

A natural flair for entertaining people, including gang shows in 'It ain't half hot' style for his comrades in WWII led to him taking to singing on the public address systems at speedway tracks during the interval of meetings. In 1949, it is reported that Howdy even made the supporting bill of a Ted Heath show at the London Palladium! Prepared to try anything he promoted speedway in Ireland as part of a consortium, competed for several months with a broken vertebrae, and appeared on the infant ATV television programme 'Tell the Truth'. Howdy suffered significant racing injuries during his career including twice fracturing his skull. These and other injuries eventually ended his career when he was unable to secure insurance to race.

Howdy cross legged with the Gang Show

Truly a great character.

PETER CRAVEN Lancashire Infantry
Riding Career: Liverpool 1951-52, Belle Vue 1952-63

Born in Liverpool 1934, Peter Theodore Craven was a speedway rider before a National serviceman. He was one of numerous riders in the 50s who had to undertake a compulsory two years in the forces, a system which continued until 1962 and had a profound affect on many sportsman of the time, whose careers had to be managed around the demands of the Army, Royal Navy and RAF.

Peter progressed from cycle speedway to the motorised version, when his older brother Brian lent him his speedway bike for a trial at Liverpool stadium. Brian had been in the Royal Corps Signals 'White Helmet' motor cycle display team. The younger Craven made his debut for the Liverpool 'Chads' in 1951 and just four years later in 1955 he won the world championship title scoring 13 pts at Wembley stadium. Peter's National service in 1952-53 was combined with his commitments for the 'Aces' with an understanding Commanding Officer, ensuring his regular appearance for the Manchester club's fixtures. Craven's individual prowess, he was a regular challenger for the Match Race Golden Helmet, was often used to great affect in England team events. In 1958 he topped the England score charts in a test series against Sweden, Australia and Poland. A second World Championship win in 1962 marked Peter as a rider in his prime. Sadly, just twelve months later he was tragically killed in a racing accident riding for Belle Vue in a challenge meeting in Edinburgh. A memorial plaque is on display in the leisure centre next to Meadowbank stadium.

JIM GREGORY Royal Corps Signals

Riding Career: Wembley 1948, Rayleigh 1949, Wimbledon 1950-52, Oxford 1952-54.

Little did Signalman Jim Gregory realise that within 12 months of riding around the streets of Cairo as a despatch rider, he would be appearing before 70,000 speedway fans at Wembley stadium as a member of the 'Lions' team. Jim started racing for the Fayid 'Dicers' in Army speedway meetings organised by the Bar-None MCC and discovered he could broad-side a bike to good effect. Before leaving the Army he qualified for the 1948 Egyptian Speedway Riders Championship. Scoring 11points he was spotted by Wembley, who took a great interest in forces speedway as a source for new blood. He was loaned out to Rayleigh and topped scored for the 'Rockets' in 1949 with 282 league points. Big time club Wimbledon came in for Jim paying a transfer fee of £50 for his signature and he was to move onto Oxford in 1952 before retiring from speedway in 1955. Jim returned to racing as part of a troupe called the 'Men in Black', who were veterans giving demonstration races on vintage machines such as the 1928 Douglas and Rudge. Jim finally retired from racing completely in 2006 aged 80.

BILL CARRUTHERS Royal Electrical Mechanical Engineers

Riding Career: Yarmouth 1948-50

Born in Forest Gate November 1911, Bill raced against 'Split' Waterman, 'Nobby' Stock and Bill Kemp at the Bari (San Spirito) circuit in Italy where crowds of 3,000 were not unheard of in 1945-46. After demob Bill joined the Speedway World magazine training school where he attracted the attention of Norwich. When Yarmouth opened in 1948, Bill was loaned to the 'Bloaters' and rode in the first ever race at the Caister road stadium. He formed a formidable pairing with the fast emerging young Billy Bales and was a leading light in the 1949 Yarmouth team that almost won the Third Division championship. Yarmouth were promoted to Division Two in 1950, with Bill scoring 111points. He suffered a compound fracture of his right leg whilst avoiding a team mate in a league match against Glasgow and this injury was to end Bill's short racing career. It was suggested that the role of Yarmouth captain had a hoodoo on it, and Carruther's injury only re-enforced the myth.

BOB FLETCHER Royal Artillery

Riding Career: Belle Vue 1947, Cradley Heath 1947, Coventry 1948-51, Belle Vue 1952-54, Motherwell 1954, Edinburgh 1954.

Born Coventry 1921, Bob served for six years in the Artillery, experiencing forces speedway in Hamburg. On demob he started as a novice at Belle Vue where he won the Eric Langton Junior Trophy. To gain experience he joined Cradley in the new Third Division scoring 110 points in thirty matches. When his home city club Coventry opened in 1948, he moved across the Midlands to captain the 'Bees' scoring 303pts from 43 matches and an average of 7.05pts per meeting.

WALLY GREEN Royal Engineers
Riding Career: West Ham 1946, Eastbourne 1947, Hastings 1948, West Ham 1949-55.

Born London 1922, Wally was a Wembley fan in 1934 when he was given the opportunity to work at Barnet grass-speedway as a track raker by Alan W Day, the renowned speedway steward who rode in the first ever High Beech meeting before taking on organisational duties at Stamford Bridge . By 1939, Wally was a 17 year old and felt ready for a riding trial himself and he duly paid his £1 to Dicky Case at the Rye House training track for some practice laps. The trial took place on the last day of August. By September 3 war against Germany was declared, Wally went away to serve his country, with all thoughts of a professional speedway career on hold.

Sgt Major Green was attached to the 7th Army in the Western desert and he fought throughout the desert campaign in North Africa. Wally was in the besieged Tobruk garrison with the Australians when Rommel's Afrika Corps attacked. On demob he invested his £70 army gratuity in a speedway machine and he revisited Rye House to see if he could catch the eye of a professional club. He was signed by West Ham then loaned out to Eastbourne to gain experience but initially could only ride in the home meetings held on a Saturday afternoon, because of his full time job as an instructor at Hendon college. Wally helped Eastbourne win the Third Division league title in 1947 before transferring to newly opened Hastings the following year. West Ham recalled him to the 1st Division in 1949 which signalled a meteoric rise in his form, culminating in Wally grabbing the runners up spot in the 1950 World Championship final behind Welshman Freddie Williams. Whilst still riding speedway, Wally utilised his mechanical skills in another form of the sport. He manufactured cycle speedway frames with great success with a Wally Green Special costing the princely some of £9-10s.

JIMMY GOOCH Royal Army Service Corps
6th Airborne Paratroopers
16th Independent Parachute brigade
Riding Career: Wembley 1950-56, Swindon 1955, Bradford 1956, Ipswich 1957-58, New Cross 1960-61, Norwich 1962-63, Oxford 1964-66, Newport 1967-68, Hackney 1969-70.

Born in Romford 1928, Corporal Gooch service no 14194859 joined the Army in 1946 after serving 12 months as a merchant seaman. He signed on as a regular and was immediately to experience the dangers of Palestine in the run up to the declaration of the state of Israel. Jimmy, who now lives in retirement with his wife of 50 years Everil, near Bradwell-on- sea in Essex still remembers his time in Palestine. *"I remember my first journey by train from Egypt to Haifa. The locals decided to blow up the train! The engine driver was killed and we were lucky to come out of it alive. On another occasion two British Sgt Majors were hung from trees in a eucalyptus grove, it really was dangerous place to be".* Jim's earliest motor cycling days started in Palestine and whilst he didn't see any forces speedway, he has memories of broad-siding a despatch riders bike on sand whilst wearing just shorts and a T- shirt, which proved no protection against a barbed wire fence when he fell off!

It was when he was posted to Germany and some level of safety that Jimmy first became aware of forces speedway. Based at Neumunster, a keen Sgt Major started organising platoon scrambles in 1947, using scrap despatch rider bikes. One Sunday a small group of these enthusiasts, including Jimmy, made the short trip aboard an Army lorry to Hanomag speedway in Hanover which had

Jimmy in Palestine

recently been opened by the REME workshops. Very quickly Jimmy's trips to spectate turned into an urge to take part and with the help of a German engineer who he worked with, a bike was prepared. *"I can't recall the name of this German POW but he was brilliant at modifying a standard WD bike into a specification suitable for speedway. He altered the frame length and angle of the forks and the bike really flew".* By 1948 Jimmy was making real progress at the Sunday Hanomag meetings and welcomed the brief visit of Wembley captain Bill Kitchen to Germany, when he was able to glean a few racing tips from the great man. Little did Jim know that within 18 months he would be riding in the same Wembley team as Bill, but more of that later. 1949 was to prove to be Jimmy's big year and with the incentive of a Wembley riding contract for the winner of that years BAOR Combined Services Speedway Championship, he set about qualifying for the September event. Winning the BAOR meeting left Jimmy in a quandary as he had 'signed on' in the Army for five years and was not due to leave until 1951.

At this point brother Tom came to the rescue by agreeing to pay the fee required to 'buy' Jimmy out of the Army, so enabling him to take his place in the Wembley line up for the 1950 season. Jimmy enjoyed a professional speedway career spanning some 20 years, the high spot being an appearance in the 1965 World Final at Wembley where he scored 3 pts . He hit the speedway headlines in 1962 when he rode for Exeter in the Provincial league before the Control Board declared his contract void and he eventually spent the season with Norwich. Since retiring, he worked for many years in a holiday park, where over a 16 year period he built a sea going boat with a concrete hull. *"At one stage I planned to sail around the world and everyone thought I was mad. I named the boat "Patient Lady" after my wife Everil who suffered the project for all that time".*

Although numerous Army riders went on to successful professional speedway careers, Jimmy holds the unique honour of being the sole Combined Services Speedway Champion to enter the professional ranks.

WILLIAM 'PADDY' HAMMOND Royal Army Service Corps
Riding Career: Birmingham 1946, Norwich 1946-47, Yarmouth 1948, Newcastle 1949.

Born Belfast 1916, William was not a stereotypical Army speedway rider, having reached the rank of Captain in the RASC when he discovered forces speedway in Hamburg whilst serving in Germany. William secured a few rides at Birmingham in 1946 before moving East to Norwich. There was tragedy surrounding Hammond's career almost from the start when, in 1947, he was involved in a crash with team mate Cyril Anderson who later died and the following year, when Yarmouth were the opposition at the opening meeting at Poole speedway in 1948. Paddy was again involved in the famous first heat, first lap, first bend accident which saw Reg Craven also lose his life. A move North to Newcastle and rides at the Santry track in Dublin was interrupted by ill health. His racing career effectivley ended in 1949. Unsuccessful attempts to promote speedway in Ireland and a reported fractured skull whilst grass track racing seems to have ended his involvement with the sport.

LEIF 'BASSE' HVEEM Norwegian Free Army
Racing Career: West Ham 1953.

For a rider who rode just four league matches in England, scoring 30 points for West Ham, the name Hveem lingers in the memory of many speedway fans from the 1950s. Norwegian Hveem first rode speedway in 1937, winning the National championship at the tender age of just 15 years 9 months old. Norway was invaded by the Germans in 1940 and he escaped to England to join the Norwegian Free Army, which had regrouped in Britain as part of the Allied Forces. Before leaving his homeland he carefully buried his bikes in sacks in the family garden, hoping to rescue them when the war ended! He had a distinguished Army career including being involved in the Normandy D-Day landings of 1944.

When peace returned and racing resumed in Norway, Basse won the Scandinavian championships of 1946 & 47 as well as the Norwegian title of 1947. By 1949 he was nominated as one of the Norwegian representatives in the World Championship qualifying rounds, some held in England. Basse qualified for the 1952 World Championship Final as a reserve rider but was not called upon to ride. He was offered a place in an Overseas team which toured South Africa and his success attracted the interest of West Ham who signed him in 1953. Hveem was also an accomplished long track racer and many argued that if he had concentrated purely on speedway he could have reached the very top. During the winter of 1955, a crash in a meeting at Durban all but finished his racing career when Basse damaged his one remaining kidney, the other having been removed after an ice racing accident.

LES HEWITT Australian Tank Battalion
Racing Career: Coventry 1949-53.

Born in Mayfield, Newcastle, Australia 1924, the teenager served 22 months in New Guinea on war service with the Australian Army, before being shot in the hip and evacuated to safety. After the war Les acquired a road bike and when stopped by a policeman he suggested he should try speedway racing so fast was he speeding! At the comparative late age of twenty four, Les started riding when he was loaned a bike by Oliver Hart who was touring Australia at the time, and was subsequently recommended by Belle Vue's Ron Mason to new league team Coventry.

Les rode in England for five years, top scoring for the 'Bees' in two consecutive seasons. He won the Brandonapolis open meeting at Coventry and broke the Fleetwood track record in successive races. Known as the 'Grin' because of his sense of humour, Les returned home to Australia with a British wife, to a job as a self employed clothes salesman foregoing his previous occupation as a pastry cook.

DON HARDY Territorials
Royal Army Ordnance Corps
Racing Career: New Cross 1947/49, Exeter 1947-55.

Born near Southampton 1921, Don was a soldier pre-war as a Territorial with the Dorset Regiment. His duties included guarding railway tunnels and manning Dover Castle, which was the target for the German long range guns from across the channel. By 1940 Don was a regular soldier and volunteered for the RAOC who were looking for soldiers with driving experience, something quite rare in the early 40s. This tour of duty gave Don vast experience to all kinds of wheeled and tracked vehicles and he was awarded an "A" license which made him a man in

Don Hardy, right, at Vomero Stadium

demand. A period of despatch riding duties was his first ever time on a motor cycle and was to be the start of his interest in bikes. Unloading vehicles from ships, convoy duties as a DR throughout North Africa and then the invasion of Italy saw Don end up just outside Naples just as forces speedway was starting at the Vomero stadium.

Speaking from his Basingstoke home, Don remembered in 2006 *"I did most of my Army speedway racing at Vomero which was an athletic track around a football pitch. I recall racing against 'Split' Waterman, Geoff Bennett, Bill Carruthers, 'Nobby' Stock and others".* His success in Italy tempted Don to have a trial at the Speedway World training school when he returned to England after the war, but when West Ham told him "no bike, no leathers, no trial" all thoughts of speedway were put to the back of his mind. It was only when New Cross contacted him by letter, which his mother responded to, that he re-considered. *"I remember meeting the Roger brothers, Cyril, Bert and Bob at the New Cross trial and I was to ride with Cyril and Bob at Exeter shortly afterwards"* explained Don *"What was annoying was that we moved to London to be near to the New Cross track and then I was told I was being loaned out to Exeter. We eventually moved to the St Thomas area of Exeter and my wife could hear the public address announcements from the kitchen window and when I returned home after the meetings, a fully marked up programme was waiting for me".* A bad back injury when he slammed into the iron fence at Exeter damaged five vertebrae in his back, an injury that troubles him to this day. When the 'Falcons' closed in 1955, Don retired, never to ride a speedway bike again.

GERRY HUSSEY Royal Artillery
Riding Career: Rye House 1953, West Ham 1954-55, Norwich 1956, Leicester 1958.

Born Hampstead 1932, Gerry was brought up in a motor cycling family, with his father having ridden at the Brooklands circuit as a young man. Despite nights out to Harringay speedway with the family as a schoolboy, Gerry preferred the road racing TT variety of racing. When his National Service papers arrived in June 1950, after training in Rhyl, North Wales, he was posted to the transport section in BAOR Germany as a DR instructor. After demob Gerry competed on the club road race scene and when he had a slack period with no meetings Jock Grierson, a family friend who rode for Birmingham, Eastbourne, Hastings and Leicester encouraged him to try speedway at Rye House. With minimum effort, Gerry qualified and won the track championship with only three weeks speedway experience, earning him a contract with big club West Ham. Within 12 months he almost qualified for the Wembley World final, a feat he was to achieve in 1955/56 and 58.

Regular winter trips to South Africa and Australia improved his form, although he did miss the 1957 season in England when he remained 'down under'. It was on his 1958-59 winter racing tour to Adelaide that he decided to try his hand at midget car racing. It was a fateful decision because on March 6 1959, just one day before he was due to fly home for another British season, his car flipped over and pinned him to the track. He died from his injuries.

AUB LAWSON Australian Infantry Force
Riding Career: Wembley 1939, Middlesbrough 1939, West Ham 1947-51, Norwich 1953-60.

Aubrey Lawson was born in Warialda, Australia 1916. His father ran a sheep station which he helped him run until, at just 15 years old, Aub ran away to Sydney and became a telegram boy for the Post Office. Finding this life boring, in 1934 Aub joined the Australian Army as a despatch rider. He might have continued soldiering had he not been selected to take part in an Army tattoo motor cycle team in 1937. Lawson proved a crowd pleaser and when ex-rider and promoter Frank Arthur saw Aub's bike riding expertise at one of these shows he suggested he take up speedway racing. Aub readily agreed and thus it was that from that small show in Shepherds Bush, New South Wales, the career of one of Australia's future test stars was born. By 1938 he was selected to represent Australia in the test matches against the English tourists. Aub won the 1938 NSW junior championship and came to England the following year with the Australian team. On his arrival he signed for Wembley, who loaned him to Middlesbrough although he returned to Wembley as a qualifier for the cancelled World Championship final in September of that year.

With the outbreak break of war, he returned to his job with the Australian Post Office, but in 1940 joined the AIF in the 8th Australian Division Signals, seeing action in Malaya and Singapore, before receiving a commission in the field as Officer Commanding despatch rider sections. He returned to England in 1947, joining West Ham and during that winter he converted from leg trailing to foot forward style, which turned him into a major star for the next decade. On the individual front he qualified for nine Wembley world finals, his best performance being in 1958, when at the age of 42, he came third behind Barry Briggs and Ove Fundin. His test record stands comparison with the best of Australian riders. He won 84 test caps for his country scoring 680 points.

JOHN 'LARRY' LAZARUS Territorial Army
Royal Electrical Mechanical Engineers
Riding Career: Glasgow Ashfield 1949-5, Glasgow White City 1953, Motherwell 1954, Ipswich 1955-56.

Born December 1918, Larry, real name John, served in the Territorial Army 1940-42 before joining REME for the remainder of WWII. It was whilst with the 7th Armoured workshop that he saw service in Burma and then Germany. Whilst in Germany he rode at the Hanomag circuit in Hanover and won the 1948 Hanover Individual Championship. One of his most memorable professional successes was winning the Ken Le Breton memorial trophy in October 1951 .When Glasgow White City re-opened in the 60s, 'Larry' was machine examiner for a number of years. John passed away in 2007, but was visited regularly by his great friend Jimmy Tannock the former Edinburgh rider up until his demise.

GORDON McGREGOR Royal Electrical Mechanical Engineers

Riding Career: Glasgow White City 1947-50, Motherwell 1951-54, Leicester 1955-56, Oxford 1957-62, Belle Vue 1963-66, Long Eaton 1967, Doncaster 1970, Birmingham 1971.

Born Dunfermline 1921, Gordon served as a despatch rider with BAOR in Germany before gaining the reputation of being the 'Vic Duggan' of the Hanomag speedway. Glasgow were the basement club of the Northern league in 1946, when promoter Ian Hoskins heard about McGregor's form on the forces speedways of Germany from another Army rider Harold Sharpe. The problem was that no one actually knew of McGregor's whereabouts, so Hoskins enlisted the help of local newspapers who ran a story to find him. When found, Gordon had no bike, just racing leathers, but the trial went well and he signed for four seasons. By 1951 he had transferred east to Motherwell and toured Australia that winter as part of the England team, even though he was a Scot! Nicknamed 'Tash' because of his large red moustache, Gordon was forced to move to England when Motherwell closed. His mechanical knowledge gained from his time in REME, enhanced his reputation as always having fast engines and he was in demand as an engine tuner for other riders.

JOHN 'KEN' McKINLAY

Riding career: Glasgow White City 1948-53, Leicester 1954-61, Coventry 1962-64, West Ham 1965-69, Coventry 1970, Oxford 1971-72, Scunthorpe 1973-75.

Born John Robert Vicars McKinlay in Blantyre, Lanarkshire in 1928 'Ken' as he liked to be known, decided to become a professional speedway rider whilst serving with the Army in Germany. Ken didn't want to wait for demob to start his speedway so he joined the Neuminster forces team which he went on to eventually captain. Corporal McKinlay came joint 6th on the 1948 Combined Services Speedway Championship before signing for the Glasgow club. By 1955 his development was such that he won the Laurels meeting at Wimbledon, defeating many of the top riders of that era. He continued his progress into a world class rider, making twelve world final appearances and regularly toured Australia with the English Lions, taking over the organisation of the whole tour in the 1960s. His racing career spanned four decades and he is a contender for the title of most successful forces speedway rider.

CYRIL 'VIC' PAGE Royal Electrical Mechanical Engineers

Special Air Services
Riding Career: Stoke 1939, Birmingham 1946, Hanley 1947, Tamworth 1948-49, Leicester 1949-51, Long Eaton 1952, Leicester 1953.

Born Walsall 1918, Cyril Victor Page, began grass track racing as a side-car driver and passenger before the war and he also competed in he World Amateur Wall of Death championships. In 1939 he signed as a novice for Stoke, but WWII came along and so started a remarkable phase in Cyril's already interesting life. Cyril joined REME and was involved in the evacuation from France in 1940. Realising that Dunkirk was under severe attack, he made his way down the coast to Brest and eventually got home to England on a coal freighter. He then became one of the first soldiers to volunteer for the Special Air Service (SAS). He volunteered to join 'L' Detachment which a short while later became 1st SAS. The SAS was formed in 1941 by David Sterling out of the Long Range Desert Group operating against Italian forces in North Africa. Cyril served under Colonel Sterling and also the legendary Col. Paddy Maine.

Captain Sterling was a visionary and proposed that small units of self sufficient, versatile and well trained specialists could target many more attack areas than the traditional larger armed forces. His theory was that this approach would cause more disruption and force opposition troops to guard installations, leaving them more vulnerable to conventional attack. Cyril's personal qualities impressed the SAS from the start. Captain Sterling established the highest standards for SAS members, with the RTU system (Return to Unit) effectively giving the almost autonomous SAS the power to refuse below standard soldiers. Members of each group had one specialist skill each as well as requiring navigational, weaponry, demolition, signals, first aid and parachuting experience. Cyril took part in Airborne and submarine raids in Sicily, Italy, Greece and Crete. On D-Day he went to France and in total saw action in fifteen countries. Demobbed in 1945, Cyril joined Birmingham as a reserve before joining Stoke as team captain. Transferred to new club Tamworth 'Hounds' and then other Midland clubs, he went on to establish himself as a speedway engine tuner, and was keen to help many up and coming Midland juniors.

ERNEST 'PEDLAR' PALMER Royal Engineers
Riding Career: Wombwell 1948, Leicester 1949-50, Long Eaton 1951-52.

Born Sheffield 1920, Ernest was introduced to speedway by his father when the sport came to his home city in the late 1920s. Nicknamed 'Pedlar', Ernest was a despatch rider and bomb disposal specialist in North Africa and Italy. One of the few riders to wear spectacles whilst riding, effectively retired from racing in 1952, but returned to the sport as team manager for the Sheffield club.

BOB OAKLEY Reconnaissance Platoon
Riding Career: New Cross 1946, Southampton 1947-50, Wembley 1950-52, Norwich 1954, Wolverhampton 1961.

Born Southampton 1922, Bob was a despatch rider in Egypt, where he experienced speedway at Tel el Kabir. On demob he joined New Cross as a novice, transferring to his home town club Southampton when the 'Saints' joined the newly formed Third Division in 1947. Coached by Mike Erskine, Bob was joined by his brother Tom in 1948 before going on to captain Southampton in 1949. First Division Wembley had been monitoring Bob's progress and payed a £1,500 fee in 1950 to make him a 'Lion'. Bob's best season was his first year at the Empire stadium when he qualified for his only World Championship final, surprising many by coming third with 12pts behind Jack Young 14pts and Freddie Williams 13pts. He retired in April 1953, before returning for a season with Norwich. After a six season gap he rode briefly for Wolverhampton in the 1961 Provincial league, but found the competition a little hot and he decided to retire from racing for good.

NELSON 'BRONCHO' WILSON Royal Electrical Mechanical Engineers
Riding Career: Wembley 1946-47.

Born Newcastle upon Tyne 1925, Nelson served six years with the Army in North Africa and Italy. He had been apprenticed as a sculptor and stonemason as a teenager before the war, but after discovering speedway racing at the Vomero stadium in Naples, he decided a career as a professional speedway rider was for him. Signed by Wembley after the war, he partnered Bill Kitchen and made slow but sure progress, but it was all to come to an abrupt end in August 1948. During a National Trophy match against Harringay, 'Broncho' was involved in a spectacular crash with one of his old Italian Army speedway rivals 'Nobby' Stock, and he died from his injuries in hospital. Amongst his off track interests were classical music and drama, and he was a regular visitor to the theatre when racing allowed. The day after Nelson's sad death, Norwich rider Cyril Anderson was also killed in a track accident to make it a very sad weekend for speedway.

RON WALTON Royal Electrical Mechanical Engineers
Riding career: California (Wokingham) 1955-56,
Aldershot 1957, Southampton 1958.

RonWalton, a National Serviceman in Germany between 1953-55 just missed the chance to compete in forces speedway (Hanomag finished at the end of the 1951 season), but this didn't stop this soldier from making a name for himself on the German circuits. Based near Rotenberg with the 31st Armoured Workshop, he became one of the very few soldiers ever to be invited to become a member of a German motor cycle club whilst serving in the British army. Ron who now lives in Bournemouth, rode primarily grass and long track with Moto Sport Enchenring throughout his German posting with REME. His links with the club were to last a lifetime and he was invited to Germany to celebrate the club's 50th Anniversary.

Back in England and working for former Wembley 'Lion' Alf Bottoms, he bought an engine from double world champion Freddie Williams and took to the British speedways. In the mid 1950's opportunities were rare for junior riders but his chance came with the California 'Poppies' in the Southern Area League *"I was relatively successful and in 1958 attempted to compete at a higher level with Southampton, but they were too quick for me. However during my time in Germany I could beat most of the locals on grass and long track. I had my 15 minutes of fame, of which I am very proud"*

SPEEDWAY SAILORS

Not surprisingly the opportunities for sailors to ride speedway during the war were very limited, their war being spent on the high seas or in some port miles from any established warzone circuit. However the warzone story would not be complete without reference to the Royal and Merchant Navy (the RAF riders were featured in *Speedway Flyers*).

Just quite what the attraction of Cradley Heath speedway was for ex-sailors in 1949 is unknown. It was however the season when three team members of the Senior Service scored 725½ points of the Heathen's season total of 1,908½ points from 44 league matches.The men involved were Alan Hunt, Gilbert Craven and Geoff Godwin, all sailors who enabled the Black Country team to secure fourth place in Division 2, the Heathens having been promoted the previous season from Division 3.

*Alan Hunt-
Chief Petty
Officer 399pts*

ALAN HUNT

Despite being a non-swimmer,Alan was a frogman in the Royal Navy. He was the star pupil at the Tiger Stevenson winter speedway school held at Birmingham's Birchfield Harriers stadium in the winter of 1946. His form secured him a team place with Cradley in 1947 and by 1951 First Division Birmingham 'Brummies' signed him for a fee of £2,500. Born in Birmingham in 1924,Alan was a Brummie to the core and was to provide the backbone of his home city's team throughout the 1950s.The year 1956 was to prove fateful year for Alan, he qualified for his fourth World Final scoring 6 pts, top scored for Birmingham with 226 league points and set out on a winter racing tour of South Africa with several of his team mates.The tour was very controversial as racing took place on unlicensed tracks.The threat of a riding ban on the parties return to England however, paled into insignificance when on February 1 1957,Alan suffered fatal injuries in a racing incident at Wembley stadium in Johannesburg. He was taken to hospital with a suspected fractured skull but passed away the following day. Mrs Eve Hunt was in South Africa with the tour and attended an Alan Hunt Memorial meeting before travelling home to Birmingham with his ashes.

GILBERT CRAVEN

Something of a globetrotter, Gilbert, brother of West Ham's Malcolm, was a ships engineer as a 17 year old in a vessel running the blockade in the Spanish Civil war. Born Ilford 1920, Gil experimented with speedway at Dagenham in 1939 and travelled extensively in Australia, New Zealand and America to gain riding experience. He finished runner up in the NZ championships of 1948-49 before signing for Cradley Heath.

Gilbert Craven-Ships Engineer 234½pts

GEOFF GODWIN

Born Hereford 1903, Geoff enjoyed a pre-war career with Rye House, Smallford, Dagenham, Birmingham Hall Green and Leeds. During WWII Geoff attained the rank of Lieutenant Commander in the Royal Navy. A broken neck sustained riding in an open meeting at Bradford in 1945, hampered his immediate post-war racing, although he did gain a team spot with Middlesbrough who won the Northern league in1946. Geoff joined Cradley, his local club for a transfer fee of £1,000.

Geoff Godwin- Lieutenant Commander 96pts

JACK GORDON

Born Bolton 1915, Jack's first race on cinders was in 1934 at Liverpool as a 19 year old. Occasional appearances at Belle Vue, Fleetwood and Bristol in the intervening years followed before he became an officer in the Royal Navy. An all round sportsman, he was an expert horseman, tennis player and boxer, Jack rode post-war for Middlesbrough, Wigan and Coventry.

MALCOLM CRAVEN

Older brother of Gilbert, Malcolm saw WWII from the deck of a ship as a Merchant seaman. A pre-war rider with Norwich, Birmingham and Wembley, in 1946 he was picked by West Ham from the pool of graded riders who were shared amongst the teams which formed the National league of that season. Malcolm qualified for a pilots flying licence and often used it to fly himself and West Ham team mates to some of the more northern Hammers away fixtures.

TONY LEWIS

Lewis was on shore leave in Sydney, Australia at the end of WWII when he and other ratings from his ship spent an evening spectating at the Sydney Sports Ground. The broad-siding skills of Aub Lawson, Max Grosskreutz and the Duggan brothers inspired Tony to try his hand at racing when he left the Royal Navy. Poole speedway opened in 1948, just up the road from Tony's Bournemouth home and this presented him with the chance to break into the sport. His first attempt faltered due to the deep cinder surface which didn't suit Tony's riding style. He tried again in 1950 when the track had been switched to the slicker shale surface and so his career took off. Tony rode in the famous 1951-52 Poole 'Pirates' team which won back to back league titles and formed a formidable partnership with ex-RAF team mate Ken Middleditch. In 1955 Tony fractured his skull but returned to the track in 1960.

SPEEDWAY'S MEN BEHIND THE WIRE

Speedway riders know all about wire safety fences when trackside, but being 'behind the wire' was an altogether different experience for some speedway prisoners of war. Howdy Byford's experiences at the hands of the Japanese, highlight one of a serviceman's worst fears in battle, that of capture and incarceration. Not surprisingly the speedway troops suffered their fare share of captures by Germans, Italians and of course the Japanese. Harry Edwards (Walthamstow), Frank Lawrence (New Cross), Bill Thatcher (Plymouth), Len Read (Plymouth), Bob Wells (Wembley), Reg Morgan (Yarmouth) and Bob Mark (Edinburgh) all spent some of their war in captivity.

Bob Mark's experience was particularly interesting, as at one stage he was held in Stalag 7A in Germany where coincidently Yarmouth's Reg Morgan (RAF) was also held but neither knew of each others presence in the camp. Bob might not even have been in Stalag 7A but for the poor condition of a boat. When Bob was imprisoned in Northern Italy he attempted to escape with a pal in a boat berthed near to where he was being kept. With the Allies advancing, he was expecting to be moved to another camp by the Germans so Bob and his pal cut through the perimeter wire and made their way to the boat mooring. They reached the boat and the plan was to make for the sector of Italy under Allied control. Unfortunately the boat sprang a leak and the duo were recaptured and transported to a camp in Germany to see out the war.

Bob Mark

Bob had joined the 8th Army serving with the Royal Artillery in the desert campaigns and took part in the invasion of Sicily and Italy before joining the garrison at Anzio. Prior to capture he had also served alongside the French Army before being evacuated from Dunkirk as part of Operation 'Dynamo'.

WAS FRED THE ULTIMATE 'FORCES' SPEEDWAY RIDER?

FRED YATES Territorials
Royal Air Force
Royal Navy

Riding career; Tamworth 1947, Hull 1948, Coventry, 1948, Glasgow 1949, Fleetwood 1949.
Warzone Speedway is documenting speedway soldiers so Fred, who joined the Territorial's as a despatch rider in 1932 has the right qualifications. He does have a unique record however, that of serving in all three Services within a fourteen year period.

Fred, a Londoner born in 1916, was academically very bright, and on leaving school he became an engineer with Rolls Royce. By 1937 he enlisted in the RAF as an aircraft engineer and during the war (1941) he transferred to Air Transport Auxiliary who were responsible for the movement of aircraft between airfields. By 1943 he was awarded an Air Engineering Commission with the Royal Navy to complete a remarkable 'hat trick'. Whilst with the Royal Navy in Sydney he saw Australian Vic Duggan in action and vowed to become a rider himself. On demob he had a trial at Belle Vue and whilst not gaining a team place he was given a job looking after the Belle Vue bikes as their resident mechanic Wally Hull wanted to ride speedway.

Fred's academic ability was to prove useful post-war as he was to become a master at the Queen Elizabeth Grammar school in Tamworth, at the same time as riding for the town's speedway team. He was a poet and wrote a poem which he later dedicated to a team mate Jack Ladd who was killed whilst riding on the continent. Adapted from "Prospice" by Robert Browning, Fred's words were a fitting tribute to all speedway riders who gave their lives for speedway racing.

Split Waterman's Rise to Fame

There are several candidates for the title 'most famous Army speedway rider'. The late Peter Craven, a twice World Champion obviously springs to mind as does Wally Green, runner up in the 1950 World Championship. Eric Boothroyd's ten club, eighteen season racing career and another twenty plus years as a speedway promoter makes him a contender. My choice however, after much consideration, must be Squire Francis Waterman.

Born in New Malden, Surrey 27 July 1923, 'Split', more of that nickname later, wanted to join the RAF on the outbreak of WWII but he was initially refused as being a toolmaker he was in a reserved occupation.

'Split' in uniform- 1942

In early 1942, he joined the Kingston area Local Defence Volunteers (Home Guard) along with his father, Waldergrave. One of Squire's earliest war time memories is of his dad fitting a machine gun to the handlebars of a 1,000cc motorcycle as part of the Kingston forces improvised armoury.

Adventurous even then at barely 19 years old, Squire wanted to join the paratroopers but as he was very young the Army required family consent. His parents refused and so the Royal Fusiliers received Waterman, Service Number 14512222 into their ranks.

Training and early war time service in Stranraer, Belfast and Omagh in County Tyrone threw up the rebel in his personality. Whilst on guard duty outside a castle garrison in Ireland he became hungry and paid a visit to the local café for egg and chips. This trip was to cost him seven days in the cook house as a penalty. The Fusiliers were subsequently posted to North Africa as part of the 8th Army. Squire saw action in Egypt, Bengazi and Libya as the Allies took on and eventually defeated Rommel's Afrika Corps in operation 'Battleaxe'. Success in North Africa for the Anglo-American force commanded by General Dwight Eisenhower (a future United States President), led to an attack on Sicily in July 1943 codenamed Operation 'Husky' and the eventual invasion of Italy via Salerno on 9 September of the same year.

"I well remember being shipped across to Salerno aboard a flat bottomed American boat and most guys were sea sick" remembers Squire, who now lives in retirement with wife Avril in Southern Spain.

Italy is geographically divided West to East by a range of mountains and Squire was deployed as an observer on one of these numbered peaks facing the famous town of Cassino and its monastery. The military importance of Cassino cannot be understated as it was an artery route through to Rome. From his observation post Squire has vivid memories of one night. *"In the darkness I saw a silhouette of a German paratrooper close by"* remembers Squire *"and it was very much a case of him or me. I shot him first but this caused an almighty barrage of gun fire and whilst not being a religious man"* admits Squire *"that night I prayed for my life! I sur-*

vived but suffered shrapnel wounds and was sent to an American hospital for treatment. The injured leg still troubles me on occasions".

Palestine -1946

But for that injury, we may never have seen the Waterman name on the speedways because his wounds were so bad that he was deemed unfit for front line action. A transfer to REME with a posting to 750 Base Workshop at Pozzuoli South of Naples, working in what had been a pre-war Armstrong Vickers factory, was to re-awaken his teenage interest in motorcycles.

His motorcycling passion had links to Squire's uncle Horace who had been a successful path rider at Crystal Palace in the early 30s. As luck would have it the soldiers in the workshop shared his interest in racing and gradually with the Germans driven out of Italy, a range of competitive scrambles, time trials and even a motorcycle gymkhana was staged. Squire, called Frank by his close friends, took great interest in these events.

Sgt Jack Uglow, a veteran in Italy at the time, recalls racing in events against this guy called Waterman and even in 1945, Craftsman Waterman had a reputation for being something special on two wheels. Recalling these events Jack, who retired to Devon and was a regular at Exeter's County Ground says *"The Pozzuoli hill climb consisted of a rough track which was level to the first left hand bend which led steeply uphill to a right hand hairpin with a sheer drop over the side. I well remember the fearless broad- siding of Corporal Waterman, who slid his machine around the edge of the sheer drop on the second hairpin. As you may have guessed he was the winner in a time of 40.2 seconds."*

On 23 September 1945 a motorcycle gymkhana and grass track meeting was held at the Casoria racecourse. The day was an inter-unit event and in addition to grass track racing other competitions included long jump, obstacle course, relay race, tilt the bucket, slow race, egg and spoon race and trick riding. Jack remembering the day over 60 years on says *"The 56 Area Motor Cycle Club organised the event and I was in the same heat as Waterman in the grass track. If I remember rightly I was first off the line, only to be passed by Craftsman Waterman as if I was standing still. He went on to win the heat and the event final along with the long jump competition."*

The natural progression to speedway came when team and individual events commenced at Vomero Stadium in Naples as part of the sporting activities organised by 56 Area Motor Cycle Club. Recalling his experiences of Vomero Stadium Squire remembers *"It was an athletic stadium with concrete stands and residential flats overlooking the stadium. It had suffered war damage so we set to rebuilding the place. The track surface was ash and cinders from the volcano and there were big holes in the running track which we had to patch up.*

Vomero Stadium- Naples 1946

Vomero Stadium- Naples 1946

"Having access to the REME 750 Base Workshop facilities I was able to regularly work on my scramble and speedway bikes. I was particularly proud of my speedway bike which was built from a basic BSA M20 despatch rider WD machine. I painted it silver and it really looked the business. This must have been 1945 and whilst the war in Italy was over, Japan was still raging so I didn't really begin to consider a professional career at this time."

These meetings at Vomero saw Squire ride against future speedway professionals including Bill Kemp, (Wembley), Nelson Wilson (Wembley), Geoff Bennett (Birmingham), Bill Carruthers (Yarmouth) and Don Hardy (Exeter).

"Before going any further into my story I would like to clear up the background to my nickname of 'Split'. The name was given to me by my Army pals, when as I became successful at racing I shared my prizes with them" says Squire *"in return they somehow acquired a pair of racing leathers for my speedway. During one meeting I fell and split the leathers right down the back . From then on they called me " Split arse" which for obvious reasons was shortened to Split when I got to Wembley!"*

'Split's' war was to have one more twist when he contracted sand fly fever which probably did him a great favour as he was originally due to be posted to Japan in mid 1945. Fully recovered, a tour of duty in Palestine, initially maintaining equipment in an Army laundry, developed into chauffeuring an officer around Jerusalem. A final deployment to Germany was to lead to the famous Wembley trial whilst on leave back in Britain.

His famous trial for Wembley at Rye House in 1946, whilst still in the Army with REME in Germany is well known. A key player in the story was Major Fenwick who was also a keen motorcyclist, who could see that 'Split' was something special on a motorbike.

The Major, 'Split's' Commanding officer, had served with Cpt Alec Jackson the pre-war Wembley manager earlier in the war and decided to contact him about a trial for the REME budding speedway star.

Major Fenwick

'Split' takes up the story *"I had been riding well in Italy winning most events I entered including an Individual Championship at Vomero in February 1946. The Major* (pictured left) *arranged things with Alec but I had to sort out my own transport from Germany to Rye House. I was due two weeks leave but wanted to get home quickly.*

I managed to convince a US Air Force officer it was urgent I get home, and in return for my Army motorcycle he sorted out a flight back to England on a Dakota. Wembley put 240 potential trialists through their paces and I am pleased to say Wembley offered me a contract. My next problem was getting back to Germany and again Major Fenwick came to my rescue arranging a train ticket back to camp in Germany so that I wasn't put on a charge for going AWOL (Absent Without Leave)."

'Split' returned home to England in early 1947 on a boat via Malta and spent his last few weeks' Army service at a tank depot in Slough whilst practising for his speedway debut.

Alec Jackson with 'Split' after his successful Wembley trial

Back in civvy street and with a Wembley contract in his pocket, 'Split' made his professional debut at Harringay in an individual event which included other prospective 'Lions' Freddie Williams, Broncho Wilson and Charlie May.

His first appearance in Wembley colours was on 19 April 1947 at Belle Vue (Manchester) when he scored 2 points in a 49-35 point away win for the 'Lions'. The Waterman name first appeared in the Wembley programme in early May, again scoring 2 points in the 41-42 defeat by Wimbledon. His debut at the Empire Stadium was interestingly made 24 hours before his official demob, so 'Split' had started his professional career whilst still in the Army! Within four meetings he was promoted from the reserve spot to a full team place, such was his form and confidence against the established stars. During that first memorable season he scored 120 pts for the Lions, broke the Wembley track record and even defeated the almost unbeatable Australian Vic Duggan, to mark him out as a star of the future.

By mid 1947, Split had established major pre-war stars looking over their shoulders and 'Split' knew there was some jealousy around regarding his success. *"I eventually replaced Bob Wells in the Wembley team"* remembers 'Split' *"and I know that did not go down well."*

An interview with Wembley captain of the time, Bill Kitchen was a measure of the impact 'Split' was having. Kitchen explained at the time *"He (Split) has developed a new method of riding. He doesn't drive and slide in the accepted way. Instead he rides around as if on the road by laying the bike over at simply alarming angles when cornering. He is also able to pull non standard gearing due to his riding style."*

Such was 'Split's' progress that by the end of the 1947 season he was short listed for a trip to Australia with the England test team. Ultimately the financial terms of the tour made it impossible for him to travel but it topped a remarkable first season for the South London boy.

Wembley 'Lions' 1947. 'Split' third from right

1948 was the real breakthrough year for the ultra confident 'Split'. A six point score for England in a test match against Australia at Wimbledon, selection as a challenger to Jack Parker for the Match race title, qualification for the Speedway Riders Championship (the equivalent of the World Final at the time) and winning the prestigious London Riders Championship, staked his claim as the first real post war star. The London title was particularly significant. Held at New Cross, Split scored 14 pts to beat Vic Duggan, Jeff Lloyd and Cyril Brine who scored 12 pts each, to break a thirteen year jinx by becoming the first Englishman to win the title since Tom Farndon in 1935.

That memorable season was recognised by the country's film makers when he was featured in a 40 minute documentary called *Speedway*, which proved very popular at the Roxys and Gaumonts of the day.

"The film was I remember black and white and one scene was shot at my mother's house. I was required to be filmed on my BMW motorcycle I brought back from Germany. We tried several times to get the right shot before I managed to drive into the local milk float. Very embarrassing" says 'Split'.

A public appearance with the Army Kinema Corps

The film proved very popular and promoted the sport to a wide audience although, with Wembley meetings attracting crowds of over 60,000 regularly, there was already a huge speedway fan base at that time. To promote the film, 'Split' made personal appearances with the Army Kinema Corporation at various Army bases (see picture above) and he particularly enjoyed meeting the serving soldiers.

Long before the days of sportsman image rights, 'Split's' crowd pulling power was immense at Wembley, with over 40% of all crowds being female. With his matinee idol looks and the famous slim moustache adding to his film star appearance he was a big draw. 'Split' demonstrated his early business acumen by approaching the Wembley Managing Director Sir Arthur Elvin requesting the concession to sell American hot dogs on the Lions Thursday race nights. *"This was deemed to be not appropriate for Wembley"* explains 'Split' *"although several years later they were introduced by the caterers and I missed out"*. By now 'Split's' name was big box office and whilst product endorsements were to follow shortly, he became a director of a Speedway magazine (*Speedway Post*) and interestingly launched a campaign for a percentage of all pictures of him sold by Wembley (of which he received not a penny) to go to the Children's Home, Dr Barnados.

'Split' had risen from raw novice to international speedway star in just three seasons at the Empire Stadium and his meteoric rise attracted interest from other clubs who saw his commercial value. It was, however, still a surprise when it was announced that for the 1950 season he would transfer across London to Harringay for a then world record transfer of £3,000. The move shocked many as the Wembley club was still drawing very large crowds and was world renowned as the premier club. His reasons for moving have never really been explained but Split agreed on my visit to interview him in Southern Spain to tell the story of the transfer.

"It all started on one of the regular trips we used to make to ride in Ireland at Shelbourne Park that whilst chatting over a drink, several of my Wembley team mates let slip the financial support their Wembley contract gave them. Whilst I largely had to pay for my bikes and maintain them" said 'Split' *"some of the older riders were receiving payments on top of their earnings. I got on very well with Alec Jackson but I felt this was unfair and tackled him on my return to England. Sadly the Wembley management wouldn't meet my demands and so reluctantly I asked for a transfer joining Harringay in 1950. To be perfectly honest I doubled my earnings overnight but I will always regret I had to leave Wembley."*

'Split' signs for Harringay- 1950

Explaining his logic in requesting a transfer 'Split', pictured signing his Harringay contract for the 1950 season says *"You only have to calculate the money raised from programme sales for a crowd of 70,000 to realise that this money alone paid the riders without taking account of admission charges and I did feel cheated when Wembley wouldn't meet me half way on a contract."*

The period 1947-50 were real boom days for speedway and 'Split' was in demand around the world. Regular trips to communist Czechoslovakia for weekend racing often meant flying out from RAF Northolt as Heathrow was then not built and was little more than a collection of Nissan huts and war time hangars.
"I often travelled with Phil Bishop and I was never paid in Czechoslovakia as you were not allowed to bring money out of the country. Pilsner, the lager people were involved, and they paid me for my racing on my return to England. In reality this was some of the earliest forms of commercial sponsorship which was unheard of at the time" says 'Split'.

On another occasion a trip to New Zealand with fellow Wembley 'Lion' Bruce Abernethy saw 'Split' become involved in car racing. Nothing straight forward you'll understand, as one winter 'Split' travelled back from down under via Honolulu and then New York where he actually raced on a speedway bike in a match race against a midget car!

Five seasons riding for Harringay were probably Split's halcyon days scoring almost 1,000 pts for the 'Racers', qualifying for five consecutive World Finals, securing runner up spot in 1951 and 1953.

Memories of those glory days remain with Split even to this day. Of particular pride was the day when he finally beat Belle Vue's Jack Parker in the British Match Race Championship, known as 'Parker's Pension' as he was almost unbeatable in this competition and received £7 per week as long as he remained unbeaten.

'Split' v Jack Parker - Belle Vue July 1951

"As I recall it was the 1951 season when I challenged Jack for his title. I lost to Jack at Belle Vue 2-1, beating him at Harringay on my birthday 27 July 2-0, before winning the deciding leg 2-1 at New Cross. Jack was 46 years old by this time and still a master at the match race competition which he first won in 1931 when he defeated Vic Huxley."

'Split' successfully defended his newly acquired title in September against Australian Aub Lawson despite a thumb injury which delayed the second leg. In typical Waterman style he interrupted a holiday in Paris to return to Wimbledon to win the third leg. Few riders alive will have as good an insight into the great Jack Parker as 'Split'. *"Jack was no doubt a very good rider although he did keep a special bike for the match races which was in fact owned and maintained by his team mate Ron Mason. In my races with him this bike seemed to have so much power. My short stroke JAP was very quick but he always seemed to go really well on this particular bike."*

'Split's' own racing career very nearly ended prematurely in 1952 when he sustained a smashed knee cap after colliding with the board fence at Bradford Odsal. His wife Avril must take the credit for preventing 'Split' having his leg amputated as a consequence of this crash.

Avril recalls *"the doctor didn't want to carry out the operation until the Monday and it was only then he suggested he may have to amputate the leg. I immediately rang Wal Phillips, the Harringay manager, who arranged for a private ambulance to take 'Split' back to London for a second opinion. Split actually rode a few days later in an important World Championship round with the leg heavily strapped and later had a false kneecap inserted which is still in working order after over 50 years use."*

The 1951 world final was probably the nearest 'Split' came to the World Championship title. Beaten into third place in his first ride, 'Split' eventually tied with Australian Jack Young and Jack Biggs on 12 pts. Biggs was unbeaten after four rides but came last in his final ride and also came third in the three man run off where Split came second behind Jack Young, the first Second Division rider ever to win the title.

Such was the high profile and charisma of 'Split' in the 50s, he was often involved in controversy, on and off the track. A prime example however of the support he enjoyed from the speedway fans of the day is shown by a group of fans demonstrating in 1952 outside the RAC offices at Pall Mall when he was attending a disciplinary enquiry. Fans carried placards calling for 'Fair Play for Split Waterman' in protest following a controversial Match Race Championship series against Jack Young.

'Split' was often in demand for product endorsements with Gillette and Black Cat cigarettes, with a newspaper column, regular bookings on radio and TV programmes, including one of the very early BBC Sports Personality of the year programmes being the norm. Socialising with film stars including Jean Simmons and Stewart Grainger and other sportsmen was part of normal life for himself and wife Avril who he met at the Wembley Pool Ice Rink.

Vic Duggan & 'Split' with the 1950 Tottenham Hotspur FC team

As the impact of the progressive introduction of television hit speedway crowds 'Split', with the help of wife Avril's father, went into business in a corner of his factory. Sheet metal working and then plastic injection moulding was to occupy 'Split' as well as racing, and such was his success he was quickly producing plastic kitchenware for retailers such as Woolworth and Betterware. If you are reading this and remember the Airfix model craze when boys would construct from plastic kits planes, boats and Army vehicles, the chances are the product was probably moulded in a Waterman factory. A solo flying licence gained in the late 50s at Surrey Flying School helped expand his business empire to Europe and beyond. 'Split' and Avril eventually married in 1970 at Caxton Hall, the venue for many high society and film star weddings of that period.

Many years after WWII, some graffiti was discovered at a German underground hospital in the Channel Islands. It read "Up the Lions. Good old 'Split' Waterman". A businessman for many years since his retirement from speedway in 1962, 'Split' ever up for a challenge, even had several wrestling bouts in the Ilford area in the early 60s but *"I was no good at all and much preferred my speedway".*

Having spent a few days in the company of 'Split' and his delightful wife Avril I feel I can now, with 'Split's' agreement, put into context the man and his reputation. A South London boy, he became a sensation within the sport at just 24 years old. The glamorous lifestyle, adulation and not inconsiderable earning power did not deter him from reaching for the stars. His approach to life is to seize opportunities and make things happen.

'Split' I know is not proud of some of his exploits in later life but, with the help of Avril he has come through some difficult times to now enjoy a contented retirement in Spain. He has few regrets and he looks back on his Army service and speedway career with obvious pride. In these more professional and sophisticated speedway times the chances of another 'Split' Waterman type rider emerging overnight are pretty slim. This man was and still is a real PERSONALITY. How much better would modern day British speedway be if we could find his like again.

THE WATERMAN RACING RECORD

TEAM	LEAGUE POINTS
Wembley 1947-49	536
Harringay 1950-54	998
West Ham 1955	186
Wembley 1956	145
Wimbledon 1957	35
Southampton 1958	26
New Cross 1960-61	252
Ipswich 1962	45
Belle Vue 1962	19

WORLD CHAMPIONSHIP FINALS

	Points	Position
1950	8 pts	7th
1951	12 pts	2nd (after run off)
1952	6 pts	12th
1953	13 pts	2nd
1954	9 pts	5th

1951 World Championship Final
Jack Biggs 3rd 12pts, Jack Young 1st 12pts, 'Split' Waterman 2nd 12pts

MATCH RACE CHAMPIONSHIP

1948	Aug-Sept	LOST v Jack Parker (Holder) 2-0, 2-1
1951	July-Aug	WON v Jack Parker (Holder) 1-2, 2-0, 2-1
	September	WON v Aub Lawson (Challenger) 1-2, 2-0, 2-0
1952	April	WON v Jack Young (Challenger) 2-1, 2-0
	May	Forfeited title to Young after being unable to defend due to injury
	June	VOID v Jack Young (Holder)

Young 'won' first race after Waterman fell. A re-run was announced.
Split won the re-run then meeting steward announced that he had awarded 1st race to Young, hence the score was 1-1!
Split refused to continue and was reported to the Speedway Control Board.

ENGLAND TEST APPEARANCES

1948	(5 caps)	v	Australia	6 pts Wimbledon, 7 pts Belle Vue, 12 pts New Cross, 7 pts Harringay, 7 pts West Ham, England won 4-1
1949	(2 caps)	v	Australia	5 pts Wembley, 5 pts Birmingham, Australia won 3-2
1950	(1 cap)	v	Australia	2 pts West Ham, England won 3-2
1951	(4 caps)	v	Australia	Nil* pts Harringay, 13 pts Wembley, 10 pts Birmingham, 17 pts West Ham, England won 4-1
1952	(3 caps)	v	Australia	7 pts Wembley, 8 pts Belle Vue, 8 pts New Cross, Australia won 4-1
1953	(3 caps)	v	Australia	8 pts New Cross, 12 pts Wembley, 11 pts Birmingham. England won 2-1
	(3 caps)	v	New Zealand	15 pts Wimbledon, 13 pts Bristol, 15 pts West Ham. England won 3-0
1954	(1 cap)	v	Australia	7 pts West Ham. England won 3-0
1956	(2 caps)	v	Australasia	11 pts Bradford, 1 pt Birmingham England won 3-0
	(3 caps)	v	Sweden	9 pts Wembley, 8 pts Wimbledon, 9 pts Norwich. Sweden won 2-1,
	(3 caps)	v	Sweden (in Sweden)	4 pts Kumla, 7 pts Osterholm, 7 pts Linkoping. Sweden won 3-0

**Split was injured in his first ride*

England 1951 team which beat Australia 4-1 in the test series. 'Split', minus moustache, second right front row

Warzone Europe Welcomes Speedway Tourists

World War II officially ended on September 2 1945 when United States General MacArthur formally accepted the Japanese surrender aboard the American battleship Missouri in Tokyo bay. How remarkable then that barely eight weeks later a party of professional speedway riders, under the banner of ENSA (Entertainment National Service Association) set out to tour Europe, primarily Germany and Belgium, to entertain British troops. ENSA's purpose was to take a little bit of England into the warzones to entertain the troops and for the Drury Lane, London based organisation to effectively sponsor a speedway tour was an indicator as to how big the sport was in the countries imagination. To attempt such a trip with Germany and much of Europe still ravaged by the affects of the war, in particular the aftermath of the RAF bombing raids on major German cities, was to say the least ambitious! To attempt the tour in the depths of winter, they left England in late October and returned in late February, was nothing short of a miracle.

And so it was that under the captaincy of Canadian Eric Chitty of West Ham fame and with the support of tour manager Frank Buckland, former Exeter rider and erstwhile promoter, a sixteen strong squad of riders set sail to bring some sporting entertainment to troops, many of whom had been away fighting since 1940. All the riders were given uniforms and an Army rank as for the duration of the tour they would effectively be seconded to the Guards Division. The party consisted Eric Chitty, Bill Kitchen, Charlie Spinks, Ron Johnson, Norman Evans, Norman Parker, 'Tiger' Hart, Alex Statham, Ron Clarke, Bill Pitcher, Fred Tuck, Malcolm Craven, Wilf Plant, Les Wotton and Mike Erskine. Arthur Atkinson was due to travel but was prevented by a family bereavement, whilst Fred Tuck incurred difficulties with the Ministry of Labour and was prevented from travelling. Illness for Charlie Spinks reduced the party to 12 riders. Manager Buckland was assisted by the Speedway Riders Association secretary Ivor Pole, these two acting as referee, starter, Clerk of the course, announcer, flag marshals and track curators.

The picture below shows the team in full Army uniform with the trucks and drivers used to transport them across what was still a dangerous Europe.

ENSA team outside German HQ prior to start of tour

A speedway tour of Europe and the warzones had been under discussion since the summer of 1945. Irregular open meetings and challenge events had recommenced in 1945, with a planned start for league racing planned for April 1946. Administrative delays, inevitable because of the travel problems which were prevalent at the time meant that Italy, the birth place of forces speedway was to miss out on a visit from Chitty and the ENSA team. The tour itinerary is difficult to accurately confirm, late switches in track availability and at one stage bad weather hampered adherence to a rigid fixture list. Fortunately 'Tiger' Hart left son John his tour memorabilia including the map which 'Tiger' highlighted in red pencil each town or city where the team appeared.

'Tiger' Hart's personal map from the tour

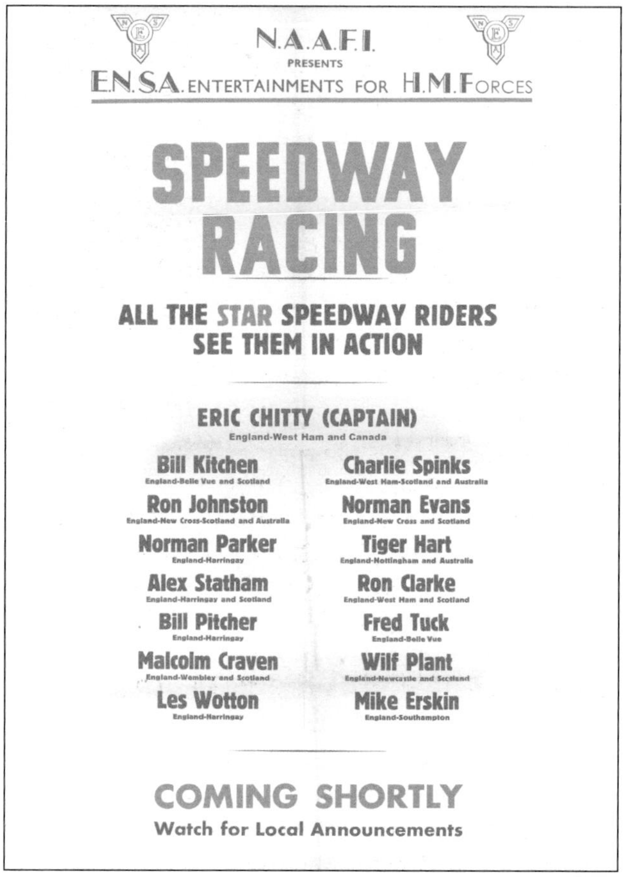

Publicity poster from the ENSA tour

At least twenty meetings were staged on a variety of track standards including circuits built in athletics, football and hockey 'stadiums' plus of course the famous impromptu tracks laid on parade grounds such as Schleiswig (Northern Germany) and St Anne's barracks (Belgium). The full list of venues from 'Tiger's' personal record is: Schleiswig, Lubek, Kiel, Buxtehude, Hanover, Bonn, Auchen, Dussledorf, Cologne, Osnabruck, Lunenberg, Celle and Hamburg whilst a three team tournament in Brussels registers Belgium as part of the tour.

'Captain' Eric Chitty in military uniform

Conditions were understandably basic at many venues and 'Major' Buckland writing in the Guards newspaper of the time graphically described some of the challenges he faced.

"We knew we would have to face the weather, this is the first time in the history of the sport that racing had been attempted in Europe throughout the winter months. We fully realised the trip would be no picnic, but we didn't anticipate having to fell trees to make a track at Lunenberg, broadside on a trials course at Celle or spin round in decreasing circles on a skating rink surface like Lubek. For that matter we did not think it possible to put up a show haring around a rope laid on the ground as on the hockey pitch at Buxtexhude nor on the parade ground at Osnabruck. Oddly enough we only had to cancel twice, once when a heavy fall of snow completely obliterated riders, bikes, track and spectators, the other occasion being when thaw turned the track into a broken sheet of frozen water".

MEMORABLE MATCH DAY

Inter Corps, Regiment and even Forces team speedway matches were regular occurrences in most warzones, with keen rivalry and the desire for victory paramount, as each team tried to maintain the 'bragging rights' over the opposition. Records show that as early as summer of 1946 the Army v RAF was staged at Qadima in Egypt with the Army coming out victorious. A Tri- service triangular match was rare indeed, but on January 1946 in Bonn as part of the ENSA tour, an historical 12 heat match between the Army 28pts, RAF 23pts & Royal Navy 19pts took place on a cold Wednesday afternoon in front of an estimated 2,000 crowd.

For the day the team captains were given military rank according to their force ie 'Admiral' Bill Kitchen, 'GOC' Ron Johnson and 'Air Vice Marshal' Norman Parker. Due to the narrowness of the Sportpark track at Gornau in Bonn it was only possible for three riders to compete in each race. Racing was reported as close, although the layer of cinders especially put down for the event was not particularly deep. Average race times of 78 seconds per race indicate a rather large circuit.

The teams were: Royal Navy- Bill Kitchen, Eric Chitty, Mike Erskine, Norman Evans

The Army- Ron Johnson, Les Wotton, Malcolm Craven, Phil Hart

Royal Air Force- Norman Parker, Ron Clarke, Alex Statham, Wilf Plant

Heat Winners: Heat 1 Ron Johnson 77.8secs, Heat 2 Ron Clarke 79.2 secs, Heat 3 Alex Statham 78.0scs, Heat 4 Malcolm Craven 78.1 secs, Heat 5 Bill Kitchen 78.0secs, Heat 6 Ron Johnson 81.6 secs, Heat 7 Mike Erskine 80.0secs, Heat 8 Ron Clarke 78.8secs, Heat 9 Bill Kitchen 80.0 secs, Heat 10 Tiger Hart 79.7 secs, Heat 11 Les Wotton 80.0secs, Heat 12 Ron Johnson 77.8 secs.

Following the 12 heat three team tournament, a two heat match race between 'Tiger' Hart and Ron Clarke was staged. 'Cinders' reporting in the army newspaper the '*Guardian*' described the races. *"The fearless riding of Phil Hart, 'Tiger' to all dyed-in-the-wool speedway fans, captured the hearts of the crowd, especially in the match races with Clarke after the Challenge match. From a rolling start Hart was chasing Ron hard when he crashed coming out of a bend. In a further race between the two, Ron Clarke came to grief when he hit a bump, riding shoulder to shoulder with 'Tiger'. In the re-run they rode neck and neck until Ron drew away going down the back straight on the last lap as Hart developed machine trouble and Clarke won by a distance".*

I WAS THERE by Len Brace

Ron Johnson leads a race on Schleiswig barracks parade ground

Len Brace, a 19 year old conscript in the 11th Air Formation Signals Regiment, has vivid memories of the ENSA teams visit to his barracks at Schleizwig in early 1945. Len had been a pre-war West Ham speedway fan, but on June 2 1944 he found himself driving through the famous stadium gates at Custom House, home of the 'Hammers', in his jeep as he prepared for the Normandy D-Day landings.

"West Ham was used as an embarkation point for D-Day and I distinctly remember being given French money and a warm meal before sleeping in the stands, very near to where I used to sit watching Bluey Wilkinson in West Ham colours in 1938" remembers Len. Of the parade ground speedway meeting, Len particularly recalls Ron Johnson who was a big star in those days and of course West Ham favourite Eric Chitty. *"The track was a loose surface, probably just dirt, spread around the drill square in an oval shape with a rope around the outside of the track being the only safety fence to protect the thousands of troops lining the track".*

The old adage, like father-like son, was certainly true for four of the ENSA tourists in 1945, with the family names of Hart, Wotton, Erskine and Plant being heard in speedway circles many years after their retirements due the exploits of their respective sons.

LES WOTTON

Bristolian Les born in 1908, rode his first ever dirt track meeting held at his local Knowle stadium in 1928, before riding for twelve clubs including Liverpool, Preston West Ham, Birmingham, Harringay New Cross and Wimbledon in a racing career which ended 23 years later when Southampton closed their doors in 1951. This unusually high number of clubs is due in part to Les's "*racing is business* "philosophy. He was successful before the war in three 'Star' championships (the predecessor to the World Championship which started in 1936), and wore the England colours at both home and abroad. According to Les' son Doug *"Dad very much ran his speedway involvement as a business proposition and few people know that our family were shareholders in Bristol Speedway. One night when he was riding for Harringay, he brought the 'Racers' team down to Knowle, but his fellow shareholders refused to pay them as they thought it was dad's responsibility."* To avoid any problems Les did in fact pay the London team riders, including himself from his own pocket!

Les, who died in 1995 aged 87 worked at Parnalls Aircraft Company during the war as a gunner instructor to RAF air crew. Time spent at the Avro factory in Chester enabled him to ride in some war time meetings at Belle Vue and this is where Les was probably recruited by Chitty for the ENSA tour. Doug Wotton's involvement with speedway started with the cycle version when he became the Somerset champion and rode in the Mars chocolate sponsored National championships, being awarded one of the rare chrome plated despatch rider helmets presented to winners. Doug had novice rides on the motorised version at Bristol in 1953, but decided not to follow his father into the professional speedway scene.

One of Doug's fondest memories of his father's career was after an England v Australia test match at Wembley when Les acquired the Lions race jackets for his son. *"Cycle speedway was very big in Bristol in those days and I rode for the Hengrove 'Bulldogs'. I thought the England race jackets would be great for St Martin's 'Lions', another Bristol based team in our league. Those jackets were used for many years by the skid kids of Bristol".*

PHIL HART

Phil Manston Hart owes his participation in the ENSA tour and in fact his whole speedway career due to a visit to Australia by the future King of Great Britain in the mid 1920. 'Tiger' was born in Balham, London 1907, but ran away to sea when he was just 16 years old, before settling in Queensland, Australia as a farmers boy.

He saved his meagre wages and eventually progressed to owning his own 200 acre farm near Toowoomba, before joining the Australian Light Horse Brigade. Phil was selected for the guard of honour for the future King and after the ceremony he went to relax at the local speedway. A riding trial alongside other Aussie pioneer riders Ron Johnson and Charlie Spinks followed and Frank Arthur the foremost Australian rider of the time recommended he sailed to England to ride professionally. Hart arrived in May 1930, many fans thinking he was an Australian, and rode for a range of teams until the outbreak of WWII. During the period 1940-45 'Tiger' was a technical representative with the Ministry of Aircraft Production. He had volunteered for RAF flying duties in 1941, was accepted as a navigator but the Ministry judged he was more useful to the war effort in his technical capacity. 'Tiger', an established yachtsman played a leading part in the ENSA tour, not only by his riding but also in his efforts to develop new riding talent for the future of the sport.

'Tiger' Hart in Australian Light Horse colours

Chief Petty Officer Kett

One such project to develop new riders for speedway was when he designed a speedway bike for the Royal Navy competitors in BAOR events in Kiel. Chief Petty Officer Kett is pictured aboard the special made by Hart. It consisted of Matchless and Norton engine parts with the frame starting life as an NSU 250cc machine. On retirement from racing due to a serious leg injury he took over as manager of Tamworth and entered the world of speedway promoting with the former Aston Villa FC owner Doug Ellis when he ran meetings at the Birmingham Alexander stadium in 1959-60. Son John followed his father onto the track riding for Cradley, Sheffield, Birmingham and Leicester in the 60s and 70s.

MIKE ERSKINE

The playing fields of Eton are more likely to produce an international cricketer or rugby scrum half than a speedway rider! However Mike Erskine, born in Westbury, Wiltshire in 1913 progressed from the famous public school to ride professional speedway pre-war for such clubs as Coventry, New Cross, Luton, Bristol and Southampton. Mike was renowned for his engineering skills and as a speedway frame maker, the Erskine Staride bike being in great demand post-war, with Freddie Williams twice winning the World Championship using Erskine frames. Mike's mechanical know how proved invaluable on the ENSA tour as spare parts were in very short supply at the time.

Post-war he rode for Wimbledon and reached test match standard in 1949. Son Jon followed father into the sport as a rider in the 60s riding for Neath, Long Eaton, Newport and Wolverhampton.

WILF PLANT

Wilf (centre) with his father and mother before setting off on tour

It is wholly appropriate that Wilf Plant took part in the ENSA tour which was to help revive international speedway, for it was Wilf who ensured that the Belle Vue war time meetings went ahead at all by supplying the required racing fuel. Born Melton Mowbray 1916, Wilf progressed to speedway from grass track racing riding on the near by Leicester 'Super' speedway before securing team spots with New Cross, Wimbledon, Middlesbrough and Edinburgh before the war. He was the subject of a £1,000 transfer deal from Middlesbrough to Fleetwood in 1948 and reached international status when he captained a British touring team in South Africa. Whilst still riding, he ran the family garage which is to this day run by his son Graham. The young Graham followed father by riding for Teeside (Middlesbrough) in the Second Division then moving on to Leicester where he was a member of their league runner up team of 1971. Father Wilf's adventures were replicated when Graham toured Rhodesia in the 70s completing his riding career with Newport and then Halifax.

ANOTHER WINTER RIDING SPEEDWAY

Monday October 28 1946 saw the second post-war European tour get underway, this time as a private venture. The plan was to run meetings in France, Belgium, Holland and Germany as part of spreading the speedway gospel to a still war ravaged Europe. Led again by Frank Buckland and Eric Chitty, the itinerary included such venues as Buffalo stadium Paris, Hanomag stadium Hanover, Liege, Antwerp, Hamburg and Heysel stadium in Brussels.

The tour team included: Frank Buckland (manager), Ivor Pole (equipment manager), Norman Parker, Eric Chitty, Geoff Pymar, Jeff Lloyd, Malcolm Craven, Frank Lawrence, Frank Hodgson, Bob Harrison, Kid Curtis, Cyril Anderson, Oliver Hart, Bill Kitchen, Ron Clarke, Bill Pitcher, Alec Statham, Mike Erskine, Ron Howes, Bob Wells (rider-mechanic), Fred Peace and Stan Seal (mechanics).

Frank Buckland

The group were based in Brussels at the Schleen hotel, the party including some rider's wives who were able to enjoy the shopping in these austere times in England. In 1946 rationing and shortages were rife with most products produced in the UK being exported to the European market and the opportunity to obtain some luxury goods was a major attraction to the ladies. The tour hit problems early on, when it became apparent that some track owners that had agreed to take the English tourists were having second thoughts, leaving Frank Buckland trying to find alternatives venues to keep the tour alive.

Meetings were held throughout November, including a memorable individual event at Heysel stadium, the scene of the Liverpool v Roma crowd tragedy in 1985. The organisers were to lay a racing oval on top of an athletics track around the football pitch when they realised they were running out of preparation time. They then had a brainwave. To speed up the process they drafted in 150 collaborator prisoners who had helped the Germans during the occupation of Belgium, to complete the work. Facilities at tracks struggled to match British standards, with some meetings being run without a starting gate, flag or green light starts being employed. In some meetings the opposition were Belgian motor cyclists who had only ridden grass track or scrambles and were riding Tiger Hudson's or Speed Triumph machines. With lack of meetings in Belgium and Holland the tour moved on to Germany (Hanover and Hamburg). The RAF had arranged three meetings for BAOR personnel in the area and they also housed the tourists in an un-named Air Force base where at least the generous hospitality made up for the lack of meetings. Records do exist for the five meetings in Germany, four in Hanover and one in Hamburg. Bill Kitchen was very much the star of this leg of the tour returning to England with the Hanover, Hamburg and German Individual Championships.

Known results:

Challenge Trophy de Bruxelles -	1st Oliver Hart 2nd Alex Statham 3rd Norman Parker
Hanover Ind Championship -	1st Norman Parker 2nd Ron Clarke 3rd Mike Erskine
Hanover Championship -	1st Bill Kitchen 2nd Norman Parker 3rd Frank Hodgson
Hamburg Ind Championship -	1st Bill Kitchen 2nd Ron Clarke 3rd Norman Parker
German Ind Championship -	1st Bill Kitchen 2nd Ron Clarke 3rd Geoff Pymar
British Riders Championship -	1st Norman Parker 2nd Frank Hodgson 3rd Frank Curtis

ENSA SPEEDWAY TOUR WINTER 1945-1946

Full Tour Squad and Officials

Three Man Racing at Sport Park Bonn

Ron Johnson and Norman Parker

Malcolm Craven racing at Cologne

Ivor Pole in uniform starts a heat in Cologne

Oliver Hart and Mike Erskine leading a heat in the ill fated Winter 1946 "Short Tour'

Entertainments National Service Association (ENSA) was formed to provide entertainment for the troops in war zones. By November 1939 they had some 700 artists on their books, staged some 1,500 shows with audiences titalling 600,000 people. The organisation followed the troops in France with George Formby and Gracie Fields being the most well known performers. Yeheudi Menuhin (violinist) Sir Adrian Boult with the BBC Orchestra and Vera Lynn were also big draws in shows from North Africa to Burma. ENSA was disbanded in 1947 with the speedway tour being just one facet of an organisation which at its peak staged 500 shows a week.

The Hanomag Speedway Story

To understand how such a professional, well equipped speedway club, which was organised to a standard and with facilities that many lower league clubs in 1947 back in Britain struggled to match, it is important to understand the immediate post-war history of a war torn and devastated Germany. The British Zone of Occupation in Germany covered by BAOR was a vast area stretching from Denmark and the Baltic in the North to the Ruhr and Rhineland in the South and from Holland and Belgium in the West to within 100 miles of Berlin in the East. The zone was bound by the Russian zone to the East and the French and American zones to the South. Also included in its confines were Polish Belgian and Norwegian contingent's. The principal cities were Hamburg, Hanover, Brunswick, Bremen and Cologne. The whole area was roughly the size of England, 300 miles North to South and 200 miles West to East.

Royal Electrical Mechanical Engineers units were deployed throughout this area, with additional smaller units in the British sector of Berlin, Copenhagen in Denmark, Brussels in Belgium and Frankfurt in the American zone. The REME units were the remnants of the organisation which formed part of 21st Army group for the invasion of the continent via Normandy. Divisional Light Aid Detachments (LAD's) were maintained at their normal scale, with workshops reduced to one brigade workshop per division. They were supplemented by sub workshops each consisting of two officers and some twenty men controlling the activities of perhaps 250 civilians. The sub workshops were the smallest element in the static organisation, which comprised Light, Medium and Heavy Workshops. Civilianisation was common in REME workshops, as they needed support for the strained resources and it was not unusual for a Heavy Base Workshop, such as Hanomag, to employ up to 3,000 civilians. Many DPs (Displaced Persons) such as Poles, Czechs, Estonians, Lithuanians, Latvians, and Ukrainians and of course Germans worked alongside British soldiers. Whilst mostly involved in mechanical repair, other vital projects such as Operation 'Woodpecker' demonstrates the significant role of REME in those harsh post-war period of rebuilding Germany. Along with Sappers from the Royal Army Service Corps and Infantry men, REME assisted in the logging of wood from forests around Luneberg, Celle and Goslar to provide crucial supplies of wood for the reconstruction programme.

Following the German surrender, the already established infrastructure of Mechanical workshops to keep the British Army mobile lost none of its importance with, thousands of military vehicles still requiring REME engineering support. As soon as was practical, German factories, previously involved in the production of equipment, arms and ammunition for the war effort, were occupied by Allied forces. Typical examples of these factories were Hamburg which was a Seaplane works, Etter a crane and steel works and of course Hanomag a commercial lorry, tractor and diesel engine factory, which was to become the home of 12 Heavy Base Workshop.

WELCOME TO HANOMAG - SPEEDWAY'S GERMAN HOME

Between 1940-45, the Hanomag factory on the outskirts of Hanover devoted most of its production capacity to the production of three quarter tracked vehicles and to large long range guns and gun mountings. A prominent feature of the works was a large shop where gun barrels up to 12 inch bore were cast, with the gun shrinking tower at the end. The tower, a large red brick construction, could be seen from many miles away but it had survived the best efforts of the RAF to destroy it. The gun barrels and tubes were suspended vertically by means of a 150 tonne crane, subjected to electrical heating and then shrunk onto one another to produce a complete gun barrel. When the first REME contingent arrived to take over the factory for 12 Heavy base workshops in 1945, the enormous main production hangar was full of partly machined gun barrels, with a large railway mounting at one end and a coastal defence mounting completely constructed at the other.

Whilst the immediate area surrounding the factory was reasonably intact, the same could not be said for the city of Hanover which along with Cologne, Hamburg and Bremen suffered grievous damage from the RAF bombings. Life for the German civilians was grim, with basic commodities such as soap, brushes and needles impossible to obtain. Fraternisation between British troops and German civilians was banned in the early stages but was gradually relaxed.
One of the early discoveries at the Hanomag site was a full blown athletics sports ground behind the factory, which fitted well with the Army's desire to provide sporting facilities for its troops. Football, cricket and athletics were the normal offering but REME had other ideas.

Speedway racing!!!!!!!

Colonel F.V. Dundas pictured at a Combined Services Championship meeting

The story of the Hanomag 'Saints', is a remarkable piece of motorcycling history stretching from 1942 in Algiers to the last season of racing in Hanover in1951. No one was more qualified than Colonel F V Dundas REME AMI Mech E to give an insight into this most famous of clubs. Apart from his role as an Officer, he held the position of President of the Hanover based club which was to produce over twenty riders who went onto the professional ranks back in Britain. I am indebted to the '*Craftsman*', the REME magazine in permitting the reproduction of Colonel Dundas' overview report on the 1949-50 season.

"The club, name and History date back to 1942 in Algiers when a REME Officer had the idea of chalking a haloless Saint on motorcycles being repaired and of adding the halo after the machines had passed their testing. The system was continually used by the Unit, and when the club was formed (1945) it took the name of 'Saints'. A.S.M 'Crash' Callaghan the present captain of the team, was one of the founder members of the club on it's formation. The Club continued its career in BAOR, all meetings being held on the Hanomag Speedway, the Sports Ground of 12 Heavy Workshops and a track which safely merits the title of the best in German, being 440 yards in circumference.

In the early months of 1949, a fully organised committee was formed having certain definite objectives, primarily to make the club pay its way on an official accounting basis, to produce the best possible standardised machines and to increase club membership, so that even allow-

ing for riders who were unable to compete every Sunday, a minimum programme containing thirty riders could normally be guaranteed. The next serious consideration was that of finance and in this sphere the club, on conclusion of a very successful season, owes considerable gratitude to its most efficient treasurer ASM Peacock of Central Inspectorate. From experience now gained it is a matter of interest to note that the total expenditure incurred on an average weekly meeting amounted to £50, such items as programme printing, in both English and German, being one of considerable expense and involving the treasurer in many complex calculations as to the rate of exchange between B.A.S.F.V(Army vouchers) and the Deutch mark. Various expedients for raising money were resorted to, and a long-suffering and hard working secretary, A.S.M Hurrell, 12 Heavy Workshops, hit on the idea of the formation of a supporters club, entailing a small charge for the privilege of membership and of the use of season tickets to cover the 21 meetings at reasonably reduced rates.

Racing at Hanomag 1946- Note no safety fence!

Other schemes resulted in raising more money for club funds, and it can now be put on record that at our opening meeting on Easter Sunday 1949, we were entirely dependent on the amount of the 'gate' to clear all our outstanding IOU's. Easter Sunday favoured us very kindly, in fact it was a glorious summer day, and our 'gate', British and German , totalled 3,000 people, exactly clearing our debt. Considerable alterations had been made to the stadium and the surrounding area specially through the assistance of 15 B.O.D, with old canvas being obtained for screening off the perimeter and finally it was impossible for anyone to see the racing unless prepared to pay a small and reasonable charge to enter the track. A drive had been made to obtain as many members (riders) as possible to the club, but owing to our limited number of racing machines, the list had to be closed on reaching seventy five members, and a waiting list was then opened. We were extremely fortunate in having an Independent Parachute Brigade Group in and around Hanover. Naturally this sport appealed to the 'red berets', and every assistance was given, and personal interest taken by Commander, Brigadier Kempster DSO. These lads produced some of our best and keenest riders, and it is with great regret that we say Goodbye to the Brigade on its departure to the United Kingdom.

Our next major problem was to obtain the requisite number of trained officials, requiring about twenty for a Sunday meeting. All these were forthcoming voluntarily, and were mostly from 12 Heavy Workshops. During the current season we held twenty one meetings and it says much for the keenness and enthusiasm of these officials that our organisation on the track never let us down on one single meeting.

In order to foster Anglo-German sport, the German employees of 12 Heavy Workshops were encouraged to learn speedway racing, and in the end a very representative team of six riders was obtained. The Hanomag 'Silver Streaks' as the German team was called, has competed against and with the riders of the 'Saints' and also very successfully in purely German races with German Speedway clubs. It is interesting to note that the German captain 'Grim' Armin, ended up almost at the top of the individual league table, and it is considered that if he continues with the sport there is no reason why he should not have a great future in German professional speedway should he decide to take this up. The 'Saints' have competed both home and away against German clubs and our riders have already proved a great attraction in these programmes. Many of the German riders are now using JAPs for the first time since the end of the war, and at the moment their riding experience is insufficient to get the best out of these machines , we have been able, therefore, to compete successfully against them on our WD machines. During the season a home and away match against the Hamburg 'Lions' was held, each club winning on its own track. Next year it is hoped to foster both the spirit of competition and friendly relationships between the two clubs, but increasing transport restrictions are likely to raise difficulties.

1947 Safety fence now in place

In each of our Sunday programmes, different match events were organised and a very considerable amount of hard work was put in by the secretary to ensure that a large proportion of main event riders were always available. Novice and junior races were included in the programme throughout the season, and a lap timing plan was devised whereby novices graduated through to juniors up to main event riders, and many of those who started as novices ended up as main event riders, with an excellent performance to their credit.

During this season the 'Saints' club has raised quite a considerable interest in professional speedway racing circles in England, and a very handsome trophy was presented for competition by the Wembley 'Lions'. As a point of interest, the winner of this trophy (Jimmy Gooch), has decided to take up professional speedway racing as a career on leaving the Army, and has received a contract with the 'Lions'. The Great Yarmouth Speedway Club also presented a trophy to the 'Saints' this to be for the rider who always competed in the best interest of sport and sportsmanship. The riders voted as to who should receive this, and after an almost unanimous vote the award went to M.S.M Brindley RASC, a rider who throughout the season has failed to win a prize at any meeting, but has always continued to ride, and in many cases to fall off, but he has always come back with a smile on his face."

Before passing on to Colonel Dundas's report of 1950 it should be recorded that apart from ex-1949 'Saints' Jimmy Gooch (Wembley) and Eric Boothroyd (Cradley Heath) who had joined the professional speedway ranks, another 19 riders were riding for clubs in England after returning to civilian life. Such was the interest in speedway racing from some Rhine Army soldiers riding at Hanomag that they decided to sign on as regulars, having completed their National Service in order that they can continue their riding careers.

"During the early months of 1950, when maintenance and track improvements were being carried out, it was discovered by accurate measurement that the circuit was only 395 yards in length this was subsequently remedied, and the track re-laid to 430 yards, ie an increase of 140 yards in a four lap race. In February, the initial committee meeting was held to decide on the policy for the season, and as the 'Big Four' of the 1949 committee were still officiating a great deal of expert knowledge was readily available. Owing to the fact that regulations governing the use of transport in the Rhine Army had been considerably tightened up, it became obvious from the point of view of riders and spectators that it would be impossible to run meetings on a weekly basis similar to 1949, and it was therefore decided to organise these on a fortnightly basis, retaining the free Sundays for fixtures against German clubs.

The German employees of 12 Heavy Workshop have again been encouraged to take up speedway racing. With the kind assistance of the German Welfare, these riders have been encouraged to compete in certain German meetings, and in August Fritz Killisch (Silver Streaks team captain) won a German meeting at Kassel, riding a normal WD machine under exactly similar conditions to British riders. On September 24 1950, a 'Silver Streaks' team of four riders travelled to Neumunster, competing in a four team tournament against Hamburg, Schleswig-Holstein, and Bremen. Killisch won the individual prize, and the 'Silver Streaks' won the team event by 28 clear points from Bremen .

The view of the third and fourth bends -Hanomag 1950

When competing in Anglo-German meetings no 'Saints' club rider is permitted to accept either 'start' or 'prize' money but appreciate a small memento of the occasion's. We have to make all our private road transport arrangements, the club receives a re-fund of these expenses and as we can only spare a Sunday for such meetings, our radius of action is considerably restricted. An Anglo-German meeting took place at the Hanomag stadium on July 9 1950 against the Allgemeiner Deutscher Autombil Club. Resultant from this meeting; considerable interest in our activities was taken by certain German enthusiasts from Ebstorf who intended to build a track. All possible expert advice was given to them by A.S.M Hurrell and an almost exact replica of the Hanomag track was produced. On Sunday August 15 1950 under our own private arrangements a team of eight riders and four reserves along with many enthusiastic supporters started off very early bound for Ebstorf. It is a matter of considerable interest to note that the Ebstorf club required 30,000 DM to open their track, a sum which was subscribed to by about twenty inhabitants of this small town, within 14 days. As the approximate 'gate' was in the region of 20,000 people, it can be seen that there is definite interest being taken by the Germans in speedway racing, and as the club charged 3 DM per seat, it is also obvious that it can be a paying concern. On our adverse rate of exchange 3 DM is the equivalent of 5s (25p today)".

After this very successful 'International' event Colonel Dundas was asked by the Brunswick club to produce a team for a similar challenge match. This meeting took place on October 1 1950 but the gate was only 5,000, this being due to various Communist demonstrations in the Western Zone which put many people of travelling. *"On arrival for practice we found that it was a 'sand track' with a loose bumpy surface. This did not unduly upset the 'Saints' although certain of our better riders were unable to settle to riding on this kind of track until they had raced in one or two heats. During this meeting we saw the famous Gunzenhauser and Marxreiter, the respective No1 and 2 of German speedway racing. Both were riding 'blown Norton JAPs', a practice which is not permitted in England under ACU rules."*

The Hanomag 'Saints' club under the Presidency of Colonel Dundas was always very careful not to use service funds to stage their meetings, an insight can be gained from the detailed running costs to enable he club to survive and prosper.

"The club accounts are audited quarterly, even to producing counterfoils for every ticket sold on a B.A.F (British currency) and Deutschmark basis. Through the Royal Army Ordnance Corps, on repayment, we obtain tyres and spares, and our speedway petrol coupon allocation on repayment is obtained through 7th Armoured Division. For each meeting the club produces a complete double sided eight page programme containing a variety of information about speedway racing in general, apart from giving fullest particulars on the actual meeting itself. This season the Rhine Army press have very kindly undertaken this work on a minimum cost basis, and 1,000 programmes are produced for £5. Prizes for each meeting are bought through the NAAFI and may appear to be a costly item. My policy has always been to give good and useful prizes. At the end of hard riding covering about three hours, a rider who may have easily incurred a bad fall or two is deserving of recognition, and undoubtedly successful winners are very appreciative of their prizes. Many club riders come from a long distance, and have been known to 'hitch-hike' in by German transport when all other means of transport has failed rather than miss a ride."

To give a few concrete figures, the following figures cover our expenditure of twelve club and three Anglo-German meetings during a season (a total of £560):

	£	s	d
Petrol and oil	30	0	0
Programmes	75	0	0
Prizes	200	0	0
Spares and Maint.	100	0	0
Loudspeaker equ.	50	0	0
Tickets and publicity	55	0	0
Travelling expenses	50	0	0

The cost for a normal meeting approximated to £30, which required a minimum 'gate' of 650 English and German spectators to balance out expenses. It can easily be understood that if given bad weather or other counter attractions on a Sunday, takings would have suffered. The club was able to cleverly balance the books over a season and went in to the 1951 season £50 in profit.

The Garrison Speedway Team

Aldershot as a garrison dates back to the 1860's and was a key training establishment in the preparations for WWII. Today the garrison holds the status of Centre of Excellence for Sport within the British Army. Its current role as a modern day sports training facility is part of the UK forces strategy of using sporting activities to deliver a physically fit soldier, sailor or airman to the front line. It does seem fitting that with the Army as early as 1944 using competitive motorcycling as a 'training' tool, Aldershot , a town synonymous with the British Army should one day have its own professional team.

An Aldershot 'Dirt track' was opened at Boxall Lane in 1929, just a year after the sport was introduced to England by the Australian pioneers. Just eight 'Open' meetings were staged in those early days but it was to be 1950 before organised team racing was introduced to the Hampshire town. Inevitably called the 'Shots' (they were briefly called the 'Poppies') a team was entered in the National League Division 3, followed by 'Open' meetings and semi-professional events in the Southern Area League.

Sadly the economics of staging the sport at the Aldershot Greyhound stadium at Tongham proved too challenging as the impact of television hit speedway crowds. The last promoter was ex-RAF man John Pilblad who struggled financially, with the tracks unusual shape, basic facilities and a refusal by the speedway authorities to allow Aldershot to join the Provincial league in 1960 all sounding the death knell for the sport .
Aldershot racing record; 1929 Open meetings, 1950-1 National league Division 3, 1952 Southern league, 1953 Open meetings, 1954 Southern Area League, 1957 Southern Area league, 1958 Open meetings , 1959 Southern Area League, 1960 Open meetings.

Forces Speedway Teams & Colours

There has long been inter-forces rivalry on a sporting level between the Army, Royal Navy and Royal Air Force. Whether its football, rugby, cricket or Speedway, wherever sport is played within the military, the pride of the Regiment, Corps or Force creates some healthy competition. To ensure those rivalries, away from the battlefields of WWII, were maintained in the world of warzone speedway, clubs, teams, colours and even programmes all competed for the right to say "we were the best". Earlier we have attempted to trace in chronological order the operating timelines of the warzone speedways. To complete the picture we examine the club structure, team racing colours, the Army hierarchy who made racing possible and finally a rider directory in tribute to all armed forces personnel who kept speedway alive in the darkest of days.

BAR-NONE M.C.C

In May 1944, a group of despatch riders and motorcycling enthusiasts deployed near Cairo decided to form a forces motorcycle club with membership open to all ranks with "no-one barred" hence the clubs name. Leading lights in founding the Bar-None at Kasr-el-Nil barracks back then were Alan Johnson of 56 DR section and Sgt Geoff Steer of 41 DR Royal Corps Signals, who had been organising unofficial time trials in the desert with competitors (on occasions 150 at a time), using their WD motor cycles.

The Army saw these reliability time trials as instructive and training aids for primarily despatch riders to improve their riding skills. With WWII reaching its conclusion, the Army top brass were actively encouraging competitive motor cycling events to occupy the many soldiers who could have found 'less appropriate' ways of spending their spare time. With the support and patronage of Brigadier J.I Chrystall CBE, MC and Brigadier H.J Hayman-Joyce DSO, a formal club with a constitution, membership cards and recognition within the Army, not unlike the Auto Cycle Union back home in Britain came into being. Club badges cast in brass or metal rescued from crashed aircraft were made by the REME workshops carrying the club insignia. Designed by Alan Johnson, a commercial artist, they started to appear on motor cycles and membership cards detailing the clubs rules were issued to all members. Branches were quickly established in Bhengazi, Alexandria, Palestine, Kassassin and the UK with members from Canada, East Africa,

South Africa and New Zealand also enjoying their motorcycling through the Bar-None activities. A formal training objective was enshrined in the club's constitution and it also issued technical regulations to ensure safe and fair racing.

By mid-1945 discussions had started within the Bar-None regarding the introduction of grass track/sand speedway racing to supplement trials and scrambling events, but of course the big challenge was the lack of suitable venues. The Bar-None newsletter of June of that year explained well the need for events " a little more dashing" to further training opportunities.

The newsletter reported "*Each Monday's club meeting during June and July has concluded with a general discussion on the next sporting event to be promoted by the Bar-None. Although reliability trials have been supported by some, the general opinion has been that something a little more dashing is required to provide advanced training for competitors, obtain splash publicity and give the spectators a new line of excitement. Presuming on forthcoming permission from Higher Authority, therefore, it is intended to put over a grass or sand meeting as soon as possible. Owing to the scarcity of grass in Egypt and the sacredness of golf courses, cricket grounds and the like, it is highly possible that "sand in my shoes" will be a popular theme song before long. A Sports committee has been elected to deal with the organisation, which will now be in the hands of C.Q.M.S Monty Terrell, Bdr Blunt and Cpls. Deeprose and Tongue.*"

We now know of course that by September 1945 the Almaza sand (speedway) meeting was held and so the snow ball had been pushed down the hill, establishing sand speedway as a major Army motor cycling activity.

BAR- NONE CLUB'S OWN WORLD CHAMPION

Some thirty two years after it's formation in Egypt in 1944, the Bar-None was able to lay claim to playing a part in producing, at that time, only the third Englishman ever to win the World Individual Speedway Championship.

Post-war, forces members of the Bar-None returned to Britain and continued their motor cycling activities through regional branches set up by the club. Fate was to play a hand in the late 1960's when as a young apprentice at a Shell oil refinery a young Peter Collins discovered that his supervisor, John Flanaghan, was involved in the local branch of the Bar-None MCC. Peter's motor cycling career, along with many other budding North West speedway riders including the Morton brothers (Dave and Chris) and his own brothers, was to start on the grass track meetings organised by the Bar-None. Some years later when Peter had developed into a world speedway star, the local Bar-None committee meetings were held in Peter's home village in Heatley, whilst John Flanaghan, by then a leading light in the club, was also a near neighbour.

Peter Collins on the grass-1970

The Collins family, Mum, Dad, five boys (Peter, Les, Neil, Phil, Stephen and their sister Anne) was to become the most famous speedway family in the sport's history, with all the boys going on to ride speedway and even Anne taking part in some lady demonstration races. Peter, the eldest brother who was to become World Speedway Champion in Poland in 1976, began spectating at Bar-None organised grass track meetings as a schoolboy combining this with his regular Saturday nights trips to Belle Vue Manchester to see his 'Aces' speedway favourites.

"I remember going to watch a Bar-None mountain grass track around 1967 when I was just 13 years old. The Baybutt brothers and Chris Pusey being my favourite riders" says Peter *"When I reached 16, and was old enough for a racing licence, I rode in Bar-None grass meetings at Pickmere. I rode on the grass for most of the 1970 season before having second half speedway rides at Crewe in September of that year. I was proud to be awarded an Honarary Life membership of the Bar-None when I won my World Speedway title in 1976 and I think it's safe to say that many young speedway riders in the area owed their interest in racing to those Bar-None grass track events in the early 70's".*

World Speedway Champion-Poland 1976

Peter Collins went on to enjoy a glittering career for club, country and internationally on grass, speedway, and long tracks. A remarkable 137 appearances for his country, ten FIM Gold medals and a host of titles may just not have happened but for his early contact with the Bar-None MCC!

PETER COLLINS' CAREER RECORD

Grass Track: 1971/72 350cc National Champion
Long Track: Qualified for World final on ten occasions
Speedway: Rochdale 1971, Belle Vue 1971- 86, British Junior Champion 1973, European Champion 1974, World Team Cup winner 1973/74/75/77/80, Inter-Continental Champion 1976/77, World Individual Champion 1976, World Pairs Champion 1977/80/83/84, World Master Champion 1978, British Champion 1979 and the Seagrave Trophy 1977.

Represented: Young England, England Under 23s, England, Great Britain, British Lions, Rest of the World.

NAPLES M.C.C (Italy)

In late 1945, Southern Italy was still divided into military sectors with Bari (San Spirito) speedway in 54 area and Naples (Vomero) stadium in 56 area. A range of motorcycle events were staged under the 'training' banner including hill climbs, scrambles, time trials in addition to oval speedway racing. Records survive which prove that a Naples club existed with a triangular badge carrying the words "Vedi Napoli at Poi Mouri" which translates into "See Naples and Die! The secretary of the club was a Sgt Dooley of the Royal Corps Signals.

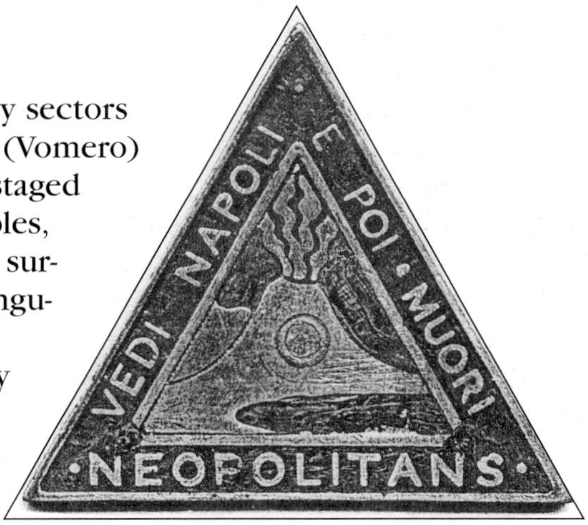

HANOMAG 'SAINTS' (GERMANY)

The 'Saints' history is well documented in this book with REME introducing the haloed saint symbol as an indication that a motor vehicle repair had been successfully completed. Undoubtedly the most organised and well supported club in warzone speedway history, its structured Combined Services Championship, season long league racing and their efforts to encourage the German population of the Heavy Base Workshops to form their own teams, mark the 'Saints' out as the premier warzone speedway club.

STYRIA DISTRICT MCC (AUSTRIA)

As the war was ending many British troops in Italy moved North into Austria as the Germans retreated back to their homeland.The Styria club, in conjunction with the 46 Infantry Division were responsible for staging the first official motor cycle event in Austria after WWII.August 5 1946 saw grass speedway staged at Gossendorf and kick started the motor cycle revival in the country.

TRIPOLITANIA SPEEDWAY RACING CLUB (LIBYA)

Rare programmes from the Seaview speedway built in the winter of 1949 to replace the Busetta racecourse gives the Tripolitania club credit for organising meetings. Local rules included helmet colours, conventional 3-2-1 points scoring system but a race jacket numbering convention rarely seen any where else. Each team was numbered and lettered ie 1A, 2 B, 3C etc with this unusual identification method carried on all the team race jackets.

The Italian Circoli Motociclistico di Tripoli ran a team in the Libyan 'league' based at Seaview speedway in Tripoli in 1950, but it appears that the driving force for the team racing came from the Grenadier , Coldstream and Scots Guards based in this historical city.The inevitable presence of the Royal Corps Signals indicates they and the Guards were behind the success of speedway which appeared to end in October 1951 when 1 Division of the Guards were moved to Fayid, Egypt.The motor cycles of 1 Div Signal Regiment were shipped to Malta, with some members who were coming to the end of their National Service riding their bikes back to the UK.

THE OFFICERS PLAYED THEIR PART!

None of the tracks would have been built, no meetings would have been held and this period of speedway history would just not have occurred, but for the support of a key group of senior ranking forces. From the very first Trani meeting in October 1944 under the guidance of Major A E Simcock, the need for senior officer support and co-operation for the staging of speedway was crucial.Authorising building work, approving the loan of equipment and manpower, providing formal structure to supply meeting officials and giving encouragement to develop Regiment, workshop and Corps teams played a significant part in the growth of the sport in the warzones. By no means a comprehensive list, but nevertheless a list which recognises some of the 'top brass' who provided the help and enthusiasm to allow the sport to grow is reproduced overleaf.

EGYPT

Brigadier Hayman –Joyce CBE, DSO

Brigadier Hayman -Joyce CBE, DSO, Brigadier W Tanner, Brigadier RA Boxhall, Sq Ldr A V Wells, Wg Cdr Rodher, Brigadier H D W Sitwell CB MC, Major Johns, Lt Col D A C Gibbs, Major C D Litteleworth, Major S E Moon, Major Williamson, Major D W Allan, Capt Kneels, Capt. Hesketh, Capt. Page, Capt. Williamson, Lt Stephenson, Lt Crowhurst, Capt. S C Harrison, Flt Lt King, and Lt Leany.

ITALY

Capt. G M Pirie, Lt Col Butcher, Col Wilson, Lt G L McCormack , Capt. Bloomfield, Lt T Gouge.
Capt. E Jameson, Capt.P.R. Davies, Lt Col H.V. Martin and Major H. D. Mills

GERMANY

Brigadier Darley, Col. F V L Dundas, Major J Lowans, FO J Hughes, Major C Browne, Major T Edwards, Major D Gershon, Lt Col K F Kinchin MBE, Capt. E Poole, Brigadier Kempster, Col. Blowey, Capt. H F Wheeler, Major Cowan, Major General J D Shapland, Major General Arkwright and Brigadier Perrger,

Major -General Shapland raises the flag on another speedway season

AUSTRIA

Major General C E Weir CB, CBE, DSO, Major General J F Combe DSO and Lt Col Vaux.

LIBYA

Lt Col E D Good, Capt. E J Woolnough, Lt Col Sir John Nelson and General H Murray CB, DSO.

PALESTINE

Brigadier Davis

CLUB COLOURS

Team racing quickly became the life blood of warzone speedway, commencing with inter-forces eg. Army v RAF, then inter-corps eg. Royal Corps Signals v REME, followed by club competitions with a 13 team league operating in Egypt in 1949 under the control of the Motor Cycle Racing Club base at Tel el Kabir. International events were also popular, appealing to the patriotism of the troops, with England facing Scotland, Ireland and Wales .

The use of team race jackets in appropriate colours bearing the team,s nickname eg, Saints, Meteors, Pirates, Lions, Dons and Tigers amongst the most common, was an exact replica of the pre-war rider identification system used in professional speedway.The equivalent of a football shirt but made in tabard style in a rugged material to stand up to the rigours of racing, the jacket was worn as a breast plate and began appearing as early as 1946, although at this time very crude in appearance with just a number identifying the wearer. Gradually the use of appropriate insignia started appearing on a race 'jacket', the Air Formation Signals being one of the earliest teams to include a forces related insignia on their bibs, which were manufactured by the local Egyptians employed in the camp tailors shop.

RAF Scotland - RAF Kabrit 1950

The RAF were even more ambitious and sets of Kabrit 'Eagles' and 'Cobras' were hand painted by skilled artists within the force.At a time when most of the professional clubs in post-war Britain were struggling due to the shortages of materials, often having to ride in a mixture of pre-war versions, crudely manufactured and often differing colours, the photograph above demonstrates just how sophisticated forces speedway had become by the end of the 1940s

Opposite page: Race jackets

EGYPT

1946-47

1947

Tel el Kabir
1946-52

Fayid Saints
1949

RAF Kabrit
1950-51

RAF Kabrit
1952

Air Formation Signals
1946

Shandur Argosy
1949

GERMANY

1946-51

1950

1949

Silver Streaks
1949

Birmingham Saints

New Cross Saints

Odsal Saints

Wembley Saints

LIBYA

Royal Corps Signals

Coldstream Guards

Royal Army Ordnance
Corps

Grenadier Guards

ITALIAN SCRAPBOOK

'Split' Waterman - Vomero 1946

Vomero stadium - Naples

Molfetta 1945/46

Practice day at Molfetta

Geoff Bennett

Don Hardy

Molfetta

Army 'stewards' - Vomero stadium

Mobile scoreboard - Naples

Don Hardy, left with trophies

Molfetta 1945

Bari at Naples 1946

Trani 1944/5

San Spirito squad Bari 1945 - 46

EGYPTIAN SCRAPBOOK

Unknown desert rider

El Ballah pits scene

El Ballah speedway 1947

Tel el Kabir

Les Mullins 'TEK' 'Dons'

Maadi - 1946

First bend at El Kabir

El Ballah speedway 1947

Practice at Tel el Kabir

Team racing at Tel el Kabir

El Ballah 'Aces' 1947

Royal Army Service Corps 1947

Tel El Kabir 'Dons' 1947 - 48

2 Base Workshop 1950

B V D E 1950

Bar None MCC 1946

Maadi 1946

Fayid 'Dicers' 1947

Suez 'Lions' 1947

3 GHQ 1947

Air Formation Signals 1946

Fayid 'Dicers' 1948

Shandur 'Argosy' 1948-49

Tel El Kabir 'Dons' 1950

Tel El Kabir 'Dons' 1951

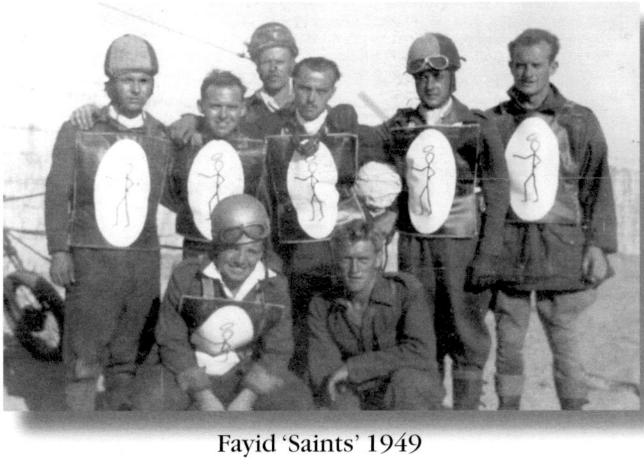

Fayid 'Saints' 1949

RAF Speedway club 1949

RAF 'Cobras' 1952

Geneifa 'Lions'

LIBYAN SCRAPBOOK

Ray Cook - Grenadier Guards 'Hellcats'

Sgt Grantham - Coldstream Guards 'Wombats'

Royal Corps Signals 'Meteors'

Pre meeting parade at Seaview speedway

Seaview speedway

Seaview speedway - Tripoli 1950

Seaview speedway - Tripoli 1950

Seaview speedway - Tripoli 1950

Cpl Brierley - Command workshop 'Tornadoes'

Cpl 'Hookey' Walker - Grenadier Guards 'Hellcats'

Royal Corps Signals 'Meteors'

Grenadier Guards 'Hellcats'

Command Workshop 'Tornadoes'

Royal Army Ordnance Corps 'Pirates'

Italian 'Black Devils' Tripoli

GERMAN SCRAPBOOK

Big crowds at Hamburg

Hanomag 'Saints' at Ebstorf

Pit scene at Hanomag

Racing in Army uniform

Championship Prizes

Hanomag v Hamburg

George Broughton

British dispatch riders take a bend at Hanomag Speedway in the meeting in Germany

1949 Combined Services Championship

Hanomag 350cc Matchless

Silver 'Streaks' (Germany) v Hanomag 'Saints' 1949

Birmingham 'Saints' 1951

Unknown R E M E team 1950

Combined Services Championship field 1950

Forces Rider Directory

GLOSSARY

ARMY

Sgmn	-	Signalman
Sgt	-	Sergeant
Cpl	-	Corporal
L/Cpl	-	Lance Corporal
Dvr	-	Driver
Pte	-	Private
QMS	-	Quarter Master Sergeant
CQMS	-	Command Quarter Master Sergeant
BSM	-	Battery Sergeant Major
Cpt	-	Captain
S/Sgt	-	Staff Sergeant
SSM	-	Staff Sergeant Major (RASC)
Col	-	Colonel
Lt	-	Lieutenant
Bdr	-	Bombadier
L/Bdr	-	Lance Bombadier
Tpr	-	Trooper
Gds	-	Guardsman
S Condr	-	Senior Conductor
Spr	-	Sapper
Rfn	-	Rifleman
MSS	-	?
Fus	-	Fusilier
Cfn	-	Craftsman
ASM	-	Armament Sgt Major

RAF

LAC	-	Leading Aircraftman
AC	-	Aircraftman
Flt/Sgt	-	Flight Sergeant
Flt/Lt	-	Flight Lieutenant
WO	-	Warrant Officer

ROYAL NAVY

AS	-	Able Seaman
PO	-	Petty Officer
CPO	-	Chief Petty Officer

Note

The directory lists riders by surname then rank. Where the rank is unknown Christian names are used. Where Christian name is unknown a riders nickname ie 'Smithy' is used.

? indicates name or rank unknown.

SQUADDIES STATISTICS

In attempting to record accurately all servicemen who rode speedway in the war zones, there is no reference book. Snippets of information covering forces racing are at best rare and very sketchy.The speedway press closed for the duration of hostilities and even post-war only the occasional foreign correspondents report from some far flung battle front reached the UK.

My only source of meeting results, competing riders and Army track matters has been from programmes kindly loaned from the very veterans who rode in these meetings.To attempt to compile a definitive rider directory is destined to fail. However I hope my efforts to create what I believe is a unique record pays some sort of tribute to the war zone speedway heroes.

It must be noted that it was possible for a regular soldier to have ridden for perhaps five seasons, whilst a National Serviceman probably only rode for two.With that in mind, any attempt to log a riders 'career' is futile. Instead the year shown indicates that the rider competing in an official meeting during that year. Over 800 armed forces personnel are represented as having competed on a warzone speedway.

EGYPT 1945

Adair	Dvr
Bailey	Cpl
Beardsley	S/Sgt
Bell	LAC
Bell	LAC
Bicker	Sgt
Blower	Cpl
Blundell	Sigmn
Boardswell	LAC
Booth	Sigmn
Boswell	LAC
Bradbury	Cpl
Bradford	Cpl
Bradley	Cpl
Brennan	QMS
Brookes	LAC
Bullock	LAC
Bullock	LAC
Bunch	Cpl
Caske	Sgt
Chandler	Sgt
Clegg	Cpl
Colley	Sgt
Cracknell	Sgt
Cross	Pte
Croston	Tpr
Cruff	Pte
Culver	L/Cpl
Daniels	LAC
Demayson	Dvr
Dickerson	Cpl
Dromsgoole	LAC
Edwards	Cpl
Finch	LAC
Fogg	F/Lieut
Fowler	L/Cpl
Gordon	Sigmn
Gower	Cpl
Grindstead	Cpl
Harding	L/Cpl
Harwood	Tpr
Heathcote	L/Cpl
Hill	Sigmn
Hodge	Sigmn
Hood	LAC
Hood	Cpl
Howard	Sigmn
Howard	Sigmn
Hufton	Sgt
Ingram	LAC
Jeacock	Sgt
Johnston	Cpl
Jolly	Tpr
Joslyn	LAC
Kassel	Sgt
Kerry	Sgt
Kerry	Cpl
Killip	F/Lt
Kimberley	Sigmn
Kirkbride	Pte
Lane	Dvr
Lloyd	LAC
Matheson	L/Cpl
Mathison	Sigmn
Matthews	LAC
May	Sigmn
McAllister	AC
McGrath	Pte

Molson	LAC	Shipley	Sgt
Moore	LAC	Sidebotham	LAC
Norcott	Cpl	Smith	F/Sgt
Owen	L/Cpl	Tantry	Sgt
Payne	LAC	Terrel	BSM
Picker	Sgt	Titterton	Sgt
Pope	Cpl	Tozer	Cpl
Prevett	Cfn	Traves	LAC
Price	Cpl	Waldock	Cpl
Reddy	F/Sgt	Wells	LAC
Reddy	WO	Wilcox	Cpl
Regan	Sigmn	Williamson	L/Cpl
Robertson	Cpl	Wood	LAC
Rowbotham	LAC	Wylde	Pte
Shanney	L/Cpl	Young	LAC

GERMANY 1945

Adams	Cfn	Kent	Cpl
Callaghan	S/Sgt	Paterson	Sgt
Dalton	Pte	Plyer	Pte
Donovan	Sgt	Randall	Cpl
Goode	Cfn	Sheather	Cfn
Gower	Capt	Smith	Gnr
Grindrod	S/Sgt	Smith	Pte
Hardcastle	L/Cpl	Stott	Cfn
Jones	Cpt		

ITALY 1945

Apsey	Cpl	Drinkall	Cfn
Andersson	Sigmn	Dudley	LAC
Baddersley	??	Edwards	Sgt
Bartlett	L/Cpl	Fletton	Sigmn
Bedford	Gnr	Fox	Sigmn
Bennett	Sigmn	Galvani	Sigmn
Bensley	Cfn	Gene	Sigmn
Birch	Capt	Guest	Cfn
Bovington	Sigmn	Hancox	Sigmn
Briley	A S	Hardy	Pte
Brewster	Sigmn	Hatch	Cpl
Brown	Sigmn	Heathcote	Cpl
Bruce	Pte	Holland	Cpl
Chapman	Dvr	Hopkinson	Sgt
Clarke	S/Sgt	Jackson	Cfn
Cook	L/Bdr	Jepson	Sigmn
Coy	Sgt	Kenny	Pte
Crowley	Dvr	Kent	Dvr
Davies	Cfn	King	Sigmn
Davies	L/Cpl	Lague	Sigmn
Dennison	Cfn	Long	Sigmn
Downham	L/Cpl	Martin	Sigmn

Maskery	Cpl
McCoy	Dvr
Morris	Sigmn
Morton	Sgt
Mumford	Dvr
Mumford	Dvr
Nesham	Sgt
Newton	Sgt
Parker	Dvr
Peak	Cpl
Pickersgill	Dvr
Peats	Cpl
Rawlins	Cpl
Rodgers	Sgt
Sacret	Sgt
Scott	Sgt
Sheppard	Sgt
Simms	Spr
Skeggs	Lt
Smith	Sgt
Snatchfod	Cfn
Stock	S/Sgt
Stone	Bdr
Taylor	Sigmn
Thurston	L/Cpl
Thompson	Cpl
Turton	Dvr
Upton	Pte
Vivian	T
Walker	Sgt
Waterman	Cfn
Weatherspoon	Sigmn
Wilkinson	Pte
Withers	Sigmn
Wildeblood	Cpl
Wilks	Sgt
Wright	Dvr
Wright	Sgt
Young	L/Bdr

AUSTRIA 1946

Ashley-Wing	Capt
Barham	S/Sgt
Bassett	Pte
Bear	Sgt
Bird	L/Cpl
Boll	L/Cpl
Burdett	ASM
Butterfield	L/Cpl
Cardozo	Cpl
Charlwood	Sigmn
Clarke	Dvr
Coulson	L/Cpl
Davies	L/Cpl
Debenham	Pte
Dennison	Dvr
Dock	Cpl
Drake	ASM
Feeney	Sgt
George	Cfn
Gloyne	Sgt
Guest	Cfn
Haig	Spr
Hardison	Dvr
Hull	Cfn
Izzland	Sigmn
James	Pte
Johnstone	Sigmn
Jones	Pte
Kneller	L/Cpl
Lamb	Cpl
Lane	Cfn
Lane	Cfn
Law	Pte
Loveless	Capt
Marquis	Cfn
Mason	L/Cpl
Mattingly	Pte
McDonald	Capt
Merrick	Pte
Ninham	S/Sgt
Ninham	S/Sgt
Nolan	Cfn
Oglanby	Sgt
Olsen	S/Sgt
Parfitt	Cpl
Parsons	Cfn
Pea	Cpl
Perry	Cpt
Phillips	Cfn
Poole	L/Cpl
Radcliffe	Dvr
Radcliffe	Dvr
Regent	Cfn
Rollings	Spr
Rooney	Sigmn
Rowlands	Capt
Seymour	Dvr
Smith	Sgt
Stout	S/Sgt
Strachan	L/Cpl

Teale	Pte	Uglow	S/Sgt
Thomas	Cfn	Vaux	Lt Col
Thompson	Sgt	Warnes	Cpl
Tuckwood	Sigmn	Woods	Sgt
Tulley	Cpl	Yiend	Sgt
Turner	Cfn		

EGYPT 1946

Allen	Cpl	King	Cpl
Amstute	L/Cpl	Large	L/Cpl
Backley	Cpl	Laycock	S/Sgt
Bird	Sgt	Lock	LAC
Brown	Capt	McManus	L/Cpl
Bullock	Cpl	Messenger	Sgt
Cleversley	Sgt	Morgan	Sigmn
Collings	Sigmn	Nelson	LAC
Couchman	S/Sgt	Oakes	Sigmn
Cunningham	Cpl	Oke	Sigmn
Dance	L/Cpl	Owen	LAC
Dungey	Sgt	Pay	Ginger
Egan	Sigmn	Pepper	Cpl
Ellis	Cpl	Pleasants	SSM
Ellis	Cfn	Plyer	Sgt
Enright	F/Sgt	Powell	LAC
Fenner	'Bronco'	Powell	LAC
Fagg	Cpl	Sealey	Sigmn
Fitton	L/Cpl	Simpkins	LAC
Good	Sgt	Steddy	Sigmn
Hannaford	F/Lt	Stemens	Cpl
Hares	L/Cpl	Stevenson	L/Cpl
Hart	Sigmn	Storrs	Capt
Hawkins	Cpl	Talbot	Cpl
Hayhurst	L/Cpl	Terrel	BSM
Henshall	Sigmn	Thompson	Sigmn
Hindmarch	AC	Townsend	Sigmn
Hipkins MBE	Cpt	Webb	LAC
Kean	LAC		

GERMANY 1946

Allison	Cpl	Callaghan	ASM
Atkins	Sigmn	Chadwicke	Dvr
Baker	L/Cpl	Claybourne	?
Ball	Tpr	Davies	Cfn
Bell	Sgt	Douglas	?
Burniston	Capt	Earle	F/Lt
Bush	PO	Edgar ??	???
Butler	Cfn	Eukings	Gnr
Buxey	Cfn	Evans	?
Buxey	Cfn	Garrod	Cfn
Byford	Cfn	Gent	L/Cpl

Gent	L/Cpl	Martin	Cfn
Godfrey	Cfn	McGregor	L/Cpl
Goode	Cfn	Morgan	Cfn
Goode	Cfn	Moss	Cfn
Gower	Major	Nash	Sgt
Grimshaw	Gdm	Nixon	?
Hadley	L/Cpl	Page	?
Hamilton	Cpl	Piquet	Cfn
Hamilton	?	Platt	Cpl
Harman	L/Cpl	Pullen	Cfn
Harper	Cfn	Pullen	Cfn
Harper	?	Ramsden	Cfn
Heaton	Sgt	Seager	Cpl
Hill	L/Cpl	Sheather	Cpl
Johnson	Sgt (Capt)	Skett	CPO
Johnson	Cfn (Res)	Stovold	Cfn
Johnson	Gdm	Tann	Cfn
Johnson	Cfn	Taylor	Cfn
Kenny	L/Cpl	Webb	Cpl
Madden	Sgt	Wilkins	Gdm

ITALY 1946

Alderson	Major	Holland	Cfn
Bastard	Sgt	Kate	L
Bennett	Sigmn	Keeling	H
Bevington	Sigmn	Kemp	Dvr
Bordderley	??	Knights	H
Bray	?	Lewthwaite	Cpl
Bruce	Pte	Rod Laudrum	??
Carruthers	Cpl	Macrae	Cfn
Clarkson	H	Marsh	?
Clissold	??	Marston	Lieut
Cross	L/Cpl	Morris	D
Crowley	D	Nickson	S/Sgt
Crowson	A	Parr	S/Sgt
Dagani	Sigmn	Pitbaldo	?
Davies	Pte	Rawlings	E
Dooley	Sgt	Rigg	E
Downham	L/Cpl	Robinson	L/Cpl
Edwards	Sgt	Robinson	??
Elves	?	Scott	?
Gayner	AQMS	Stock	S/Sgt
Gray	Sigmn	Vaux	Lt Col
Hancox	John	Waterman	Cfn
Handcox	Sgt	Wheeler	?
Hardy	Pte	Wilkinson	L/Cpl
Harman	Sgt	Wilson	Cpl
Heath	Pte	Winfield	Fus
Heathcote	Cpl		

EGYPT 1947

Abbot	Joe
Amstute	Sigmn
Angell	L/Cpl
Balmer	Pte
Beaumont	Sigmn
Bendle	Cfn
Bennett	Lofty
Bibby	Tich
Biggs	"Besa"
Bind	Dicky
Biscoe	Bob
Blower	Sgt
Bri ??	Cpl
Briscoe	Bob
Brown	Cpl
Brown	Doug
Brown	Pte
Brytherick	Sgt
Carrow	Cpl
Christie	Pte
Collings	Sigmn
Cooper	Sigmn
Cooper	Nobby
Cox	Cpl
Craddick	L/Cpl
Cruickshanks	L/Cpl
Cuppleditch	Lt
Dean	"Crash"
Dix	L/Cpl
Doland	Freddie
Duncan	Pte
Dungey	Sgt
Egan	Sigmn
Ellis	Cpl
Emmerton	Cfn
Farrow	'Plough'
Fenner	'Broncho'
Fitton	L/Cpl
Flockhart	Ron
Flour	'Split'
Flower	'May'
Gilbert	Herbert
Goodie	'Blondie'
Goody	Cpl
Gregory	Jim
Grindle	Cpl
Hake	Ken
Hanman	Jock
Hanswell	Tpr
Harkus	Tpr
Hart	Ron
Hartley	Bryan
Hastie	Sigmn
Hayhurst	L/Cpl
Hempstead	Cfn
Henrotto	George
Henshaw	Sigmn
Herridge	Bill
Hickman	'Band'
Higerty	Sgt
Hitchenson	Cfn
Hogg	Ct
Holgate	Cpl
Ide	Cpl
Jennings	John
Jolley	Cpl
Jones	L/Cpl
Jones	Tom
Joyce	L/Cpl
Kelly	Reg
Kett	Eric
King	Cfn
Knight	S/Sgt
Latter	Tom
Lucas	'Spiv'
Mappin	'Happy'
Matten	'Mountaineer'
Matten	'Legs'
McDowall	Howard
Melville	Jock
Mercer	Gnr
Meredith	'Taffy'
Miesen	Mick
Millar	Dusty
Millen	Jock
Mitchell	Dvr
Morgan	Sigmn
Morris	Alfie
Morton	'Brasses'
Moull	Pte
Mullins	'Mad'
Murfin	Cpl
Normansen	Cfn
Oakley	Pte
Oakley	'Snozzle'
Ogden	Pte
Orange	Vic
Paget	'Boy'
Paxman	Johnnie
Pay	'Ginger'
Pearson	Cpl
Peel	Sgt
Percival	Sigmn
Pleasants	SSM

Poyner	Sgt
Pridy	Cpl
Prignell	Tpr
Ravenscroft	F/Sgt
Roberts	Sg
Rockall	Cpl
Seadon	L/Cpl
Short	'Slim'
Sibbley	Harry
Smith	Tpr
Smith	T
Stacey	Flash
Stacy	Flash
Stag	Dvr
Steddy	L/Cpl
Stevens	Cpl
Stewart	Jimmy
Stripp	Cpl
Taggard	Cfn
Talbot	Cpl
Taylor	Pte
Thompson	Sigmn
Thorn	R
Towler	Sigmn
Townsend	Sigmn
Twine	Pte
Vallance	Cfn
Walker	Sigmn
Walker	'Hookey'
Walley	?
Waters	Cpt
Watts	Dvr
Wells	H
Wood	Cpl
Wileyman	Tpr
Wright	Cfn

GERMANY 1947

Ball	Cfn
Callaghan	ASM
Carey	Pte
Charges	Lt
Gant	S/Sgt
Ingham	Cfn
James	Sgt
James	Cfn
Laudrum	Rod
McCabe	Lt
Osbourne	CQMS
Piquet?	Cpl
Pullen	Cpl
Ratcliffe	Pte
Stanton	Cfn
Webster	Sigmn
Wooldridge	Cpl

PALESTINE 1947

Cuppleditch	Lt
Cooper	?
Jolly	?
Hitchensen	?
Freeman	Ray
Blowes	?
Ogden	?
Twine	?
Taylor	?
Kitchener	Jack

EGYPT 1948

Barry	Sgt
Callaghan	ASM
Copper	?
Dorland	?
Fillis	Cfn
Fountain	S/Sgt
Gregory	Jim
Hart	T
Hart	R
Husband	Cpt
Kerr	?
Moody	?
Morris	?
Morris	R?
Oakley	?
Price	?
Salmen	?
Scragg	Cfn
Shaw	T
Sibbly	?

Smart	?	Walker	?
Thomas	Dvr	Witham	Pte
Thompson	Cfn	Yeadon	?
Turner	?		

GERMANY 1948

Pullen	Cpl	McKinlay	Cpl
Lazarus	Jock	Fulljames	Sgt
McCarthy	Speed	Brindley	S.Sgt
Callaghan	ASM	Scragg	Cfn
Lancaster	S. Condr	Moody	Pte
Datridge	Cpl	Taylor	Sgt
Fountain	S.Sgt	Farr	Tiny
Whatling	Cpl		

EGYPT 1949

Armstrong	?	Jacobs	'Spike'
Baldwin	Sid	Jewel	'Tiny'
Bales	B	Johnstone	'Jimmy'
Bannerman	?	Keast	?
Beaumont	'Chic'	Kirk	?
Bell	?	Krappy	?
Bennett	?	Lightfoot	?
Berchard	?	Lyes	?
Bollington	Sid	Masson	?
Brundle	?	Mayes	'Shorty'
Bullen	?	Miles	?
Burrows	?	Miller	'Max'
Calaghan	?	Nicholls	?
Cameron	?	Nicholson	?
Cannon	Bob	Owen	Cliff
Cathcart	?	Partington	?
Chapman	?	Plant	?
Claxton	?	Plews	?
Collins	Dan	Porteous	'Jock'
Cooper	'Vin'	Pugh	Roy
Cummings	'Chubby'	Pymeon	?
Davies	D	Redfern	?
Davies	T	Robinson	?
Eade	?	Saunders	Ray
Eustace	?	Shepherd	?
Eyre	?	Sing	?
Flannery	?	Smith	?
Fox	?	Stephenson	?
Francis	D	Stevens	?
Goodhead	Vic	Sturton	?
Greenaway	?	Theo	?
Harding	Reg	Tinline	?
Hesketh	?	Turner	?
Ironmonger	'Chico'	Walker	?

Ward	?	Whitehead	?
Watson	?	Wiffen	?
Wheeler	'Mutt'	Wilson	?

GERMANY 1949

Boothroyd	Eric	Hessel	Cyril
Boughton	George	Husbands	'Jack'
Brewster	Ray	Jones	'Flyer'
Brindley	'Busty'	Jones	'Teddie'
Burrel	'Flash"	King	'Ace'
Burrow	'Digger'	Lahey	'Ted'
Butchart	'Bluey'	Logan	Pat
Callaghan	'Crash'	Marshall	'Pip'
Cook	Harry	Meacher	'Micky'
Cooper	'Chick'	Miller	'Micky'
Cottam	'Cobb'	Moody	'Geoff'
Darwin	Cpl	Morrison	'Drew'
Davey	Reg	Primrose	'Bud'
Fookes	'Skid'	Rowden	"Darkie"
Fountain	'Splash'	Scott	'Wally'
Fullsames	Sgt	Smith	'Trailer'
Gift	'Lofty'	Vincent	Bob
Gooch	'Jimmie'	Ward	'Nippy'
Hall	'Nobby'	Wilkes	'Johnny'
Halligan	'Grit'	Williams	'Happy'
Harris	Jenny	Yard	'Kit'
Haydock	Charlie	Zamitt	'Zip'

LIBYA 1949

Allen	Sgt	Mantolani	Sigmn
Bailey	Sigmn	Mazzoni	Sigmn
Ball	Cpl	Miens	Dvr
Banbera	Sigmn	Morrison	Sigmn
Barla	Sigmn	Palmer	T
Bonaccorso	Sigmn	Pattison	SQMS
Brierley	Cpl	Smith	Gdsn
Burgess	Sgt	Taylor	Sgt
Busetta	Sigmn	Thomas	Sigmn
Chance	Sgt	Townsend	Gdsn
Cook	Cpl	Turner	?
Holmes	Gdsn	Walker	Cpl
Jackson	Gdsn	Wallace	C

GERMANY 1950

Ambler	L/Cpl	Beasley	Pat
Audsley	L/Cpl	Boughton	L/Cpl
Bainbridge	Sigmn	Braithwaite	Pte
Baver	Bernhard *	Brindley	S/Sgt

Bluck	AC	Mason	Pte
Callaghan	ASM	McDermott	Cfn
Carroll	Spr	McIligrew	Cfn
Chrystal	L/Cpl	Meacher	Cpl
Clark	Cfn	Miller	Cpl
Coe	Cfn	Mills	Pte
Cottam	Sigmn	Moody	Cpl
Dawson	L/Cpl	Morgan	Cfn
Decker	Walter *	Morgan	Dvr
Drage	L/Cpl	Murray	Sigmn
Elliot	AC	Noble	Pte
Fookes	Cpl	Ottley	Lt
Fountain	S/Sgt	Pagan	Pte
Grove	MSS	Payne	Sigmn
Haynes	Sgt	Przybilla	Gunter *
Hearne	L/Cpl	Puttergill	'Splits'
Heffey	Spr	Ramolla	Alfred *
Hicking	Spr	Ramsden	L/Cpl
Hole	Sigmn	Raspini	Pte
Holland	Cfn	Rowden	Dvr
Howard	Cfn	Schlossel	Fritz *
Hudson	Rfn	Sheppard	F/Sgt
Ireland		Simmons	'Squibb'
Jenkins	Cpl	Singer	Cfn
Johnson	Cpl	Slawinski	Heinz *
Johnson	S/Sgt	Smith	Sigmn
Jones	Cpl	Suckley	S/Sgt
Killisch	'Cinders'	Sumner	Cpl
King	Sigmn	Swaine	LAC
Kirchner	Alfred *	Symonds	Cpl
Lakin	Dvr	Thompsett	F/Sgt
Leather	Sigmn	Thompson	Sigmn
Lee	L/Cpl	Wain	Cpl
Lidell	Cfn	Walby	Spr
Lunn	Pte	Wilke	Walter *
Lunt	L/Cpl	Williams	MSS
Mandeville	Pte	Winterscale	LAC
Marsh	Cpl	Yard	Sgt
Marshall	Cpl	Zammitt	L/Cpl

* German riders. Members of 'Silver Streaks' Team.

LIBYA 1950

Aaron	Gdsn	Chapman	'Young'
Adams	Gdsn	Cook	J
Allen	Sgt	Cook	Ray
Andrews	'Spanner'	Curtis	L/Cpl
Bates	Bodger'	Devells	Gdsn
Bales	?	Evans	'Killer'
Brierley	S/Sgt	Grantham	Sgt
Burgess	S/Sgt	Grindley	Sgt
Chance	Jim	Hanman	'Spiv'

Harris	Gdsn
Jackson	Maurice
Kelly	Sgt
Killington	'King'
Maddocks	Sigmn
Marriot	L/Cpl
McClaren	Sigmn
Millan	Lt
Miller	L/Cpl
Mitchell	L/Cpl
Morris	Larry
Noakes	'Nodder'
Palmer	P
Parker	Cpl
Peacock	Sigmn
Stead	Ernie
Taylor	Sgt
Thrussel	F
Tillotson	L/Cpl
Turner	?
Vanstone	Gdsn
Walker	Baldy'
Walker	'Cyril'
Wallace	'Wobble'
Willetts	Dave
Williams	'Shaky'

MALTA 1950

Cawdell	Ron
Burgess	Taffy
Allen	Ken
Bonner	Ken

GERMANY 1951

'BIRMINGHAM SAINTS' (Hanover)

Jones	Cpl 'Flyer' (Team Capt)
Smith	Sgt 'Smudger' (Vice Capt)
Voges	Herr 'Kid'
Ireland	L/Cpl 'Jimmie'
Clark	Cfn "Nobby"
Schlosser	Herr 'Fritz'
Elliott	ACI 'Olly'
Hurn	Tpr 'Tanky'
Kraut	Herr 'Kurt'
Heffey	Spr Bill
Randall	Cpl Geoff
Wally	Herr 'Helmut'
Pickering	Pte Ray
Jeffries	Sigmn Johnnie
Knauer	Herr Gunter
Jones	Cfn Terry
Knigge	Herr Wolfgang
Sturdy	Spr Billy
Clark	Sigmn 'Dart'
Klamet	Herr Erich
Gresty	L/Cpl Fred
Paul	Herr Victor
Smith	Sigmn David
Metzner	Herr Herbert

'WEMBLEY SAINTS' (Hanover)

Zammit	Cpl 'Zipp' (Team Capt)
Fountain	S/Sgt 'Splash' (Vice Capt)
Killisch	Herr 'Cinders'
Smith	Mr 'Trailer'
McDermott	Cfn Dennis
Ramolla	Herr Alfred
Payne	Sigmn Arthur
Williams	Mss 'Slide'
Neumann	Herr Harry
Ambler	Cpl 'Bennie'
Chrystal	L/Cpl 'Rusty'
Plackowski	Herr Konrad
Harness	Dvr 'Yorky'
Drage	Sgt 'Ginger'
Przikling	Herr Gunther
Meese	L/Cpl Ewan
Spannberg	Herr Otto
Wright	Pte Jerry
Bateman	Sigmn 'Hawk'
Almstadt	Herr Hans
Johnson	S/Sgt 'Speedy'
Decker	Herr Walter
Raven	Cfn Len
Frank	Herr Alfons

'NEW CROSS SAINTS' (Hanover)

Boughton	Cpl George (Team Capt)
Sheppard	F/Sgt 'Bas' (Vice Capt)
Pryzbilla	Herr Gunter

Fookes	Cpl 'Skid'	Simmons	Mr 'Squibb"' (Vice Capt)
Sumner	Cpl Ted	Slawinski	Herr Heinz
Neu	Herr Gunter	Meacher	Sigmn 'Mickie'
Grove	Sgt Ron	Leather	Sigmn Warren
Marsh	Cpl 'Arty'	Schelm	Herr Bruno
Eisermann	Herr Gunter	Shannon	Sigmn Joe
Evershed	Pte 'Slim'	Moody	Cpl Geoff
Sharpe	L/Cpl Don	Heitmann	Herr 'Willi'
Prosenbauer	Herr Michael	Davies	ACI 'Dia'
Kirk	Sgt 'Paddy'	Miller	Cfn Mick
Stamp	Sigmn 'Sticker'	Winkler	Herr Paul
Rieseberg	Herr Richard	Kempster	L/Cpl 'Kim'
Johnson	Cfn Bill	Wilson	S/Sgt 'Bronco'
Tendryssek	Herr Siegfried	Schnarewski	Herr Hans
McIlgrew	Cfn 'Ricky'	Dawson	Sigmn Peter
Greaney	L/Cpl Bert	Matschuck	Herr Heinrich
Venus	Herr Horst	Morgan	Sigmn Tom
White	Cpl 'Chalky'	Derbyshire	Sgt Eddie
George	Herr Otto	Wendisch	Herr Gottfried
Godden	L/Cpl 'Allan'	Checksfield	Cpl Charlie
Hamburger	Herr 'August'	Schink	Herr Berndt
'ODSAL SAINTS'	**(Hanover)**	McNiven	Spr Duncan
King	Sigmn 'Ace' (Team Capt)	Volkoi	Herr Walter

EGYPT 1952

Baker	'Doughy'	Huggins	Joe
Bennett	'Slip'	Duffy	'Jock'
Burton	'Spurton'	Ewin	Sgt
Butler	Tich	Longstaff	'Brummie'
Collett	Dave	Luck	Reg
Davidson	'Dude'	Lunn	Jeff
Duqusman	'Duke'	McDonald	Mal
Free	'Swede'	McGregor	Keith
Fisher	'King'	Rowe	Art
Griggs	Cliff	Tose	Cpl
Hartland	Johnnie	Johnstone	Johnnie
Hayward	Ken		

British Armed Forces Motorcycling

The Modern Era

Army motorcycling still continues in the modern era, under a Tri-Service (Army, Royal Navy, and RAF) frame work. Away from the public profile of the motor cycle display teams such as the 'White Helmets' (Royal Corps Signals) training and competitive motorcycling within the Armed Forces is still employed to ensure that troops are combat ready. Lt Colonel (Retd) Bob Birrell secretary of the BAFMA explains the current state of motorcycling today to continue the thread of military history covered by *Warzone Speedways*.

The Army Motorcycling Association was formed in the 1930s, the exact date is obscured by time, but an Army team took part in International Six Day Trials (ISDT) well before WWII. In 1939 the ISDT was held in September , the Army Team were leading until day five when a military attaché led them out of Austria just 24 hours before war was declared.

After the war, an annual 'Army Championships' took place; much of the silverware awarded then is still competed for today, including the magnificent Graham Walker Cup (Father of TV commentator Murray Walker). A programme from a Motor Cycle Sports meeting held at Maadi in Egypt(1946), reveals that the services had taken delivery of 100,000 BSA M20s, that would be one each for every man in the Army today.

Meanwhile the Army teams in the ISDT continue to thrive, particularly during National Service, when professional riders such as John Giles rode in the Army team. The ISDT became the International Six Day Enduro in the 80s, this saw a gradual diversity in design of trials and enduro bikes, similarly derivatives of Service machines became uncompetitive and unsuitable. To overcome this, the Army Motorcycling Association managed to borrow competition machines for importers and manufacturers. The in-service bikes were the BSA M20 which survived until the mid 60s, when they were replaced by the side valve Triumph TRW. A plan to have Greeves mass produced bikes for the Army was rejected on the grounds of unsuitability of two strokes, not a wonderful bike for the Army which soon gave way to the BSA M40, probably the last 'off the peg' machine used by the British Army. In the early 80s we finally went two stroke, with the Bombardier Can Am and then the Armstrong 500cc which was an addition of disc brakes. Later the loss of 150cc provided Army with the current Harley Davidson model we use today.

The future of motorcycles in the current operational environment is questionable, to say the least, future bikes are likely to be far fewer in number and bought 'off the peg'. In 2003 the Army Motorcycling Association became the British Armed Forces Motorcycling Association, this change of title merely recognised the increased participation of RAF riders in military competitions. The current activities provide a ladder of opportunity for young Service riders. We run a series of Short Course Enduro events, culminating in 'Exercise Hard Ride', the Armed Forces championship. This is a mixture of map reading, mechanical tests, trial sections and Enduro with classes for Military machines and competition machines ridden by Servicemen. The best rider's progress to the British Enduro Championship series where they used privately owned and Regimentally owned competition machines. The 'best of best' can be selected for the ISDE, held in a different country each year, New Zealand in 2006 and Chile 2007. The BAFMA regularly earn Gold and Silver medals and we have riders selected for the Great Britain teams (Senior and Junior Trophy). For these more gruelling events we need the support of a major manufacturer to supply new bikes, we have used Yamaha in recent years, they are highly competitive and even more importantly, 100% reliable.

Although the trials discipline has diversified, it has not been neglected, our major exercises contain a large trials element and each year we enter a four man team in the Scottish Six Day trial, the Army also provide the resources for refuelling the 280 competitors, a frequent occurrence as a modern trials bike carries only 2.5 litres of fuel. We also run a 24 hour charity enduro for military bikes, 'Exercise Enduring Help', which has for the past 10 years raised over £15,000 each year for Service and Children's charities. Motorcycling is very much alive in the Army. Military requirements are bound to decrease but enthusiasm will not, the proportions of military bikes to competition bikes will alter but the patient is very much alive.

Military Miscellany

- Alfred Rumrich believed to be the only Luftwaffe pilot to hold down a team place in a British team, had his career cut short thanks to a German Air Force eye test. Alfred was signed by Wimbledon in 1937 to replace American Miny Waln in the 'Dons' National league team. A British career of just eight weeks was interrupted when Alfred was required to return home to Germany for an eye test as part of his duties as a pilot reservist. He arrived back in Germany 24 hours late for his appointment and the matter was taken very seriously by his superior officers. They instructed the German equivalent of the British ACU to revoke his licence, which effectively banned him from riding for the rest of the season.

- Talking of Germans, Wigan promoter Peggy Waxman signed a 27 year old Naval officer Horst 'Eric' Szworski in 1947 to bolster her 'Panthers' team. Eric was the star novice on the Ainsdale Sands training school run every Sunday on the beach near Southport in Lancashire.

- In the build up to war, the German philosophy that Germany was for the Germans had an impact on a speedway tour of the 'Fatherland'. Australian Max Grosskreutz and a party of riders opened a track in Hamburg in the mid 30s just as Nazism was taking a hold. Unfortunately Hitler's supporters picketed the stadium causing Max and his backers to lose all their investment.

- In 1938 following an Air Ministry and Civil Guard plea to assist the RAF in emergencies, the Herts &Essex flying club, owned by Wembley riders Buster and Roger Frogley, were inundated with some 1,200 applicants from prospective pilot wishing to learn to fly. Pre-war riders who were taught to fly by the Frogley brothers included Billy Lamont, Frank Arthur, Buzz Hibberd, Ray Tauser, Claude Rye, Morian Hansen, Vic Huxley, George Greenwood, Lionel Van Praag, Wally Kilminster, Frank Charles, Jack Parker and Jack Ormston.

- A St Austell meeting against Aldershot in 1952 turned into a tragedy when an RAF helicopter giving a demonstration of a night landing on the centre green, crashed when a rotor blade flew off onto the crowd. The pilot Fl Lt Minnifi and a spectator were killed as a result of the accident.

- When Crystal Palace exhibition centre caught fire in 1936, a huge tangle of metal remained from the glass construction. With war clouds gathering it is amazing to learn that the authorities sold the scrap metal to Krupps of Essen, who were producing steel for the German impending war effort.

- Maurice Morley, team manager for Newport, Hackney, Romford and others was only 15 years old when he joined the Army in 1940. He was post-war an oil and fuel man for the great Jack Parker before riding himself for New Cross, Bradford and Long Eaton.

- In 1969, a Rochester, Kent team was due to enter the fledgling British League Second Division. They were called the 'Bombers' and wore the RAF roundel on their race jackets in recognition of the Sunderland Flying boats in which promoter Pete Lansdale flew in WWII. The Sunderland, built by Short brothers was built on the nearby Medway, where the proposed Rochester speedway was to be constructed.
- Whilst racing at New Cross ceased in 1939 along with other London clubs, the stadium did open during the war years. One such occasion was on September 20 1943 when the Deptford Beautification and Social Affairs committee arranged a family and sports day, including a small fair on the speedway centre green.

- Willem Shey, a Czechoslovakian racer who was a Major in the Polish Army was involved in a spectacular crash during his debut meeting at Newcastle. Willem lost three fingers in his first ride and also wrecked a new bike which he had been loaned.

- Post-war Harringay speedway announcer Major L F G Anthony was well qualified for the job. The Major was a leading light with the Army charity show 'Khaki Kapers' which toured North Africa entertaining the troops.

- Ron Johnson, the New Cross captain caused quite a stir when he was invited to make a personal appearance at the REME Army camp at Arborfield near Reading. The occasion was a screening of '*Speedway*' the 1948 film about speedway and the Globe cinema on the camp was swamped with hundreds of squaddies wanting to meet Johnson.

- Vitek Formanek the renowned Czechoslovakian speedway historian tells me that an ex speedway rider from Austria/Germany, Sepp Giggenbach was the engine driver on Adolf Hitler's private train.

- The Wembley club, under the management of Alec Jackson, assisted the Middlesex Army cadets to form a motor cycle unit. The unit was formed from 'Lions' fans who were able to carry out their pre-National Service training as despatch riders before formally entering the ranks.

- Vic Gent, who progressed from BAOR speedway in Germany to ride for Exeter & Plymouth, used his fathers' undertaking business store room to tune his bike and it was not unusual for 'occupied' coffins to hear the roar of his highly tuned JAP machine.

- Les Marshall's efforts to open Birmingham speedway in 1946 are indicative of the building difficulties of the time. The stadium had only been de-requisitioned in late February and had been used in the war as an Army training ground and as an Italian POW camp. One of Les's biggest problems was his car park, which had been converted into a maze of trenches, rifle ranges, assault courses and barbed wire entanglements. A safety fence was required and with wood at an absolute premium, he used wood from packing cases used to transport Jeeps to build the wooden construction.

- One day in March 1946, Arthur Atkinson the West Ham co-promoter unearthed a small object from the track whilst preparing for racing. It proved to be a German Iron cross. As the stadium had never been used as a POW camp, the only feasible explanation was that the Medal must have fallen from the air when a German aircraft was shot down in the vicinity.

- George Hunter, Scottish star with Edinburgh in the 1960s had the British Army to thank for his speedway career developing quicker than might otherwise have been the case. The 21 year old former grass tracker was rejected for National Service on medical grounds. Explained George *"The medics took one look at my grass track injury record and decided I wasn't fit for active service".*

- The Halifax 'Dukes' team that entered the 1949 Third division were so named after the Duke of Wellington regiment which was garrisoned in the Yorkshire town. The speedway club even adopted the regiments maroon and French grey colours and the elephant insignia on their race jackets.

- Fred Whitehead, the Harringay manager after WWII, offered special rates to all ex-servicemen using the training facilities at the Green Lanes circuit in North London. Enquiries from soldiers requesting a riding trial came from as far a field as Rome, Cairo and Hong Kong, all keen to take part in the Wednesday morning sessions.

- Professor A M Low, who for a time was Chairman and vice-president of the Auto Cycle Union, was an engineer in the Royal Flying Corps in 1916. He was Commander of the RFC experimental unit and invented electronically guided rockets some 20 years before Hitler's V1 flying bombs.

- Post-war Bradford Odsal promoter Bruce Booth flew a small light aircraft to away team matches.

- Exeter's County Ground stadium, now demolished for housing was commandeered for military use in WWII. It became home to thousands of American GIs preparing for D-Day. Included amongst the temporary residents in tents on the centre green was World Heavy weight boxing champion Joe Louis.

- In 1959, Norwich speedway purchased an RAF refuelling three wheeled vehicle. It was adapted by club mechanic Les Mullins and was used for track preparation at the Firs stadium.

- Nigel Boocock, 'little boy blue' of Coventry fame, was riding for Ipswich in the late 50s when he had to decline a racing trip to Australia due to his imminent call up for National Service. Apparently it was an offence to leave the country whilst awaiting call up. Nigel eventually joined the Royal Corps Signals, but he was back in Civvy Street within 28 days of signing on, due to speedway injuries which made him unfit for soldiering.

- During the war time meetings at Belle Vue, the traditional two minute siren warning used by the steward warning riders of a time allowance was dropped. It was felt it might have been confused with an air raid siren which warned of a German bombing attack.

- Through the years there have been some very strong links between Matchless motor cycles and the armed forces. The post-war Sales manager for the AMC (parent company of Matchless) was Jock West who was a Wing Commander in the Royal Air Force Volunteer Reserve. He was to present Douglas Bader, the famous tin legged pilot with a Matchless motor cycle for Outward Bound organisations supported by Bader.

- West Ham's Canadian Eric Chitty applied to join the RAF, Army and Royal Navy on the outbreak of WWII. Unfortunately for Eric, his aircraft factory work was deemed as a reserved occupation. He was accepted after interview for each of the services, but the authorities judged his skills as an engineer were more useful than putting him into uniform.

- Walter Brown, a Scotsman who was awarded the Military Cross and the Croix de Guerre (Belgian) in WW1, lost his life whilst riding at a speedway meeting at Marine Gardens Edinburgh in May 1929.

- In 1955 a West Ham team toured Austria to ride against a team called the 'Continentals'. The two matches were watched by a large contingent of Russian and British troops, who celebrated the Hammers' victories by carrying the team around the track shoulder high on a victory parade.

- Jack Barnett who rode at High Beech in the late 1920s joined the Army as a despatch rider under the motor cycle training recruitment scheme initiated by Graham Walker, father of Formula 1 commentator Murray Walker.

- When Hull opened for speedway in 1948, the track was constructed on the site of Hedon airfield which was used as a rocket battery site in WWII. The club used the old hangar as a grandstand, the safety fence being made from Morrison shelter panels and Nissen huts around the site being used for workshops, rider sleeping quarters and a first aid room.

- In September 1938 the New Cross stadium in South London was used as an anti-aircraft battery site complete with high frequency listening equipment.

- Phil Bishop, who started riding speedway at High Beech as a 16 year old in 1928-29, worked as a tank ferry driver throughout the war.

- During the war Wembley officials received a request from a German POW camp for a supply of 'Lion' supporter's scarves. It turned out that a group of British POWs had formed a Wembley supporters club within the confines of the prison camp.

- One of the most unusual of candidates for warzone speedway status came in 2006, when Redcar beach was chosen to be a re-creation of the Dunkirk beaches for a £36 million budget film. Starring Vanessa Redgrave, the beach scenes were filmed within an exhaust note distance of the newly opened Redcar Bears track.

- In 1954, Glasgow promoter Ian Hoskins announced he was giving a trial to a former Army paratrooper who rode at Hanover on the BAOR Army speedway. The rider went by the name of 'Leap' Primrose and he became the fifth 'Saints' team member to ride at the Glasgow White City track, the others being Ken McKinlay, Gordon McGregor, Larry Lazarus, and Angus McGuire.

- The Rye House war time meetings were organised by the Harringay Speedway Motor cycle and Light Car club. The meetings were used to raise funds for the Prisoners of War Parcel Fund, co-ordinated by the British Red Cross. Ever conscious of the dangers of running meetings, the meeting programme issued the following warning *"In the event of an air raid an announcement will be made over the loudspeakers. Patrons should proceed at once to one of the exits and disperse quickly. Do not run."*

- Brigadier H Hayman Joyce, a major patron of the Bar-None club activities was a despatch rider himself in WW1, riding a Triumph in Mesopotamia.

- The track of Sittingbourne 'Crusaders' in Iwade, Kent is built on the location of a WWII gunnery school overlooking the Thames estuary. The MoD vacated the area in the late 50s but it was not until 1971 that the Thomas brothers Barry and Ivor opened the Marshbank farm site as a training track. Underground bunkers still exist at the track and have been used as workshops, changing rooms and even the referees box is sited on a previous gun emplacement.

- One of the keenest speedway fans of 1959 must have been RAF airman Steve Collins. A Londoner, Steve was serving a 12 year term with the RAF based in the North of England, near Newcastle. Such was his enthusiasm for speedway that he regularly dashed home when on a week-end pass to spend time helping Aldershot promoter Ted Payne prepare the race track at the Tongham stadium.

- During the two seasons of racing at Eastville stadium in Bristol (1977-78), riders were brought under starters orders and flagged at the finish of races by American Lee Harris an ex-United States Air Force pilot. Extravagant Lee wore a top hat, white trousers and a Union Jack waistcoat when carrying out his duties.

- With war over, on December 1 1947, all competitive motor cycling events were banned as part of the Governments edict for fuel saving. A demonstration by the long forgotten Brands Hatch Speedway was to influence the re-introduction of a 'Standard' fuel allowance by the spring of 1948, which allowed all forms of motor cycling to recommence.

- Cliff King ,the West country ACU referee who officiated at the 1951 & 52 Wembley World finals, played a leading role in the formation of the Air Raid Protection (ARP) despatch riding unit in Bristol which served the city throughout the bombings in WWII. C H King was the secretary of the ACU Wessex Centre at the time and he was able to enlist the right trained motor cyclists for the job.

- New Cross Director and announcer Cecil Smith took a commission with the Territorial Army as a Major and spent most of his war in East Africa training the native troops.

- The Right Hon. Lord Howe of Aberavon CH QC, former Chancellor of the Exchequer and Deputy Prime Minister was plain Lt Geoffrey Howe with the Royal Corps Signals. Lt Howe spent his Army career in Kenya and possessed a Matchless G3L. Sadly no evidence exists of Lord Howe competing in the forces racing in Nairobi!

- 1976 World Champion Peter Collins often calls into a German motor cycle shop in Holzwickede. It is owned by Josef Joy who enlisted in the Royal Engineers as a despatch rider and MT recovery Sergeant in 1947. Leaving the Army in 1953 Josef decided to stay in Germany, making his home near Dortmund and became a regular competitor in trials, scrambles, grass/longtrack and for three years on the 1960s speedway racing. PC and Josef became good friends when Josef began running a racing spares service at the tracks. With Josef fluent in German he was often called upon to act as translator for the English riders including Peter.

- Rick France (Coventry), Dave Younghusband (Halifax) and James Bond (Wolverhampton) almost certainly hold the honour as the last serving British soldiers to ride professional speedway. France and Younghusband were DR instructors at Rippon where Bond met them and all were in one of the very last intakes before National Service was abandoned in the early 1960s.

- Evidence exists of the Local Defence Volunteers, renamed the Home Guard, acting as 'promoters' for grass speedway events in the summer of 1944. The Hawks MCC (Cheltenham) and the XHG Tiger club of Poole are believed to have been particularly active in running events as part of the 'Holiday at Home' programme of that year.

- In July 1944 the firsy recorded competitive forces motorcycle event in Italy was staged at an unknown venue by the Molfetts MCC. Races were held over 2, 4 and 10 laps and the meeting contained a five heat 'Test Match' between England and United States, England were represented by Fred Smith, H. George, "Nobby' Clarke and Bob Kent. America fielded Don Riley, E. Studinsky, Gerry Brown and Dorsey Davies running out winners by 13pts to 11.

And Finally...

Readers of '*Speedway Flyers*' the first in this series of armed forces speedway books will remember my appeal for any further nominations of Royal Flying Corps and RAF personnel who rode speedway professionally. I am indebted to all who have contributed and am pleased to further complete for posterity, this unique piece of speedway history:

'Duke' Bell- Plymouth

Dave Hankins – Norwich / Leicester

John Pope- Glasgow Ashfield

Tony Robinson- Belle Vue

Dick Fisher -Belle Vue

Laurie Schofield- Cradley Heath

Maurice Littlechild - Kings Lynn promoter

Ernest Mason

Ernie Price - Belle Vue

Bill Wilson- Middlesbrough

Eric Salmon - Bristol

Gus Khun - Stamford Bridge (RNAS)

Lionel Pugh – Stoke / Swindon

Charlie Barrett - Middlesbrough

Bill Wilson survived WWII with the RAF but was killed aged 32 years old whilst riding for Middlesbrough in a National Trophy match at Norwich.

Squadron Leader Ernest 'Imshi' Mason DFC, Commanding Officer of 94 Squadron is recorded as having ridden dirt track speedway in 1928. Born in Darlington in 1913, Imshi was a legend in the Desert Air Force .